The GI's Rabbi

THE GI's RABBI

World War II
Letters of
David Max Eichhorn

Edited by

Greg Palmer

and

Mark S. Zaid

With an Introduction by

Doris L. Bergen

University Press of Kansas

©2004 by the University Press of Kansas

Published by the University Press of Kansas (Lawrence, Kansas 66049), which was organized by the Kansas Board of Regents and is operated and funded by Emporia State University, Fort Hays State University, Kansas State University, Pittsburg State University, the University of Kansas, and Wichita State University

Library of Congress Cataloging-in-Publication Data

Eichhorn, David Max, 1906–1986
    The GI's rabbi : World War II letters of David Max Eichhorn / edited by Greg Palmer and Mark S. Zaid ; with an Introduction by Doris L. Bergen.
        p. cm. — (Modern war studies)
        Includes bibliographical references and index.
        ISBN 0-7006-1356-0 (alk. paper)
    1. Eichhorn, David Max, 1906–1986 — Correspondence.   2. United States. Army — Chaplains — Correspondence.   3. World War, 1939–1945 — Chaplains — United States.   4. World War, 1939–1945 — Personal narratives, American.   5. World War, 1939–1945 — Personal narratives, Jewish.   6. World War, 1939–1945 — Campaigns—Europe.   7. Chaplains, Military — United States — Correspondence.   8. Rabbis — United States — Correspondence.   I. Palmer, Greg.   II. Zaid, Mark S.   III. Title.   IV. Series.
    D769.375.E43   2004
    940.54'78'092—dc22   2004008733

British Library Cataloguing-in-Publication Data is available.

Printed in the United States of America

10 9 8 7 6 5 4 3 2 1

The paper used in this publication meets the minimum requirements of the American National Standard for Permanence of Paper for Printed Library Materials Z39.48-1984.

Contents

A photo section follows
page 222.

In the fall of 2001 I began work on a four-part documentary series about World War II for public television. *The Perilous Fight: America's World War II in Color* is based on two successful British series and, like its predecessors, uses only color film shot before and during the war years. Our goal was not to present another battle-by-battle history of the conflict but to explore the experience of those at home and those overseas whose lives had been changed forever by the war. My particular program of the series, "Wrath," focuses on the European theater of operations from D-Day to V-E Day and was originally broadcast nationwide by PBS in February 2003.

Many people assume that there is little color film of World War II, but in fact hundreds of hours of sometimes spectacular color footage can be found in the archives of the combatants. Private collectors have color film too, often shot by their fathers or grandfathers and stored away for decades in attics and garages. In the first month I spent working on the series, it seemed like I watched all that film, sitting in a dark room in Seattle, taking notes and trying to figure out who was who in the movies, as well as when and where they had been filmed.

One day I was looking at silent color footage shot by Hollywood director George Stevens during the April–May 1945 liberation of Dachau, the oldest concentration camp in Germany. And there, for eleven seconds, was a uniformed GI conducting some kind of religious service in the camp. Stevens's film logs are haphazard at best, because he was shooting the color film for his personal use, not as part of his duties as director of the army's European Signal Corps units. But on the log for this particular footage, someone had written in pencil, "This may be a Rabbi Eichorn, identified by his grandson, Mark Zaid."

When I found Mark Zaid at his law firm in Washington, D.C., he confirmed that the man was his grandfather and told me that the event was the first Shabbat service at Dachau, which took place a week after the camp had been liberated by Allied troops — troops that included his grandfather. David Max Eichhorn, chaplain, XV Corps,

U.S. Army, was the first rabbi from the outside world to confront the horror of Dachau and minister to those who had survived it.

Perilous Fight includes no retrospective interviews. People's thoughts and feelings are expressed through readings of their wartime letters and journals. I originally made contact with Mark to confirm his grandfather's identity, but also to find out whether any of the rabbi's wartime letters — especially concerning Dachau — still existed, to use in the soundtrack of my program. Mark said that he would check with the family about any letters, including asking his grandmother, Zelda Socol Eichhorn, the rabbi's widow. In the interim, he sent me some pieces that had been written about the event, including his grandfather's own account from a collection of wartime reminiscences of a group of rabbi-chaplains titled *Rabbis in Uniform* (1962). It was from this piece that I learned that George Stevens had shot more than just a little color film for his own use at the service. His Signal Corps photographers had documented the entire ceremony on black-and-white film, with synchronized sound. This meant that in *Perilous Fight,* for the first time in more than fifty years, an audience would be able to hear some of that historic event as it had happened — if we could find the black-and-white film.

We are still looking. A few reels of the raw footage were located in the U.S. National Archives and Records Administration, so we were able to use part of the sound from the proceedings, including a portion of Rabbi Eichhorn's Prayer for the Dead (El Male Rachamin), his sermon, and "God Bless America" sung by a choir of Hungarian Jewish girls under the rabbi's direction. But neither the rest of the raw footage nor the final edited film has been found. We believe that copies of this documentary record were made and sent to interested organizations across North America, and we continue to hope that somewhere, sometime, that film will be rediscovered. It should be seen and kept safe forever, as a tribute to those who died and those who survived in all the camps. It is powerful evidence that in the midst of almost unbelievable horror, there was faith and hope and communion.

For now, we have Rabbi Eichhorn's letters. David Max Eichhorn was a devout man committed to giving everything he had to the war effort — even his life, if need be. He was a scholar and a patriot. He provided comfort and solace to thousands of soldiers and their families. But he was also a GI and, as he signed many of his letters, a "husband, daddy, brother, and son," trying in every possible way to maintain a connection to Jon, Mike, Jerry, and Judy, his four children growing up without him, and to Zelda, the wife he left behind to go on a great adventure. In that, he was like almost every other GI during the war — an ordinary person in extraordinary circumstances.

Like so many of his comrades, he rose to the occasion in ways that still speak to us of honor and compassion, of death and life, and of hope for us all.

Greg Palmer

Acknowledgments

In preparing this book, we received invaluable help from many people and organizations. In particular, we would like to thank Martin Smith, producer of the documentary series *The Perilous Fight*, without whom this book would not exist; TWI, KCTS/Seattle, and Carlton, creators of the television series, and their executive producers Alastair Waddington, David Rabinovitch, and the late Polly Bide; Rina Nicholson and Rivy Kletenik for their assistance with the glossary; researchers David Boardman, Blair Foster, Kari Basford, Mercedes Yeager, Cecilie D. Keenan, and Marcie Finnila; the staffs of the U.S. Holocaust Memorial Museum in Washington, D.C., and the Yad Vashem Archives in Jerusalem; Alex Grobman, author of *Rekindling the Flame: American Jewish Chaplains and the Survivors of European Jewry, 1944–1948,* for helpful leads; several of Rabbi Eichhorn's former colleagues and their children and grandchildren; and especially Michael Briggs and his staff at the University Press of Kansas.

And of course, we cannot thank enough the Eichhorn family — in particular, the rabbi's widow, Zelda, and their son, Rabbi Jonathan Eichhorn, who saved the correspondence in this book for nearly sixty years. Thanks also to Rabbi Eichhorn's daughter, Judith Zaid, and niece, Dawn Eichhorn, for access to numerous photographs.

Introduction

Rabbi David Max Eichhorn, chaplain, XV Corps, U.S. Army, participated in some of the pivotal events of the last phase of World War II in Europe. He landed at Omaha Beach on July 10, 1944, just weeks after D-Day, and accompanied the Third, the First, and finally the Seventh Armies as they fought their way through Normandy, endured the Battle of the Bulge, crossed the Rhine River, and advanced into Germany. Chaplain Eichhorn arrived at Dachau on April 30, 1945, one day after the first American troops, and organized the first Jewish religious service at the concentration camp site. He witnessed the refugee crisis that preceded and followed V-E Day in Germany and did what he could to help displaced persons, especially survivors of the Holocaust. In the course of his duties, he encountered Generals Dwight D. Eisenhower, George S. Patton, Alexander M. Patch, and Omar Bradley, as well as the British ambassador in Washington, Lord Halifax.[1] For Rabbi Eichhorn, these historical experiences were shaped by his professional standing as a military chaplain with the U.S. Army — and not just any chaplain, but a Jewish chaplain. His correspondence, collected and edited in this volume, offers an articulate, opinionated, and immediate view of what it was like for him to be a chaplain — in his words, "a good soldier and a good rabbi" — in the midst of a war of unprecedented scale and destruction.[2]

Eichhorn's letters, like the man himself, are frank, astute, eloquent, and well informed. Like him, too, they are discreet. Restricted by wartime censorship, bound by a well-honed sense of propriety, and sensitive to his worried family back home, Eichhorn omitted certain details — place names, most conspicuously — and passed over some key conflicts and developments. Wisely, the editors of this volume have supplemented the wartime letters with selections from Eichhorn's other writings: sermons, radio addresses, reports, and excerpts from an unpublished autobiography he completed in 1969. These materials fill in gaps in the letters and highlight the significance of specific references, allusions, and silences.

One incident that Rabbi Eichhorn left out of his letters but recounted in his autobiography illustrates how he fit into the broader contexts of

World War II, the development of the military chaplaincy, and the history of Jews in the United States. On January 30, 1945, by command of General Eisenhower, a firing squad drawn from the U.S. 109th Infantry executed Private Edward Donald Slovik on the charge of desertion to avoid hazardous duty.[3] Eddie Slovik was the only American soldier put to death for desertion during World War II; indeed, his was the only such execution since the Civil War. (The German Wehrmacht, in contrast, killed an estimated 30,000 of its own men between 1939 and 1945, most of them in the last phases of the war.)[4] In a typically terse and understated manner, Rabbi Eichhorn's account reveals a little-known yet crucial aspect of the Slovik case.

Eichhorn describes what and how he heard about the background of the Slovik affair.[5] According to him, General Eisenhower had been outraged in December 1944, during the Battle of the Bulge, when thousands of inexperienced U.S. troops had panicked and fled to the rear. With the intention of making an example, Eisenhower instructed his staff to search military prisons for American soldiers who were repeat offenders for abandoning their arms and deserting before the enemy. Six candidates were identified, among them a Jewish soldier from Philadelphia. One of Eisenhower's aides contacted Rabbi Eichhorn, the nearest Jewish chaplain, to inform him that if the Jewish soldier were chosen, in accordance with tradition, Eichhorn would be responsible for ministering to the condemned man, to help prepare him and be present at his execution.

Eichhorn's brief account reminds us of the contingencies of war, even a war that, in hindsight, appears to have been decided long before the end of 1944. General Eisenhower and his advisers deemed it necessary to take drastic action — a military execution to prevent future desertions — because, in their minds, the war was far from over. It is easy in hindsight to presume the inevitability of German defeat — and Allied victory — and to read that knowledge backward to the Battle of Stalingrad in 1943 or even earlier, perhaps to the German invasion of the Soviet Union in 1941. Rabbi Eichhorn's account of the Slovik case shows us that the situation looked and felt much more uncertain — even desperate — to the American leadership and U.S. troops at the time.

Eichhorn said little about his feelings, but his dread was evident. Still, he could hardly refuse to do as he was asked: the right to spiri-

tual care before a military execution had a long history in the chap-
laincies of Europe and North America. Herman Melville's novella *Billy Budd* depicts such a scene from the late eighteenth century, and even Nazi Germany permitted such pastoral attentions, although admittedly, many executions in the chaotic final days of the war were hasty affairs with no time for niceties.[6] As a chaplain, then, Rabbi Eichhorn was obligated to do his duty.

Eichhorn certainly recognized the horrific irony of what he might be ordered to take part in: the execution of an American Jew in the midst of a landscape deep in the blood and ashes of the victims of Nazism, many of them Jewish. Although not yet aware of all the details of the Holocaust, Eichhorn understood very well that the Germans had been systematically murdering Jews for several years. Indeed, a sermon of September 28, 1943, and letters dated from mid-1944 to early 1945, reproduced in this volume, leave no doubt as to his knowledge of the genocide.[7] A task that would be difficult for any chaplain, anywhere, would, in the specific context of World War II in Europe, have brought terrible pain to Rabbi Eichhorn.

Eichhorn's involvement in the Slovik case also provides a window into the situation of Jews in the United States in the 1940s. From our position decades after the Holocaust, we see the heroism of liberation and read memoir accounts of Jewish survivors meeting champions and helpers — and even future husbands — among the U.S. armed forces, especially its Jewish members.[8] The contrast between the deadly antisemitism of Nazi Germany and Nazi-occupied Europe and the safe haven of a pluralistic United States is stark — and comforting for those of us on the right side of what Studs Terkel and many others have called "the good war."[9]

Yet Eichhorn's careful formulations and controlled anxiety serve as a reminder that even in the United States, Jews and other minorities were vulnerable. According to some observers, notions of Jews as shirkers in wartime drew on popular stereotypes and persisted within the U.S. armed forces, particularly among officers.[10] The execution of a Jewish soldier on charges of desertion would have lent a dangerous sheen of credibility to such charges. The idea that only certain kinds of Americans could be effective, courageous fighters was widespread during World War II: African Americans, segregated in special units and generally kept far from combat, rarely had a chance to prove their bravery and value to the cause.[11] Rabbi Eichhorn saw connections between the situations of Jews and African Americans. Back in Arkansas in 1937, he had spoken out in his synagogue to prevent the lynching of an African American, who became the first black man in the state to be acquitted on charges of murdering a white person.[12] Now, however, as a chaplain, Eichhorn was prepared to do as he was ordered.

Happily, Rabbi Eichhorn never had to bear that burden. According to his account, Eisenhower ordered psychiatric examinations for the six candidates for execution. Those tests determined the Jewish soldier to be of unsound mind, unfit to accept responsibility for his actions. Thus, it was not a Jew but the Roman Catholic Eddie Slovik who faced the firing squad on January 30, 1945. And it was not Chaplain Eichhorn but his Catholic counterpart, Father Carl Patrick Cummings, who told the twelve riflemen to do their duty, prepared the accused for his death, and offered him the comfort of his religious tradition.[13] Nevertheless, Eichhorn's account of his brush with the Slovik affair serves as a powerful introduction to the value of the correspondence presented in this book, writings that guide readers into the world Eichhorn inhabited and, in his own way, helped shape.

Eichhorn and the War: The Military Context

Eichhorn's letters both reveal and conceal many important details about the U.S. effort in World War II. In Eichhorn we see embodied the deep commitment of many Americans to the anti-fascist cause, even before U.S. entry into the war. Through his eyes, however, we catch only glimpses of the isolationists, opponents of American involvement, and critics of President Franklin D. Roosevelt. For Eichhorn, Winston Churchill was a hero, and the British, Poles, and Chinese were indisputably on the side of right.[14] Accordingly, when the Japanese attacked Pearl Harbor on December 7, 1941, and the United States declared war on Japan, Eichhorn immediately offered his services as a chaplain.[15] His weak eyes notwithstanding, he was accepted and spent the next twenty-two months at Camp Croft Army Infantry Replacement Training Center in South Carolina. There he took part in training and provided religious services for troops awaiting deployment to Europe and

Asia. This chapter of his career, though less dramatic than what would follow, is represented in some of the letters and documents here. These materials speak to the value of such work stateside and prepare us for Eichhorn's subsequent references to the importance of his South Carolina days when it came to making contacts and learning the ropes of the military.

In March 1944, Rabbi Eichhorn received notice that he was being sent overseas, where he would be stationed with a combat unit in Europe. By early June 1944, he was en route to England, and at the end of the month, he received his assignment to the headquarters of the XV Army Corps, under the command of Major General Wade H. Haislip. After the fact, Eichhorn would describe his appointment as "an experiment to determine whether a Jewish chaplain could function effectively at the corps level."[16] That sense of unpredictability, of being part of an endeavor whose outcome was unknown, pervades Eichhorn's correspondence and reminds us of the chronic uncertainty and upheaval in wartime.

Chaplain Eichhorn's assignment to a corps rather than a division added to the instability of his situation. A corps is constantly in flux, taking on and dropping divisions and artillery units as needed. During its more than nine months in combat on the Continent, the XV Corps was part of the Third, First, and Seventh U.S. Armies. It ranged in size from one to six divisions and from twelve to twenty-seven battalions of artillery. All told, twenty-seven different divisions fought under the XV Corps, and at times, the corps strength reached 150,000 men.[17] No wonder there was so little continuity in the cast of characters with whom Eichhorn interacted and so much physical and mental exhaustion evident in his correspondence.

Not only was the XV Corps extremely mutable; it was almost unbelievably mobile during its months in combat. Such rapid movement presented enormous challenges to Chaplain Eichhorn, but it also makes his letters an extraordinarily useful source on the American experience in wartime Europe. Few other chaplains could boast that their units traversed France, Germany, and Austria, for a total advance of 1,200 miles, on an almost continual offensive. According to the "General Summary" of corps activities prepared by its headquarters for the period July 31, 1944, to May 11, 1945, "In the course of its operations, the XV Corps crossed twenty three major rivers, four mountain ranges and made deep penetrations into the Austrian Alps. Those natural barriers were all defended by the enemy."[18]

By other measures as well, the XV Corps was a resounding success. It participated in some of the most dramatic and significant triumphs of the U.S. effort in Europe: it helped clear the Parroy Forest in northern Alsace and broke through the natural fortification of the Vosges. It took Strasbourg, Zweibrucken, and Saarbrucken and, in the words of U.S. General Jacob L. Devers, "plunged across" the Rhine, "once considered an important military barrier," with "almost no pause." It encircled and captured Nuremberg and then Munich, "one of the most sacred of German cities to the Nazis." Its men were among the first liberators of Dachau, and with the subsequent entry into Austria and capture of Salzburg, they "broke the last remnants of German resistance."[19] Eichhorn was present for all these events, and although prudence and censorship often dictated that he conceal his precise location, subsequent correspondence and the records of the XV Corps enable us to retrace his steps without difficulty.[20]

Eichhorn's letters, written on the spot and in the heat of the moment, reveal the human details of events that we too easily assume we already knew. Who realized that, when the golden swastika atop the speakers' platform at Nuremberg was blown sky-high — a scene immortalized in the film *Judgment at Nuremberg* — the throng of cheering spectators included seven American Jews, who, together with five soldiers from Palestine, "were clustered around the little jeep with the big Magen David." The jeep, of course, carried one proud XV Corps chaplain, Max Eichhorn.[21] Seen through his eyes, the ruins of Nuremberg take on a satisfying — almost delightful — quality whose irony was only enhanced by the fact that the XV Corps took the city on April 20, the Führer's birthday. At the opposite end of the emotional spectrum, Eichhorn's description conveys the horrors of Dachau in vivid, powerful ways. The naked bodies lying everywhere did not smell, he wrote: "There was no meat left on them to rot, just skin and bones."[22]

Eichhorn was not one to mince words or to flinch from the destruction and misery he witnessed. As a chaplain, however, his concern was first for the living, then for the dead. His letters say little about the casualties the XV Corps experienced and inflicted; for that information, we need to turn to corps records. According to the first report after V-E Day, "Even disregarding the many thousands of Germans killed and wounded by the XV Corps, the total battle losses of the Corps (28,710) remain less than one-twelfth of the total number of German prisoners taken by the Corps (352,536)."[23] Instead, Eichhorn writes of the small groups of Jewish survivors he found in France; the sometimes amusing encounters with locals; and the services he organized, such as the Yom Kippur service at Lunéville in October 1944, when the city was still behind German lines.[24] These and many similar passages speak to his energy, resilience, and courage in the midst of violence and disorientation.

Most of Eichhorn's letters only hint at the difficult conditions he and the soldiers around him faced as they fought their way through western Europe. The Battle of the Bulge alone claimed more than 70,000 Allied casualties; for U.S. forces, it was the most costly battle of the entire war.[25] No wonder Eichhorn became impatient when his correspondents back home grumbled about shortages and other hardships.[26] His own life was in jeopardy every day. Indeed, one of Eichhorn's recurring themes was the uncertainty of his situation and of the war as a whole. "Don't expect me to guess when the war will end," he wrote in the fall of 1944. "I'm too busy trying to help win it to engage in foolish theorizing."[27]

Eichhorn's awareness of the unpredictability of his situation reminds us of the difference between the way he and others experienced the war and the way we tend to think about it after the fact. His corps commander, Major General Haislip, recounted an incident that reinforces the same point. In August 1944, the XV Corps set out to capture Le Mans. Intelligence reports indicated an unspecified but large number of German forces in the area. And as Haislip recalled, there was even worse news:

> We were told that there were 800 tanks in our front. Now, in my opinion, that is a hell of a thing to tell a corps when you order it into battle. Believing that this figure was excessive, I told my G2 (intelligence) to pass the word to the divisions that there were 80 tanks to our front. Later, I revised this number downward to about eight tanks. After the first few weeks of fighting, we had destroyed 120 tanks so maybe there were 800 tanks after all.[28]

By March 29, 1945, Eichhorn and the XV Corps had crossed the Rhine River.[29] Although the advance through Germany was rapid,

Eichhorn witnessed opposition of various kinds — from members of the Volkssturm, the citizens' militias formed in the last months of the war,[30] and from residents of the towns and villages the Americans entered.[31] Eichhorn, whose parents were both German immigrants, had some familiarity with the culture and the language, but he made no effort to conceal his dislike of the Germans, whom he contrasted with the more congenial British and French.[32]

The most powerful experience of Eichhorn's time in Germany was his encounter with the concentration camp at Dachau.[33] Like other eyewitnesses, Eichhorn described what he saw, including the piles of corpses, the barracks of the almost-dead, and the acts of vengeance carried out by surviving inmates against guards and capos.[34] As a chaplain, Rabbi Eichhorn played a key role in organizing the first Jewish religious service at Dachau on May 5 — an event that was captured on film and inspired this volume's coeditor, Greg Palmer, to seek out Eichhorn's grandson, Mark Zaid, for documentation. That service can be interpreted as a pivotal moment for U.S. forces in Europe, a point of transition from the role of combatant-conqueror to occupier-rebuilder. Certainly from that point on, Rabbi Eichhorn's own role changed, as did the focus of much of his work — from the American troops to the survivors of the Holocaust, the displaced persons.[35]

Eichhorn's letters in the weeks and months following V-E Day shed light on the nature and challenges of U.S. military occupation. He remained in Europe until October 1945, including a stint in May and June 1945 with the XV Corps in Austria as chief rabbi, a position that he described as "plenty of headaches." His duties there included "caring not only for the thousands of American Jewish soldiers . . . but also the tens of thousands of wandering Jewish civilians."[36] One of Eichhorn's "unpleasant" experiences occurred at Ebensee, Austria, where he supervised a delivery of food to survivors of a concentration camp. The hungry inmates rushed the trucks, and Eichhorn, certain that someone would be trampled to death, ordered the guards to surround the vehicles with fixed bayonets. The mob retreated.[37] Dealing with the locals presented other kinds of problems. Eichhorn's personal feelings about the Germans notwithstanding, he spoke out against the policy of nonfraternization, because he considered it unenforceable and counterproductive.[38] Although he hoped to go home to his family, he was prepared for reassignment to Asia, a possibility that seemed very real to him until he received orders to return to the United States in August 1945.[39] He finally made it in December.

Through the eyes of David Max Eichhorn, we see World War II, American style, not only as the unambiguous triumph of the "greatest generation"[40] but also as a series of events and contingencies where heroism coexisted with fear; where uncertainty, confusion, and disagreement sometimes produced positive results; where loneliness, death, and despair plagued the victors as well as the vanquished and their victims; where everyone involved was a human being, with human failings. Eichhorn's war was no less impressive for its human dimensions — on the contrary, through his eyes, we see the war not as a game of chess but as a drama of real people.[41]

Eichhorn and the Military Chaplaincy: The Professional Context

Max Eichhorn experienced World War II from a particular perspective: that of a military chaplain. Throughout his correspondence he emphasized the importance of that professional designation to his understanding of himself and his purpose. As a chaplain, he believed that his duty was to his country, its cause, and the men in his charge, above all but not exclusively the Jews among them. The Slovik case indicated that Eichhorn's position as a chaplain was not without challenges and contradictions; there were times when he had to swallow his misgivings and defer to the military hierarchy and occasions when he encountered skepticism and even hostility from friends as well as foes.

As a military chaplain with U.S. forces in World War II, Rabbi Eichhorn was heir to a long tradition. Chaplaincies in the United States and western Europe trace their origins back to antiquity, although admittedly, they choose different forebears — from the early Celts to the biblical Hebrews[42] or the ancient Romans.[43] Many of the functions — even the specific tasks — that Eichhorn performed would have been recognizable to chaplains in very different contexts. He exhorted fighting men to courage and sought to provide comfort and meaning in the midst of fear and danger through the maintenance of religious tradition.[44] His predecessors in medieval Europe did so as well.[45] He buried soldiers from his faith, tried to make sure that their graves were marked appropriately, and sent condolences to members of their families.[46] His Christian counterparts from Canada in World War I did the same.[47]

In addition to such recognizably pastoral tasks, Chaplain Eichhorn served as a kind of all-purpose counselor and go-to man: he mediated between soldiers and their wives,[48] supervised German prisoners of war as they cleaned up desecrated synagogues,[49] provided liaison between U.S. armed forces and local populations, censored letters, and distributed cigarettes and reading material. Such utility has a long tradition in the chaplaincy, as attested to in the American Civil War, when chaplains served as scribes, mailmen, medics, and even cooks.[50] Indeed, the combination of religious and practical, earthly functions has been a hallmark of the military chaplaincy in western Europe and North America since at least the early modern era.[51]

If Rabbi Eichhorn shared the tasks and duties of generations of military chaplains before him, he also embodied many of the contradictions and tensions inherent in the position. As shown by the close call with the Jewish soldier who could have been executed instead of Eddie Slovik, a chaplain could find his multiple loyalties — to his military superiors and to his religious community and principles — in conflict. Even for someone like Eichhorn, who had no doubts about the rectitude of the cause for which he stood and the war he supported, such clashes were possible, even unavoidable. How much tighter were the tensions for chaplains in wars that must have seemed, at least to the more open and honest of them, morally ambiguous or even wrong? Civil wars, particularly between coreligionists, genocidal wars, "dirty wars" against civilians, wars to preserve racist domination — all of them have involved chaplains, whether in seventeenth-century England, Germany in the 1940s, or South America and South Africa more recently.[52] Rabbi Eichhorn's experiences allow a glimpse into the complexity of the chaplain's position, even under the best possible conditions.

Eichhorn's letters point to another feature of military chaplains' work in many national and chronological contexts — its emotional intensity. Memoirs by and about chaplains in settings as diverse as the Franco-Prussian War of 1870 and the Korean War almost a century later point to the close — and sometimes painful — relationships between chaplains and the soldiers they serve.[53] Eichhorn wrote of what the men meant to him, how much he appreciated a familiar face and words of gratitude, how it felt to hold religious services for a group of men one day and hear of their deaths the next.[54] He also hints in places of the emotional strain as he was stretched to the breaking point by demands on his time, energy, and goodwill while surrounded by death, destruction, and confusion. Even a chaplain, he admitted, had to get drunk at least once in a while, had to find trusted friends in whom he could confide, had to collapse from exhaustion.[55] Rarely did Eichhorn given in to such human frailty; much more characteristic were his determination, strength, and stoic acceptance of his situation. Still, in poignant ways, his correspondence reminds us of a dilemma of the military chaplain: who cares for the caregiver?[56]

A specific incident related in Chaplain Eichhorn's correspondence captures some of the tensions and opportunities inherent in his position. In the fall of 1944, as the XV Corps moved into France, the Jewish holiday of Yom Kippur approached. Rabbi Eichhorn spoke to the commanding general, Wade H. Haislip, about organizing services for Jewish personnel.[57] Haislip insisted that Eichhorn use the large synagogue in the nearby city of Lunéville. There was only one problem: Lunéville was still in German hands. Eichhorn recounts how he and his assistant nevertheless managed to reach the synagogue one day before Yom Kippur to prepare the site for services. They found the city deserted, with the exception of an American MII (military intelligence) team consisting of an officer and two men. Just that morning the Germans had retreated to the Forest of Parroy, about a mile to the west.

The MII lieutenant greeted the chaplain with incredulity: what did he think he was doing there? Eichhorn explained that Haislip had authorized — indeed, ordered — him to hold Yom Kippur services in Lunéville. And the service took place. Local people cleaned out the synagogue and helped decorate it with lights and flags. Even more surprising, some 350 men arrived, as Eichhorn related, "mostly from the 44th and 79th Divisions, on foot, by jeep and by truck 350 battle-grimed Jewish fighters came to the synagogue for Kol Nidre." For Rabbi Eichhorn, it was the most moving service he had ever held and the only time he had cried since landing in Europe. It was the last religious service for many of the men, who left straight into a "bitter firefight" with the Germans in the Forest of Parroy.

Afterward, the MII lieutenant thanked Chaplain Eichhorn for his "great contribution to military intelligence." He had learned something important from the service, the officer told Eichhorn: The Germans surely had detected the movement of American vehicles and men. If they could have, they would have shelled the synagogue. Since they did not do so, they must have withdrawn their artillery to the middle of the forest.[58] From this exchange, Rabbi Eichhorn discovered that his Yom Kippur service, in addition to being a powerful emotional and spiritual experience, had been bait for the enemy. Fortunately for him and the 350 Jewish soldiers present, the Germans had not bitten.

Eichhorn's account of Yom Kippur at Lunéville points to a perennial challenge of military chaplains: their quest for credibility. The intelligence officer had been willing to risk the life and safety not only of the chaplain but also of hundreds of soldiers in order to establish with certainty the Germans' position. With the words "duty before friendship," he had joked at his disregard for Eichhorn, whom he respected but considered dispensable. From the point of view of military planning, chaplains might be useful, but their importance was secondary; they were nonessential personnel who needed to prove their worth over and over again. One sees this reality reflected in Eichhorn's correspondence, with its combination of pride in his role and occasional evidence of a defensive posture. Rabbi Eichhorn emphasized the courage and significance of his fellow chaplains and noted those who had been decorated for bravery and those killed on duty as a way to prove his own credentials as a "good soldier" to anyone who might have doubts. And indeed, the *Saturday Evening Post*'s 1944 article "Are the Chaplains Doing a Job?" raised these very challenges:

> On the whole, servicemen demand more of a chaplain than that he be a preacher. If he is only a preacher, or is a sissy or if they suspect him of being a hypocrite, or if he nags them about petty things and narrow dogma, they will barely tolerate him; and sometimes they will be downright vicious toward him. But if he can prove to them that he is a man — as in a vast majority of instances — and show them by example that there is no inconsistency between living cleanly, worshiping God, and manliness he can do perhaps the most valuable work being done today toward preserving our civilization.[59]

This issue of credibility is familiar to anyone who has studied chaplains in other contexts, particularly in the modern world. German chaplains in World War II, faced with hostility from the Nazi regime and charges that churches were somehow implicated in the German's defeat in the previous world war, responded with frantic efforts to prove their value and the magnitude of their sacrifice.[60] Literary depictions of chaplains are almost universally negative: Melville's impotent cipher in *Billy Budd;* the alcoholic cynic in Jaroslav Hasek's *The Good Soldier Svejk,* a biting satire of the Habsburg empire in World War I; Joseph Heller's noble but pathetic chaplain in *Catch 22;* and the ineffectual buffoons in *M*A*S*H* and the comic strip "Beetle Bailey." Soldiers' memoirs, at least in the twentieth century in North America, have often been bitterly critical of chaplains. For example, Canadian veterans of World War I described chaplains as "brass hats" who used fancy talk of God to send men "over the top" to their deaths.[61] U.S. veteran and influential scholar Paul Fussell derided chaplains as at best, irrelevant; at worst, offensive. According to Fussell, his only contact with a "real" chaplain in World War II came six weeks before the end of the war in Europe, when he was wounded by a German shell. At the battalion aid station, the chaplain, a first lieutenant, considered himself the men's ethical consultant. According to Fussell, he cheered people up when they got their morphine by "telling them the lie they had done well, and the battalion was proud of them."[62]

World War II marked the high point of the status of military chaplains in the United States. Critical voices would explode during the Vietnam War, as some soldiers came to consider chaplains, like military psychiatrists, their worst enemies, ready to sell them out to the authorities if they could not patch them up sufficiently to go out and kill and risk death for their country.[63] Rabbi Eichhorn faced nothing comparable in World War II, but his correspondence does hint at attacks on his credibility. As a result, he followed with keen interest any public attention given to the chaplaincy, as evidenced by his references to coverage in the popular press.[64]

In the epilogue, Mark S. Zaid mentions the four most famous American chaplains of World War II: Fox, Goode, Poling, and Washington. These men died in February 1943, along with almost 700 other people, when the USS *Dorchester* sank. Their story, one of the great tales of wartime heroism and sacrifice, is also a testament to ecumenism and perhaps an indication that the ultimate proof of a chaplain's value is his death. Chaplains George Fox (Methodist), Alexander Goode (Jewish), Clark Poling (Dutch Reformed), and John Washington (Catholic) were among the first on deck after a German torpedo struck the ship. They calmed the men and distributed life jackets, giving away their own when supplies proved inadequate. Witnesses recall last seeing the "four immortal chaplains" standing arm in arm, praying as the ship went down. At the dedication of the Chapel of the Four Chaplains in the Pentagon, President Harry S. Truman quoted from the New Testament: "Greater love hath no man than this, that a man lay down his life for his friends."[65]

A Good Rabbi and a Good American: Eichhorn and the History of Jews in the United States

Max Eichhorn was not just any chaplain; he was an American Jewish chaplain in World War II. As such, he experienced a particular moment in the history of the military chaplaincy from a specific perspective. His letters reflect this particularity even as they speak to his commitment to ecumenism and his participation in the pluralistic society of the United States. Eichhorn never forgot that he was responsible to his country as a whole and to every one of its soldiers, regardless of their religion. But his work was shaped by his own devotion to Judaism, by his training as a rabbi and a scholar, and by his experiences living and working as a Jew and with Jews in the United States, especially in the South.

Half of the active rabbis in the country — some 500 men — volunteered to serve as chaplains in the U.S. armed forces during World War II. Of those, 311, including Eichhorn, received commissions and entered active service.[66] This remarkable number constituted a first. In World War I, although many volunteered, only 23 Jewish chaplains received commissions, and they were the first official Jewish chaplains in the country.[67] Michael Mitchell Allen, who served Union troops in the Civil War, is sometimes named as the first American Jewish military chaplain, but Allen never achieved formal status. In one of his postwar publications, Eichhorn recounts Allen's story as follows:

> In July 1861, the 65th Regiment of the 5th Pennsylvania Cavalry elected as its Chaplain a young Philadelphia Hebrew teacher, Michael Allen. . . . The Commanding Officer of the 65th regiment,

Colonel Max Freedman, and many of the officers and men of the Regiment were Jewish. Allen handled his assignment in an exemplary manner. His sermons, excellent in tone and content, were obviously intended for a mixed audience of Christians and Jews. In September, a worker from the Young Men's Christian Association visited the camp near Washington, where the 65th Regiment was stationed, and discovered that its Chaplain was neither a Christian nor an ordained clergyman. He raised such a commotion that Allen was forced to resign.[68]

Until World War II, the military chaplaincy in the United States, like its counterparts in Britain, Canada, Australia, and elsewhere, was more or less limited to mainstream Christian groups.[69] There were Catholic chaplains and chaplains from the major Protestant denominations, but very few Jews; those Jews who did serve, for example, in World War I, either had no official standing (the situation in Germany in 1914–1918) or were given positions on the periphery (the U.S. case). Other religious groups had no representation in the military chaplaincy at all.[70] Thus Eichhorn and his counterparts were pioneers who embodied the progress that Jews had made in America over the previous two centuries. Eichhorn never mentioned this fact in his letters; on the contrary, he emphasized the normalcy of his position. Still, he was keenly aware of the novelty of his calling: in his history of Jewish military chaplains, he demonstrated precise knowledge of the names and dates of his predecessors and the conditions under which they broke through the barriers to take their place alongside Christian clergy.[71]

Eichhorn's work as a Jewish chaplain with U.S. forces is all the more remarkable when one considers a topic he himself rarely raised, and never explicitly: antisemitism. In his extensive study of antisemitism in the U.S. military, Joseph Bendersky traces the stubborn persistence of old stereotypes about Jews, even in the "land of the free." As late as 1918, the Army Manual of Instructions for Medical Advisory Boards claimed that "the foreign born, and especially Jews, are more apt to malinger than the native born."[72] The 1930s and 1940s marked the low point, Bendersky suggests, as members of the American officers corps, trained by outspoken conspiracy theorists and critics of Jews, carried negative assumptions out of the classroom and into active service.

In his wartime correspondence, Eichhorn never cried antisemitism, but he did indicate that he detected certain negative ideas about Jews. For example, the notion of Jews as shirkers and cowards was one that he combated actively, presumably because he considered it widespread enough to be dangerous.[73] Similar accusations of Jewish cowardice had rumbled through the German military in World War I, aided by an official inquiry into their veracity, the results of which were never released. Those who carried out the study hinted that the outcome was so devastating that they did not want to be responsible for the anger that gentile Germans might express toward their Jewish countrymen when they found out the truth. In fact, the study showed that Jewish Germans served their nation in at least equal proportions and at an even higher cost in lives than did their non-Jewish counterparts.[74] During World War II, the same kind of rumors circulated in the Soviet Union about the Red Army. Jews supposedly enjoyed the fruits of the war from safe positions behind the lines, where many of their countrymen believed they functioned as profiteers and parasites.[75]

The experiences of American Jewish chaplains in World War II remind us of both the similarities between antisemitism in the United States and elsewhere and the uniqueness of the U.S. situation. The lies and innuendoes might be the same — Jews as cowards, profiteers, and even Christ-killers — but Eichhorn and his counterparts had official standing and institutional support. Thus, when Eichhorn ran into trouble with General George S. Patton, whose attitude toward Jews the chaplain described as "none too friendly," General Haislip intervened on the side of his Jewish chaplain,[76] something unimaginable in the Red Army and beyond inconceivable in Hitler's Wehrmacht.

One example may suffice to illustrate both the presence and the limits of antisemitism in the U.S. military of Eichhorn's day. Floyd L. Parks graduated from the Army War College in 1940, rose to the rank of general, and later became military governor in Berlin. Parks had served as aide-de-camp to former U.S. chief of staff Malin Craig in the 1930s, at which time General George Van Horn Moseley had caused a scandal with his open profession of eugenic ideas, vulgar racism, and blatant antisemitism. Publicly, Craig distanced himself from Moseley, but in private, he showed that he attached little importance to the matter.[77] Certainly Parks would have heard many antisemitic slurs, and he used such stereotypes himself in a joking way, describing a man "with a rather Semitic Cast of Countenance" and his wife as possessing a nose he would know "anywhere." Nevertheless, during the war, Parks had a good relationship with Hersh Livazer, the Jewish chaplain under his command. On occasion, he even attended Jewish services, a practice that deeply impressed Livazer but struck Parks's old boss, General Craig, as hilarious.

In late 1943 and into 1944, at a time when information about Nazi genocide was reaching the United States from many sources and pressure was mounting on the military to take action, Craig continued to rib Parks about what he called "my Hebrew friends," the rabbis with their gift of the gab, who performed "baptism with a 'pair of scissors,'" wore "straggly long black whiskers in which the bats hung," or had "no hair" on their chests at all.[78] Such notions must have played some role in shaping U.S. policies and practices regarding Jews — as potential immigrants and seekers of asylum prior to 1939, as victims of prejudice and mass murder prior to 1945, and as displaced persons after the war ended.

Antisemitism, both blatant and subtle, also affected the work of Jewish military chaplains. Some of Eichhorn's counterparts, for example, reported problems with their gentile colleagues, who had been known to denounce Jews as "Godless Communists." At least one American Christian chaplain described the antisemitic Father Charles Edward Coughlin in Detroit as "the greatest Catholic priest in the world." In response to a request that Jewish troops be excused from an Easter service, another chaplain retorted, "Why shouldn't all men regardless of creed or race pay homage to our Savior? Don't they all come out when a famous general goes by our area? And as to the Jewish men, they have a choice of either the Catholic or Protestant services."[79]

Rabbi Eichhorn, in contrast, reported nothing but harmony with his fellow chaplains. The worst he admitted was Christian ignorance about Jews and Judaism, which could produce uncomfortable situations, even when the intentions were good. In December 1944, Eichhorn and two other Jewish chaplains organized a service for Erev Hanukkah. The XV Corps chaplain, Colonel Gustave Schellhase, a Lutheran, preached "with oratorical brilliance," and an all-Protestant choir sang. "As a special treat," Eichhorn wrote, they had learned what they had been told was the traditional Chanuka hymn, i.e., "Rock of Ages." Unfortunately, no one told them that this was not the same "Rock of Ages" as we use but the one which is sung in Christian churches and when they began to give out with "Rock of Ages, cleft for me, let me hide myself in Thee," I was forced to halt the choir before they shocked our Orthodox constituents by telling them of "the water and the blood, from his wounded side which flowed." It was an embarrassing moment but we managed to smooth it over very quickly.[80]

Eichhorn's anecdote about the wrong "Rock of Ages" provides a glimpse into the challenges of genuine ecumenism and the opportunities the military chaplaincy presented for furthering interfaith relations. As U.S. troops discovered, living together amid shared dangers tended to reduce antisemitism and other forms of prejudice. According to many Jewish soldiers, "there were no anti-Semites at the front line"; in combat, the "Jew shared the same fox hole with his Christian buddy."[81] Many chaplains felt the same way. Rabbi Max B. Wall, who, like Eichhorn, served in Europe in World War II, put it in simple terms: "It started when chaplains got to know one another as human beings."[82] That sense of a common purpose, of contributing to a worthy and vital cause, and being accepted as valuable members of the group boosted the confidence not only of chaplains like Wall and Eichhorn but also of American Jewish soldiers and their families back home. As Eichhorn reported to his wife and children in October 1944, "I don't know how long it will last but, for the time at least, our men are more intensely and proudly Jewish than I have ever known a similar group to be in the States."[83]

Prior to being accepted into the chaplaincy in 1942, Rabbi Eichhorn held a number of positions in the American South. In 1935, he accepted a post as rabbi in Texarkana, a town on the border of Texas and Arkansas. Subsequently, he directed the Hillel at the University of Florida in Gainesville and the Florida State College for Women in Tallahassee. At the same time, he served as rabbi of Tallahassee's Temple Israel. In those locations, Rabbi Eichhorn witnessed a society that included both opportunities for Jews and certain limitations.

Max Eichhorn's father arrived in the United States from Germany in 1893, his mother in 1899. They numbered among the 1,694,842

Jewish immigrants who moved to this country between 1890 and 1914, accounting for 10 percent of all immigrants during those years.[84] Most of the new arrivals moved to the major cities of the Northeast and Midwest — New York, Chicago, Cleveland, and Pittsburgh — and to smaller urban areas such as Columbia, Pennsylvania, where David Max Eichhorn was born in 1906. Of course, there were also Jews in the South, as there had been since 1733, when forty-two Jews of German, Spanish, and Portuguese descent landed in Georgia.[85]

The Jewish communities that grew up in the South were smaller and less confident than their counterparts in the North. According to historian Leonard Dinnerstein, Jews in the South were "particularly concerned about their image in the Christian community,"[86] above all, in the white Christian community. Before the Civil War, southern Jews seem to have accepted the institution of slavery with little ambivalence, which no doubt helped them keep a low profile. Nevertheless, negative attitudes toward Jews carried into the Reconstruction era and the twentieth century, when Jews often became convenient scapegoats in times of social and economic crisis. Some of those tensions came out in 1915 when Leo Frank, a Jewish industrialist originally from Brooklyn, was lynched in Atlanta. Although the evidence against him was practically nonexistent, Frank had been accused and convicted of the 1913 murder of one of his employees, Mary Phagan, a thirteen-year-old white girl.[87] Less than thirty years later, when Eichhorn landed in Europe, the memory of that violence could not have been so distant, particularly in a society where lynchings, Jim Crow, and other injustices against African Americans must have served to remind Jews of their own vulnerability.

Against this backdrop, Rabbi Eichhorn's willingness in 1937 to deliver a sermon calling for his Texarkana congregants to demand justice for a black man charged with murdering a white person and, moreover, to assist a Jewish lawyer in the defense of the accused stands out as all the more courageous and remarkable.[88] The young rabbi had not only his white Christian neighbors to worry about but also the Jews in his community, some of whom no doubt resented the attention he drew to them. It is no coincidence that after the war, when many American Jews became active in the civil rights movement, far more activists came from the North than from the South.[89] Max Eichhorn's hatred of Nazism and every form of intolerance was based not only on firsthand observations of the deadly results of such ideas in Europe but also on experience with institutionalized racism back home.

The correspondence of David Max Eichhorn brings to life a pivotal moment in American history — a time replete with glory, idealism, and success in a "good war," but a time that also had its threatening side. Eichhorn, a patriotic American, a "good soldier and a good rabbi," did not dwell on the dangers, but he saw them all the same. His vision of a better America — the vision that he shared with his family — was based not on naivete but on a clearheaded, realistic appraisal of the state of the world and a profound understanding of the power of an individual to shape his or her destiny, albeit within certain limits and only with a tremendous effort of will. It is this combination of acknowledgment of reality and its ravages, confidence in the future, and eagerness to engage in the process of rescuing, rebuilding, and improving the lives of fellow human beings that makes Rabbi Eichhorn's letters such compelling and inspiring reading.

Max Eichhorn was a scholar and a writer as well as a man of action. In 1931, Hebrew Union College in Cincinnati bestowed on him the title of rabbi. Before the war, he wrote a dissertation on a fifteenth-century Jewish text from Prague and earned the degree of doctor of divinity.[90] During the war, he contributed articles, sermons, prayers, and reports to various publications, mostly Jewish, and contemplated a postwar literary career.[91] Afterward, he authored not only an autobiography, which remained unpublished, but also historical works on Jewish military chaplains in the United States, books of folklore, and reflections on a range of issues from the Book of Ecclesiastes to Jewish intermarriage and Arab-Jewish relations.[92] In all this activity, however, one topic fell by the wayside. Sometime before 1941, Eichhorn began an essay on the biblical Rachel. That project followed him into the war in Europe but apparently not out of it.[93]

Like the editors of this volume, I have not read Rabbi Eichhorn's reflections on Rachel. I can only speculate as to why that character appealed to the serious, politically engaged American rabbi. What did he see in the beautiful young shepherdess who caught the eye of Jacob at the well and, eventually, after being overlooked by her father in favor of her older sister Leah, married that son of Isaac to become one of the matriarchs of Israel? Was it her independence, her refusal to leave her father's home without taking with her the household gods and concealing them even from her husband? Was it the tragedy of her life, a woman who died without seeing her second child and without entering the land promised to her line? Or was it the fact that she is, in biblical terms, an unusual figure: not good, but good enough? Imperfect and unremarkable, but nevertheless desired and chosen, Rachel lived at a crucial moment and therefore played a vital role in events that changed the world.[94] Perhaps it is not so strange that Rabbi David Max Eichhorn might see in Rachel a kindred spirit.

I am grateful to Steven Schroeder of the University of Notre Dame for his expert assistance with the research and preparation of this prologue. A Faculty Research Award from the Graduate School of the University of Notre Dame provided much-appreciated funding. Thanks as well to Rabbi Michael Signer for his advice, to the editors Mark S. Zaid and Greg Palmer for their input, and to Michael Briggs of the University Press of Kansas for his interest and encouragement.

Doris L. Bergen

[1]Eichhorn's August 14, 1944, report to the Jewish Welfare Board (hereafter JWB) noted that he landed on Omaha Beach on July 10, 1944. Details on Eichhorn's experiences in Normandy appear in a letter dated August 19, 1944. On the Battle of the Bulge, see the letter of January 7, 1945. On his entry into Germany, see the letter of March 31, 1945; on Dachau, see especially the letter dated first week of May 1945. Regarding contacts with Generals Eisenhower and Patton, see the excerpt from Eichhorn's report titled "Contacts with the Great and Near Great," describing events in the first half of August 1944 at the so-called Falaise Gap; on General Patch, see excerpt from the same report describing events in October 1944; for his encounter with General Bradley in Verdun, see the letter of October 2, 1944; on Lord Halifax, see Eichhorn's postwar report to the JWB titled "Contacts with the Great and Near-Great," describing events of May 29, 1945.

[2]In a letter dated August 6, 1944, Eichhorn wrote to his wife and children: "I am happy to know that my children are proud of their daddy and I hope that I shall never do anything to make them ashamed. I want them to know and to feel that I am doing as much as my limited abilities allow to be a good soldier and a good rabbi."

[3]William Bradford Huie, *The Execution of Private Slovik* (New York: Dell Publishing, 1954).

[4]See Jürgen Thomas, "'Nur das ist für die Truppe Recht, was ihr nützt . . .' Die Wehrmachtjustiz im Zweiten Weltkrieg," in *Die anderen Soldaten. Wehrkraftzer-*

setzung, Gehorsamsverweigerung und Fahnenflucht im Zweiten Weltkrieg, ed. Norbert Haase and Gerhard Paul (Frankfurt am Main, 1995), 48.

[5]Excerpt from Rabbi Eichhorn's 1969 autobiography (unpublished), describing events of December 1944–January 1945.

[6]The most famous account of a Wehrmacht chaplain accompanying a condemned man to his execution appears in a work of fiction: Albrecht Goes, *Unruhige Nacht* (Hamburg: Friedrich Wittig, 1950). Goes, a Protestant pastor, served in the Wehrmacht.

[7]See the sermon of September 28, 1943, in which Rabbi Eichhorn said, "One-fifth of our number lie in martyrs' graves. The lights of freedom and happiness and mercy have completely extinguished for millions of Jews in Germany and Poland, in France and Roumania." Eichhorn described the use of gas vans in mass killings in a report sent from France to the JWB dated August 14, 1944, and he relayed accounts from Jews who survived Auschwitz in a letter of April 24, 1945.

[8]Examples of Jewish survivors who met their future husbands among their American liberators include Gerda Weissmann Klein, *All but My Life* (New York: Hill and Wang, 1957), and Judith Magyar Isaacson, *Seed of Sarah: Memoirs of a Survivor* (Urbana: University of Illinois Press, 1990). It seems likely that the same Gerda Weissmann Klein wrote the May 15, 1945, "Letter from a Polish Survivor," trans. Chaplain Herman Dicker, in Louis Barish, *Rabbis in Uniform: The Story of the American Jewish Military Chaplains* (New York: Jonathan David Publishers, 1962), 111–13. The author of the letter, listed as "Gerda Weissman of Bielitz, Poland," wrote shortly after her liberation to thank "the soldiers who liberated us to new life, to a future of beauty and joy" (113).

[9]Studs Terkel, *"The Good War": An Oral History of World War Two* (New York: Pantheon Books, 1984). For a discussion of the phrase itself and two possible meanings — a war "good" for American prosperity and beneficial to certain elements of U.S. society, or a morally "good" war against fascism and tyranny — see John W. Jeffries, *Wartime America, the World War II Home Front* (Chicago: Ivan R. Dee, 1996), 8–15.

[10]See Leonard Dinnerstein, *Antisemitism in America* (New York: Oxford University Press, 1994), 136–41; also Joseph Bendersky, *The "Jewish Threat": Anti-Semitic Politics of the U.S. Army* (New York: Basic Books, 2000), esp. 259–347.

[11]For an analysis of one all-black unit in World War II, see William Alexander Percy, "Jim Crow and Uncle Sam: The Tuskegee Flying Units and the U.S. Army Air Forces in Europe during World War II," *Journal of Military History* 67 (July 2003): 773–810.

[12]Excerpt from Eichhorn's unpublished autobiography, describing an incident in Texarkana in 1937.

[13]A detailed description of the role of the Catholic chaplain, Father Cummings, appears in Huie, *Execution of Private Slovik,* 212–33.

[14]Eichhorn explicitly praised Churchill, the British, and the Chinese in a sermon dated October 3, 1940, given at Temple Israel, Tallahassee, Fla. He spoke

movingly of the suffering of children — Chinese, Polish, Belgian, Russian, Dutch, Norwegian — in a radio address of January 3, 1944, at Camp Croft, Spartanburg, S.C.

[15]Regarding Eichhorn's application to and acceptance into the chaplaincy, see letters to Eichhorn: June 22, 1942, from War Department, Office of the Chief of Chaplains; July 6, 1942, from Abram Leon Sachar, national director B'nai B'rith Hillel Foundation at American University, Chicago; and July 7, 1942, from Julian Morgenstern, president, Hebrew Union College, Cincinnati.

[16]See the excerpt from Eichhorn's autobiography dealing with events of June 28, 1944.

[17]Wade H. Haislip, "Corps Command in World War II," *Military Review* (May 1990): 22–23.

[18]Section IV, General Summary, July 31, 1944–May 11, 1945, signed Wade H. Haislip, Lieutenant General, U.S. Army, Commanding, in Headquarters, XV Corps, United States Army, "Action against Enemy, Report After," June 1, 1945, 18–20.

[19]Letter of commendation from Headquarters, Sixth Army Group, Office of the Commanding General, Jacob L. Devers, to Commanding General, XV Corps, May 10, 1945; attachment to "Action against Enemy," June 1, 1945.

[20]For brief coverage, see "XV Corps Leaders Receive Awards," *Stars & Stripes*, March 14, 1945, 8.

[21]Eichhorn to JWB, April 24, 1945.

[22]Eichhorn's report dated first week of May 1945, Dachau.

[23]"Action against Enemy," June 1, 1945, 20.

[24]For Eichhorn's discussion of locating Jewish refugees in France, see report to JWB, August 14, 1944. On his humorous encounter with a French mayor who was eager to please, see Eichhorn to Zelda et al., August 19, 1944. Eichhorn's description of events surrounding the Yom Kippur services in Lunéville in 1944 appears in a letter to the JWB, October 2, 1944.

[25]See David M. Kennedy, *Freedom from Fear: The American People in Depression and War, 1929–1945* (New York: Oxford University Press, 1999), 741–42.

[26]In a number of letters, Eichhorn chastised those back home for complaining about wartime conditions. For example, in a letter to his family dated August 19, 1944, Eichhorn wrote: "Too many letters from back home reflect an unwarranted optimism over the course and possible length of the war and an unwarranted self-pity over the enduring discomforts that, from this particular neck of the woods, seem quite bearable." See also letters to his family dated August 30, 1944, and January 7, 1945: "From far too many of the letters that we get, we can easily discern how psychologically unprepared too many people back home are for making real sacrifice. The complaints that we find in our letters are tragically laughable."

[27]Letter to Zelda et al., October 8, 1944; see also letter of August 14, 1944.

[28]Haislip, "Corps Command," 23.

[29]The *Stars & Stripes* covered the Rhine crossings in front-page detail. See "First Army Crosses Rhine," March 9, 1945, 1, 8; and "7th Army Crosses Rhine," March 27, 1945, 1, 8.

[30]On the Volkssturm, see David K. Yelton, *Hitler's Volkssturm: The Nazi Militia and the Fall of Germany, 1944–1945* (Lawrence: University Press of Kansas, 2002).

[31]Eichhorn described German women throwing grenades down on U.S. troops from second-story windows in a letter to Zelda et al., March 31, 1945. Eichhorn reported the same behavior, this time from both men and women, in another German city in his Passover Diary to the JWB, April 6, 1945.

[32]In Eichhorn's words: "Scenically, I like Germany and Austria better than England or France, but I like the people in the other countries more." Letter to family, May 26, 1945, Salzburg.

[33]See Robert Abzug, *Inside the Vicious Heart: Americans and the Liberation of Nazi Concentration Camps* (New York: Oxford University Press, 1985).

[34]For Eichhorn's descriptions of Dachau, see report dated first week of May 1945, Dachau. For another version, see Eichhorn, "Dachau," in *Rabbis in Uniform*, 63–70.

[35]On the care of displaced persons in the Allied zones, including some useful primary documents, see Abraham S. Hyman, *The Undefeated* (Jerusalem: Gefen Publishing, 1993). In Eichhorn's assessment, the American armed forces, "officially and through the individual GI and the Jewish chaplain," did a "superb" job of acquiring and distributing food and other supplies to displaced persons, "and it is high time that this fact be made known in the history books." Letter sent to Rabbi Judah Nadich after the war.

[36]Letter to Jonathan and Zelda, June 7, 1945, Salzburg.

[37]Report, first week of May 1945, Dachau.

[38]For Eichhorn's stand against the nonfraternization policy, see excerpt from "Contacts with the Great and Near-Great," regarding events of May 29, 1945.

[39]Eichhorn frequently expressed the view that he would be redeployed to Asia. See, for example, letters to family, April 27, 1945, and May 26, 1945.

[40]The phrase comes from Tom Brokaw, *The Greatest Generation* (New York: Random House, 1998).

[41]A deliberate attempt to get away from the war–as–chess game approach is Gerhard L. Weinberg, *A World at Arms: A Global History of World War II* (New York: Cambridge University Press, 1994).

[42]Even the *Saturday Evening Post* of 1944 ventured a theory as to the origins of the military chaplaincy: "There have been chaplains with armed forces ever since Aaron and Hur upheld the hands of Moses at the Battle against Amalek, and among the pagans before that." David G. Wittels, "Are the Chaplains Doing a Job?" *Saturday Evening Post*, December 16, 1944, 92.

[43]Scholarship indicates that the connections between the modern military chaplaincy and the situation in ancient Roman armies are loose at best. See Ralph Mathisen, "Priests, Bishops, and Monks: Military Chaplains in the Roman

World," in *The Sword of the Lord: Military Chaplains from the First to the Twenty-first Century,* ed. Doris L. Bergen (Notre Dame, Ind.: University of Notre Dame Press, 2004).

[44]For example, in a report to the JWB dated October 2, 1944, from somewhere in France, Eichhorn described how his work boosted morale: "After the service, a high-ranking officer who was known to be Jewish but who had tried to conceal his Jewishness and who had made a poor showing in combat, came up to me and swore that, from here on out, he would be a faithful Jew and a good soldier. . . . He would be a better man because of this day's worship. I pray that this will be so and I believe that it will be so."

[45]On chaplains in late antiquity and medieval Europe, see Michael McCormick, "The Liturgy of War from Antiquity to the Crusades," in *The Sword of the Lord;* Michael McCormick, *Eternal Victory: Triumphal Rulership in Late Antiquity, Byzantium, and the Early Medieval West* (Cambridge and New York: Cambridge University Press, 1986); and David S. Bachrach, *Religion and the Conduct of War c. 300–1215* (Woodbridge, 2003).

[46]For example, in letter to Zelda et al., August 30, 1944, Eichhorn wrote that he "visited our cemetery [near Le Mans] and said Kaddish at the grave of each Jewish soldier buried there." Also see the list of graveside services dated October 12, 1944.

[47]See Duff Crerar, *Padres in No Man's Land: Canadian Chaplains and the Great War* (Montreal: McGill-Queen's University Press, 1995).

[48]See Eichhorn's letter to Catherine Maas, January 22, 1944.

[49]Eichhorn got ten German prisoners of war to help clean out the synagogue in Verdun and prepare it for Rosh Hashanah in September 1944. Letter to Zelda et al., September 20, 1944; see also report to the JWB, October 2, 1944, where Eichhorn says that the "erstwhile 'super-men' really did a super job."

[50]For details, see Gardiner H. Shattuck Jr., "Faith, Morale, and the Army Chaplain in the American Civil War," in *The Sword of the Lord;* also Gardiner H. Shattuck Jr., *A Shield and Hiding Place: The Religious Life of the Civil War Armies* (1987).

[51]On early modern chaplains and their duties, see Anne Laurence, *Parliamentary Army Chaplains, 1642–1651* (Suffolk, England: Boydell Press, 1990), and Anne Laurence, "Did the Nature of the Enemy Make a Difference? Chaplains in the English Civil War," in *The Sword of the Lord.* For a view from Prussia, see Hartmut Lehmann, "In the Service of Two Kings: Prussian Military Chaplains, 1713–1918," in *The Sword of the Lord.*

[52]On chaplains in morally compromising situations, see Doris L. Bergen, "Witnesses to Atrocity: German Military Chaplains and the Crimes of the Third Reich," in *In God's Name: Religion and Genocide in the Twentieth Century,* ed. Omer Bartov and Phyllis Mack (New York: Berghahn, 2000). For another case, see the Report of the South African Truth and Reconciliation Commission, which devotes considerable time to discussion of the military chaplaincy and its role in lending legitimacy to the apartheid regime.

[53]An example of the intense relationship that develops between chaplains and their men is William L. Maher, *A Shepherd in Combat Boots: Chaplain Emil Kapaun of the 1st Cavalry Division* (Shippensburg, Pa.: Burd Street Press, 1997).

[54]Regarding Eichhorn's relationship with his men and the intense nature of his work, see letter to Zelda et al., February 24, 1945: "It is no use dwelling at too great length on the horrors of war because only those who have gone through and are going through these things fully comprehend. . . . [for example:] Finding a boy who had been with me at Croft and had been a loyal follower of mine all through France in a hospital with an arm off and both legs crushed. . . . I have an inner urge to work and work and work for these fellows until I can work no more."

[55]See, for example, letter to family, May 26, 1945, in which Eichhorn describes an occasion near Nuremberg when "five of us were so danged tired of moving and being shot at and living like little pigs that one day, . . . we sat down and drank our lunch. We drank and drank." See also letter to family, July 16, 1945, in which he admits that he worked himself "to a frazzle" and was diagnosed by a doctor with a "plain case of nerves caused by overwork and inability to relax properly."

[56]The question of who cares for the chaplain is poignantly raised in Joseph O'Donnell, "Clergy in the Military — Vietnam and After: One Chaplain's Reflections," in *The Sword of the Lord.*

[57]On the factors leading up to the Yom Kippur service in Lunéville (General Haislip's insistence; Rabbi Eichhorn's preparations), as well as a description of the service itself, see report to the JWB, October 2, 1944. A short version of Rabbi Eichhorn's account of the Yom Kippur service in Lunéville appeared in *Jewish Chaplain* 1, no. 1 (February 1943): 9–11. The 1943 date does not accurately reflect the contents of the publication.

[58]According to Eichhorn's report of October 2, 1944, the MII lieutenant explained that he had not informed the chaplain of his plan before the service because, "if perchance you had refused to hold the service, I would not have found out what I wanted to know."

[59]Wittels, "Are the Chaplains Doing a Job?" 13.

[60]For more information, see Doris L. Bergen, "German Military Chaplains in World War II and the Dilemmas of Legitimacy," *Church History* 70, no. 2 (June 2001): 232–47.

[61]See Duff Crerar, "Where's the Padre? Canadian Memory and the Great War Chaplains," in *The Sword of the Lord.*

[62]Comments of Paul Fussell are from a conference on military chaplains, held at the University of Notre Dame in March 2000, quoted in Doris L. Bergen, "Introduction," *The Sword of the Lord.*

[63]For a discussion of how the Vietnam War challenged and changed the U.S. military chaplaincy, see Anne C. Loveland, "From Morale Builders to Moral Advocates: U.S. Army Chaplains in the Second Half of the Twentieth Century," in *The Sword of the Lord;* also interesting are opening sentences of the preface

(dated 1970) in Philip S. Bernstein, *Rabbis at War: The CANRA Story* (Waltham, Mass.: American Jewish Historical Society, 1971): "Against the background of Viet Nam, it is hard to recall that there once was a popular war, but there was. The American people overwhelmingly gave their support to the Allied cause in World War II."

[64]Eichhorn's letters show that he was well aware of public-relations issues for military chaplains, especially Jewish chaplains. See letter to Zelda et al., February 5, 1945, in which he mentions with approval the "SatEvePost article" [Wittels, "Are the Chaplains Doing a Job?"]: "It is one of the very few articles which I have seen which gives a fairly true picture of the work of the chaplains without laying on the goo an inch thick." The only mention of Jewish chaplains in the article comes in the last stanza of a poem by Joseph Auslander: "Accept this praise, O priest and pastor / And rabbi, who in peril strive / To keep the conscience from disaster, / To keep the soul alive!" (90). In a letter to his family dated March 12, 1945, Eichhorn responds to something one of his correspondents said or wrote: "I don't know what it should be that Catholic chaplains are mentioned more in public print than the others, except perhaps because they may have more expert publicity agents."

[65]On the "four immortal chaplains" and, in particular, Rabbi Goode, see Eichhorn, "One of the 'Four Chaplains' Was a Rabbi (1943)," in Eichhorn, *Joys of Jewish Folklore: A Journey from New Amsterdam to Beverly Hills and Beyond* (Middle Village, N.Y.: Jonathan David Publishers, 1981), 184–87. One of Chaplain Alexander D. Goode's sermons, "Toward Eternal Peace," appears in *Sermons and Addresses by Jewish Chaplains in the Armed Forces of the United States*, ed. Committee on Army and Navy Religious Activities (New York: National Jewish Welfare Board, 1944), 18–20. A photograph of Rabbi Goode is in Dov Peretz Elkins, *God's Warriors: Dramatic Adventures of Rabbis in Uniform* (Middle Village, N.Y.: Jonathan David Publishers, 1974).

[66]Eichhorn, "A History of the American Jewish Military Chaplaincy," in *Rabbis in Uniform*, 20. For more on Jewish chaplains, see Julian N. Jablin and Azriel Louis Eisenberg, *The Jewish Military Chaplain* (New York: Jewish Education Committee of New York, 1962); Bernstein, *Rabbis at War;* and Albert Isaac Slomovitz, *The Fighting Rabbis: Jewish Military Chaplains and American History* (New York: New York University Press, 1999).

[67]In 1917, there were 400 English-speaking rabbis in the United States. Of those, 149 volunteered as chaplains during World War I. Eichhorn, "A History of the American Jewish Military Chaplaincy," in *Rabbis in Uniform*, 9–10. See also Bernstein, *Rabbis at War,* iii, which gives the number of Jewish chaplains appointed in the United States during World War I as 26 and specifies that 6 served overseas. Bernstein identifies Rabbi Elkan C. Voorsanger, commissioned in November 1917, as "the first Jewish chaplain to wear the uniform of a commissioned officer."

[68]Eichhorn, "A History of the American Jewish Military Chaplaincy," in *Rabbis in Uniform*, 3.

[69]On the Canadian situation, see Gershon Levi, *Breaking New Ground: The Struggle for a Jewish Chaplaincy in Canada*, ed. David Golinkin (Montreal: National Archives, Canadian Jewish Congress, 1994).

[70]In this regard, the U.S. military chaplaincy has changed dramatically since World War II. There are now chaplains from many, often small, Christian denominations, as well as from religions other than Christianity and Judaism, most visibly, Islam. The war with Iraq brought U.S. Muslim chaplains into the public eye in various contexts. For one example, see Eric Schmitt, "Ex-Chaplain with Detainees Is Charged," *New York Times*, October 11, 2003.

[71]Eichhorn, "A History of the American Jewish Military Chaplaincy," in Rabbis in Uniform, 1–33.

[72]Quoted in Bendersky, The "Jewish Threat," 38.

[73]For Eichhorn's efforts to combat the notion of Jews as cowards and shirkers, see his sermon of October 3, 1940, at Temple Israel, Tallahassee, Fla. Also relevant, but not included in this volume, is his sermon "We Must Fight!" in Sermons and Addresses by Jewish Chaplains in the Armed Forces of the United States, 10–11.

[74]Discussion of the World War I German inquiry appears in Saul Friedlander, *Nazi Germany and the Jews*, vol. 1, *The Years of Persecution* (New York: Harper-Collins, 1997).

[75]In fact, according to historian Zvi Gitelman, "It is estimated that half a million Jews served in the Soviet armed forces in World War Two and that about 180,000, more than a third, died in combat. There were about 150 Jewish Heroes of the Soviet Union (they ranked fifth among the nationalities in this respect, though Jews were eleventh in population)." Gitelman, "Internationalism, Patriotism and Disillusion: Soviet Jewish Veterans Remember World War Two and the Holocaust" (paper presented at "Remembering for the Future: The Holocaust in an Age of Genocide," Oxford, July 2000).

[76]Eichhorn, "Contacts with the Great and Near Great," describing an incident from the first half of August 1944. Patton's antisemitism has been widely documented. See, for example, his description of Jewish displaced persons as "animals," and "a sub-human species without any of the cultural or social refinements of our time." Patton diaries, September 21, October 21, [1945], quoted in Bendersky, The "Jewish Threat," 352.

[77]For an account of the General Moseley scandal, including Chief of Staff Craig's reaction, see Bendersky, The "Jewish Threat," 249–58.

[78]Ibid., 301.

[79]Dinnerstein, *Antisemitism in America*, 138–39. Memoirs by Jewish chaplains provide insight into relations with Jewish and gentile counterparts in various settings. For examples, see Aaron Landes and George M. Goodwin. *The Reminiscences of Rabbi Landes* (Providence, R.I.: Temple Beth-El, 1943); Hersh Livazer, *The Rabbi's Blessing: From the Memories of a Chaplain in the U.S. Army (1943–1965)* (Jerusalem: H. Livazer, 1980); Leon S. Rozen, *Cry in the Wilderness: A Short History of a Chaplain: Activities and Struggles in Soviet Russia during*

World War II (New York and Tel Aviv: Om Publishing, 1966); Max B. Wall, "We Will Be: Memories of a Jewish Chaplain with U.S. Armed Forces in World War II," in *The Sword of the Lord*. Rabbi Wall's account, drawn from an interview with the Shoah Foundation, describes a postwar encounter with an openly anti-semitic British officer who tried to obstruct relief efforts for Jewish displaced persons.

[80]Letter to Zelda et al., December 14, 1944. For more information on relations between American Protestants and Jews, see Egal Feldman, *Dual Destinies: The Jewish Encounter with Protestant America* (Urbana: University of Illinois Press, 1990).

[81]Quoted in Bendersky, The "Jewish Threat," 299.

[82]Wall, "We Will Be," in *The Sword of the Lord*, 190.

[83]Letter to Zelda et al., October 25, 1944.

[84]See statistics in Dinnerstein, *Antisemitism in America*, 58.

[85]Leonard Dinnerstein, *Uneasy at Home: Antisemitism and the American Jewish Experience* (New York: Columbia University Press, 1987), 84.

[86]Ibid., 93.

[87]See Leonard Dinnerstein, *The Leo Frank Case* (New York: Columbia University Press, 1968).

[88]Excerpt from Eichhorn's unpublished autobiography, describing an incident in Texarkana in 1937.

[89]Dinnerstein, "Southern Jewry and the Desegregation Crisis: 1954–1970," in *Uneasy at Home*, 133–45.

[90]David Max Eichhorn, "Anti-Christian Elements of the 'Sefer Nitsachon'" (dissertation, Hebrew Union College, 1931).

[91]Frequently in his letters, Eichhorn mentioned short pieces he was working on for publication. For example, in the letter to Zelda et al., August 14, 1944: "I have written up a number of interesting little anecdotes for the Jewish press and, in due time, you may see them printed somewhere or other." Some appeared in *Jewish Chaplain* (e.g., in the February 1943 issue), a sermon was published in *Sermons and Addresses by Jewish Chaplains in the Armed Forces of the United States*, and a number of pieces were reprinted after the war in *Rabbis in Uniform*. Rabbi Eichhorn is also acknowledged as playing an important role in reading the manuscript and making suggestions for Elkins's book *God's Warriors: Dramatic Adventures of Rabbis in Uniform*, ix. See also letters to Zelda et al., January 7, 1945, on his hope to see an article to which he had contributed appear in *Harpers;* and to Zelda et al., April 27, 1945, on plans for a postwar literary career.

[92]For example, David Max Eichhorn, *Musings of the Old Professor: The Meaning of Koheles, a New Translation and Commentary on the Book of Ecclesiastes* (New York: Jonathan David Publishers, 1963); *Jewish Intermarriages: Fact and Fiction* (Satellite Beach, Fla.: Satellite Books, 1974); *Evangelizing the American Jew* (Middle Village, N.Y.: Jonathan David Publishers, 1978); *Joys of Jewish Folklore; Hagar and Ishmael: A Study in Arab-Jewish Relations* (Merritt Island, Fla.:

Temple Israel, 1985); *Cain, Son of the Serpent* (Chappaqua, N.Y.: Rossel Books, 1985); *Jewish Folklore in America* (Middle Village, N.Y.: Jonathan David Publishers, 1996); and Eichhorn, ed., *Conversion to Judaism: A History and Analysis* (New York: Ktav Publishing House, 1966).

[93]See Eichhorn's reference to a project on Rachel in letters to his family dated June 21 and August 19, 1944: "To give my mind an occasional rest, I work on my 'Rachel' article in the rare moments when I have a little time to spare."

[94]For the biblical account of Rachel, see Genesis 29–35.

UNITED STATES ARMY

Somewhere in England
June 21, 1944.

Dear Zelda, Jenny, Mike, Jerry, Judy, and all,—

In my last letter to you I carried the account of my peregrinations up to the time we got on the boat. In this letter, I shall tell you what I can of the trip across and, perhaps, something of our early days in the United Kingdom.

We were very, very fortunate in that we came across on a big, fast, and beautiful liner — the most gorgeous hunk of metal that I have ever seen. Even though the steamer had been stripped of its pre-war fineries in order to accommodate as many soldiers as possible, it still was a grand looking sight, inside and out. Eight of us, all chaplains, occupied a state-room on the Main Deck, normally meant to accommodate two people, but there was still plenty room to move around. We had an English steward who made our beds and brought us hot water and drinking water, both of which were strictly rationed, whenever we needed them. Our going across was quite without danger and quite smooth.

Most of the letters and reports written by Rabbi David Max Eichhorn while he served as a chaplain in the U.S. Army during World War II were typed, a few were handwritten, and all are transcribed here with as few deletions as possible and largely as they originally appeared. We have corrected minor spelling errors, especially of European place names, but it is worth noting that although Rabbi Eichhorn was sometimes writing under battlefield conditions, in candlelight, on a typewriter balanced on sawhorses or on the hood of a jeep, his spelling, punctuation, and syntax are astonishingly precise and accurate.

The correspondence is presented here in chronological order. In addition to the wartime letters and reports, we have included other materials — from before, during, and after the war — that we hope illuminate Rabbi Eichhorn's character, background, and beliefs, beginning with a 1940 sermon he delivered to his congregation at Temple Israel in Tallahassee, Florida. These additional materials are, with few exceptions, inserted chronologically, based on the date of the event they describe, regardless of the date of the actual document. Among such supplemental materials are excerpts from Rabbi Eichhorn's unpublished autobiography, completed in 1969; letters he received from family, friends, colleagues, and other soldiers; and contemporary media reports that provide a context for his work and the times. The appendix is a transcription of Rabbi Eichhorn's daily log for his last thirteen months in uniform. Also provided is a glossary of the Hebrew and Yiddish words and expressions he uses throughout the letters.

October 3, 1940
Rosh Hashana eve, 5701
Sermon at Temple Israel, Tallahassee, Florida

CAN WE TAKE IT?

There has never been an hour in Jewish history more fateful and more solemn than this. There has never been a Rosh Hashana when the advent of the New Year found a more affrighted or a more unified Israel. There has never been a time when the hearts of a whole people were more hungry for a message of courage, of hope, of assurance that the dangers which beset us on every side will be overcome.

Heavy is the responsibility which devolves upon him who seeks to bring his people a message in such a time. Great is the temptation to shirk that responsibility, to mouth pleasantries and platitudes, to let words of syrupy smoothness flow forth to cover up the ugliness and tragedy of the hour. Perhaps there are those who, on this night, will succumb to such temptation. Perhaps there are some of our spiritual leaders who, on this night, will indulge in a policy of spiritual "appeasement," who will force their lips to utter optimistic prophesies which, in their heart of hearts, they know are empty delusions.

I do not intend to follow such a policy of appeasement. I shall not seek to comfort you with vain hopes or to beguile you with false prophesies. I shall permit myself, for a moment, to put on a cloak of that greatest of all contemporary statesmen, the honorable Winston Churchill, and to paraphrase the honest words with which he announced his war program to the British people. Like him, I shall, on this Rosh Hashana eve, make you no promises of personal happiness or well-being. Like him, I shall predict, for the year 5702, only blood, tears, and sweat. Like him, I firmly believe that the role of the Jew, in the year which lies ahead, will be one that will demand the severest measure of personal sacrifice.[1]

This is undoubtedly quite a digression from the path of "sweetness and light" that is traditionally associated with Rosh Hashana. It may not be the sort of message which some among us want to hear. If that be so, I must say, in all frankness, that those who feel this way need the message of this evening most and that to them especially is this particular sermon directed.

The world today is filled with an admiration and a respect for the British people which has not been felt for many a year. The remarkable courage which has been shown by the English and Scotch and Welsh, from the youngest to the oldest, their determination to stand firm in the face of every threat and brutality, their dogged efforts to keep their chins up and their morale unshattered, all these things have won for them the warm affection of their friends and the grudging compliments of their enemies. Those among us who, before the war, spoke of the British as a "nation of shop-keepers," a cowardly, spineless, decadent people, feel somewhat ashamed of ourselves. To use a very homely phrase, which the British themselves are fond of using, the men, women, and children of Great Britain have shown that they can "take it," and, whether their final role in this world conflict be that of victor or vanquished, there will be none who will deny that the common people of the British Isles have met the military might of Hitlerism gallantly and gloriously.[2]

The simple and direct question which I should like each one of us to ask himself or herself on this Rosh Hashana eve is this: Are we, too, as individuals and as a people, prepared to "take it"? Out of the centuries of tradition of British pride and stubbornness and honor has come this dramatic spectacle of a united people, fighting for its life against tremendous odds, fighting with a valor unexcelled in all of history. We, too, have thousands of years of a noble and honorable tradition back of us. We, too, speak boastfully of our heroes and martyrs and prophets. We, too, have been branded as a race of shop-keepers. We, too, have been accused of cowardice. What will be our answer in the fateful hour when we may be called upon to endure all manner of hardship and to make all manner of sacrifice? Shall we respond to the call with every fibre of our being nerved for battle? Shall we feel the blood of Judah the Lion-hearted surging through our veins? Shall the age-old rallying-cries of our people and our religion rise unbidden to our lips? Or are we destined to fail in such a venture, to prove to be a weak, degenerate, and unworthy remnant of an ancient and noble race? Will we write a new and glorious chapter in the annals of Jewish history or will it be our sad fate to have our short-comings listed on the last page of the last chapter of that chronicle?

Every race and every religion, like every individual, has a definite life-cycle. Like human beings, races and religions are born, grow, live, and die. In their childhood, they lead automatic, artificial existences. Obedience and conformity are their chief virtues. Their distinction between right and wrong is a matter of law rather than of spiritual values. Their religious preachments and practices are on a low ethical level. Their folk-lore is filled with superstitious nonsense. Their God is a man, only bigger. He lives somewhere in the sky. His chief task is to satisfy the whims and fancies of mankind, both here and hereafter. Man does not exist to fulfill the will of God so much as God exists to fulfill the will of man. Religion is, for them, entirely a matter of supernatural power and external observance. The individual feels no inner sanctification, no inner consecration. Races, religions, and human beings, in their childhood, talk much about faith — but it is a simple, blind, unreasoning faith. Judaism passed through such a naïve child-hood and there are some Jews today who, in their religious thinking, have not outgrown that childhood.

Then come the years of adolescence, a great formative period, when new psychic forces are at work. These years are filled with intense physical and mental activity. They are years of questioning and of doubt, years of brooding depression and morbid introspection. The dogmatic infallibility of the childish law-makers is contested and many individuals demand the right to think for themselves. Adolescence is, essentially, a process of mental clarification. It marks the beginning of a larger and finer spiritual consciousness. It is the time when ideals are formed and expounded. It contains an intimation of a more nearly per-fect way of life; but adolescence has one outstanding weakness, in reli-gious thought as well as in the development of the individual: it talks more effectively than it acts. It knows what it should do but it lacks the confidence and the willingness and the ability to do it. Judaism went through a period like that. And we still have with us, in consid-erable numbers, "adolescent" Jews, adolescent not in the number of years they have lived but in the attitudes with which they approach religious and world problems. There are so many Jews who want to be leaders before they have even learned how to be good followers, so many whose mouths are continually open and whose pockets remain shut, so many who are quite willing to teach their fellow-Jews how to sacrifice and to struggle and to endure but are quite unwilling to set their words to the music of sacrificial and useful actions.

In the course of time, races, religions, and individuals reach the years of maturity. This stage is attained when the doubting, wishy-washy attitude of adolescence disappears and is replaced by a posi-tive, constructive, manly philosophy of living. The change comes about mainly through the assumption of responsibilities. In the indi-vidual, these responsibilities take the form of citizenship, of marriage, and parenthood. In the nation and religion, the end of adolescence is symbolized by the use of numerous catch-phrases, such as "helping men to reach the kingdom of God," "building a more just and right-eous social order," "saving the world for democracy," etc. Such matu-rity of thought and action, wherever it is found, contains within itself the sum-total of the experiences and wisdom of some part of the hu-man race, plus the desire to change that which is already good to an even higher good. It is basically unselfish, in direct contradistinction to the thinking of childhood, which is basically selfish. It marks a philosophy of life which moves away persistently from values which are ego-centric toward those which are centered in society and in that Supreme Ideal whom we call "God."

A very young girl, asked by a psychologist to describe her ideal in life, replied: "I would like to be thirty years old, to be beautiful in form and feature, to have a wonderful voice, and to be very rich." A mature woman, when the same query was put to her, answered: "If I reached my ideal, I would like to be what I am, only in a better and finer way; I would like to be a better wife and mother; I would like to be a tower of strength to the suffering and discouraged and an inspiration to those who seek to serve humanity."

The motto of childhood is "Obey! Conform!" The motto of youth is "Be yourself!" And the motto of maturity is "Forget yourself!"

The ideals of the mature person and race and religion may be listed as follows: First, to desire knowledge and to seek the truth. Second, to strive for perfection of body and mind. Third, to use these gifts for the service of man and the glory of God.

These are the ideals of Judaism. These are the goals which have been set before us by Isaiah and Akiba and Maimonides and Spinoza and Einstein.[3] These are the Jewish "Stars of Bethlehem," the lights which beckon us toward a distant, unknown future. They did not appear in the formative period of our history nor were they perceived in our people's youth. They were first seen in the days of our great literary prophets, when Judaism came of age, and, for more than twenty-five centuries, they have been the key-stones of that unselfish and mature philosophy of life for which generation after generation of Jews have suffered and died.

There are some who maintain that the days of Judaism's manly vigor have passed and that the life-cycle of the Jewish people is almost completed, who say that our race will soon go the way of the ancient Roman and Greek and Persian. Perhaps they are right. Perhaps, unheralded and unperceived, the weaknesses of old age have set in and, in a not-far-distant time, the death-knell of Judaism will be sounded. Perhaps we have entered the decay of second-childhood and are attempting to ward off an inevitable end. Perhaps we are not worthy of carrying on the precious philosophy which has been handed down to us. Perhaps so. We shall soon know. For we live in a day of grave decision, in a day when, once again, "God has sounded forth the trumpet that shall never call retreat; He is sifting out the hearts of men before his Judgment seat."[4]

"Verily the Lord knoweth the ways of them that are whole-hearted," declares the Psalmist; "and their inheritance shall be for ever. They shall not be ashamed in the time of evil, and, in the day of trouble, their strength shall increase. For the Lord loveth righteousness, and forsaketh not His saints; but the seed of the wicked will He destroy" [Psalm 37].

We shall soon know. Each one of us will know whether his own philosophy of life is based upon the selfishness of childhood, the indecision of youth, the weakness of age, or the courage and wisdom and consecration of mature Jewish manhood and womanhood. In their bitter hour of trial, the people of Britain and the people of China have shown themselves to be fit bearers of a great tradition. We, too, are being given a like opportunity. The challenge has come and the spirits of countless saints and sages march by our side as we go forth to meet that challenge. We shall, here and now, prove ourselves spiritual giants or spiritual weaklings, craven cowards or lion-hearted sons and daughters of Judah.

> For at least our country takes her rightful place with men.
> Never shall the seas divide her from the world's great
>   need again.
> The old dream has fled forever, that we dwell, serene and far,
> With God's special smile to light us, on some private,
>   separate star.
> All we are the Old World made us. Where it lost we learned
>   to gain.
> We have triumphed through its failures, built our joy upon
>   its pain.
> Toiling centuries have struggled upward on a stony way
> Just to set the torch of freedom where it flames aloft today.
> Shall we, children of the ages, fail them in this mighty trust,
> Let their beacon pale and dwindle, quench its beauty in
>   the dust?
> Rather let us hold it higher, shake its splendor through the sky,

Searching out each nook of shadow till the things of
    darkness die.
Where a woman still is vassal, where a child is still a slave,
There shall rise our instant bivouac, there be digged a
    tyrant's grave.
All the old forlorn lost causes, every fair forbidden dream,
The prophet's hopeless vision and the poet's flitting gleam,
All the hopes of subject peoples, all the dreams of the oppressed,
Must be ours, our hopes, our visions. We can never stay or rest
Till our beacon pales above us, dies into the level ray
Painting every peak and valley with the light of golden day,
Till the rounded earth together, to the last isle of the sea,
All our many-languaged brethren shall be free as we are free.

Praise to all the past that made us in the heat of its desire;
Glory to our elder brothers, those swift runners with the fire
From the dimmest edge of distance, who have perished
    far away,
Far beneath the light we live in, many years before our day.
We are standing in the dawn of a day they did not know,
On a height they only dreamed up, toiling darkly far below;
But our gaze is toward a summit loftier, fairer, mist-encurled,
Soaring skyward through the twilight from the bases of the world.
Other feet than ours may stand there on that mountain's
    lonely crown;
We may faint upon high trails, fall and lay our burden down;
Yet, enough to fill one lifetime is this joy Death cannot touch . . .
Right and faith and hope of freedom! These are ours, and these
    are much.
Wondrous day to be alive in when, with furious might and main,
God is fashioning the future on the anvil-horns of pain!
Every life, however humble, takes a touch of the sublime
From the light that bathes our yearnings in this grey and
    tragic time.
Forward, then! And onward, upward, toward the greater days
    to be,
All the people join the chorus of our hymn of liberty.

Up and up, achieving, failing, weak in flesh but strong of soul . . .
On the march toward Truth Immortal! Truth Immortal is our goal![5]

Amen.

[1]Speaking before Britain's House of Commons on May 13, 1940, three days
after becoming prime minister, Winston Churchill said, "I have nothing to offer
but blood, toil, tears, and sweat. We have before us an ordeal of the most griev-
ous kind. We have before us many, many long months of struggle and of suffering. You ask: 'What is our policy?' I will say: 'It is to wage war by sea, land,
and air with all our might, and with all the strength that God can give us; to
wage war against a monstrous tyranny, never surpassed in the dark and lam-
entable catalogue of human crime.' That is our policy."

[2]Just weeks before Rabbi Eichhorn delivered this sermon, Hitler decided to
delay indefinitely an invasion of the British Isles, shortly after the Royal Air
Force (RAF) defeated a major Luftwaffe raid on London. German bombing raids
continued, with heavy losses on both sides, but the RAF had effectively won
the Battle of Britain.

[3]Isaiah was an eighth-century B.C.E. Hebrew prophet. Akiba (or Akiva) ben
Joseph (50–135 C.E.) was a Talmudic scholar, considered one of Judaism's greatest teachers. Moses Maimonides (1135–1204) was the leader of Cairo's Jewish
community during the Middle Ages and wrote about Jewish history and sacred
texts, including *Guide of the Perplexed* and *Thirteen Principles of Faith*. Baruch
Spinoza (1632–1677) was a Dutch philosopher whose pantheistic doctrine advo-
cated an intellectual love of God. Albert Einstein (1879–1955), the German-born
theoretical physicist who created the theory of relativity, was probably the most
famous Jew living at the time of this sermon.

[4]The first lines of the fourth verse of "The Battle Hymn of the Republic" by
Julia Ward Howe.

[5]The source of this poem is unknown. Some family members contend that
Rabbi Eichhorn wrote it.

*Approximately a third of all the American soldiers who fought in the
European theater during World War II were, like David Max Eichhorn,
of German ancestry. The following excerpts are from the first pages of
his unpublished autobiography.*

I . . . was born on January 6, 1906, at Columbia, Pa., the eldest child and
only son of a men's clothing merchant, Joseph Eichhorn, and Anna (Zivi)
Eichhorn. My father migrated to the United States in 1893 . . . from
Richelsdorf bei Gerstungen, in the province of Hesse, Germany. His

father was a cattle dealer. The original Jewish Eichhorn, centuries ago, must have been a Bavarian Hof-Jude [court Jew] who adopted the surname of his noble patron. I surmise this because: a) Eichhorn is a common name among Bavarian Roman Catholics and uncommon among Jews and b) our family has a coat of arms, which, so far as I know, no Jewish Eichhorn ever uses. My father's mother was a Bacharach. Her brother Joseph was for many years parnas of the very pious Jewish community of Hersfeld in Hesse. He died in the Dachau concentration camp, at the age of 81, shortly after being convicted of "rassenschande."[1] He was accused of having seduced an 18-year-old Christian housemaid!

My mother came to the United States in 1899 . . . from Muelheim-am-Rhein, Baden, Germany, part of the Black Forest country. Her father owned a vineyard.

Also from the autobiography:

In my early years in the rabbinate, I was an ardent pacifist but, as the menace of Hitler loomed larger and larger, my position changed radically. During the summer of 1937, I attempted to enlist in the Abraham Lincoln Battalion,[2] which was being organized in the United States to fight on the Loyalist side in the Spanish Civil War. The recruiting officer in New York City turned me down with the statement that I could do the Loyalists more good supporting their cause as a rabbi in Arkansas than by adding one more soldier to the Loyalist Army.

On January 1, 1935, David Max Eichhorn was elected rabbi of Mount Sinai synagogue in Texarkana, a town on the border of Texas and Arkansas. He held that position at the time of the Spanish Civil War and volunteered for service in that conflict, so it is no surprise that four and a half years later, he volunteered to be an army chaplain immediately after the Japanese attack on Pearl Harbor.

[1]Literally, "racial dishonor." Jews and eventually all non-Aryans were prohibited from having sexual contact with gentiles as part of the Blutschutzgesetze (Blood Protection Act) of the 1935 Nuremberg Laws.

[2]An estimated 3,000 men — 30 percent of them Jewish — fought in the Abraham Lincoln Battalion, sustaining heavy casualties. One-third of all the American volunteers were killed.

June 22, 1942
War Department
Office of the Chief of Chaplains
Washington

Dear Rabbi Eichhorn:

Your application papers for appointment as Chaplain in the Army of the United States have been received in this office.

The Surgeon General has found you physically disqualified by reason of defective vision right 20/200 corrected to 20/15, and left 20/400 corrected to 20/20, for which waiver is recommended for limited service only. It is necessary for all applicants who are found qualified for limited service only to execute a waiver of their physical defects. Inclosed [sic] herewith are forms for your use in executing the necessary waiver. These should be filled out in triplicate, sworn before a competent military authority or Notary Public, and returned direct to this office.

You are under consideration for appointment as Chaplain (1st Lt.) in the Army of the United States and assignment to immediate active duty, and upon receipt of these forms in this office properly executed further consideration will be given to your application and you will be notified of our action at that time.

> For the Chief of Chaplains,
> Carl L. Wilberding, Chaplain, Assistant
> Incl. Waiver for Physical Defect (in trip.)

July 6, 1942
B'nai B'rith Hillel Foundation at American University[1]
Chicago, Illinois

Dear Max:

Your telegram announcing your induction as chaplain was not unexpected. I know how anxious you have been to be of service to your

country and to our people and how anxiously you have been awaiting the induction call. We join in the prayers of all your good friends
and your dear ones, in wishing that the interruption of your career
will be a short one and that you will return to the normal routine of
peace in health and in strength. I know that the experience will be
very valuable for you and will make you all the more valuable to the
ministry.

There will be a spot for you at Hillel if you want it when you come
back to civilian life. Please keep in touch with us, for you know how
interested we are in your welfare.

I am grateful to you for so promptly notifying Rabbi Lorge.[2] It will
be of tremendous help to have him come from Florida while you are
still there so that the work can go on without interruption. Will you
let me know what kind of impression he makes on the community. I
have every confidence that he will be quite successful, especially
when you make his way so much easier.

> With all good wishes, cordially yours,
> Abe
> Abram Leon Sachar, National Director[3]

[1] B'nai B'rith, founded in 1843, is the oldest Jewish charitable organization
in the United States. B'nai B'rith started Hillel — the Foundation for Jewish Campus Life — in 1923 as a network of Jewish student organizations on college cam-
puses worldwide. At the time of his induction, Rabbi Eichhorn was serving as
the first Hillel director at the University of Florida in Gainesville and Florida
State College for Women in Tallahassee (later Florida State University), as well
as rabbi of Temple Israel in Tallahassee.

[2] Rabbi Ernst Lorge (1916–1990) succeeded Rabbi Eichhorn as Hillel director
at the University of Florida and eventually followed him to Europe as an army
chaplain. Rabbi Lorge served Temple Beth Israel in Chicago from 1947 to 1985.

[3] Abram Leon Sachar (1899–1993) became the national director of the B'nai
B'rith Hillel Foundation in 1928. He would eventually become one of the
founders and the first president of Brandeis University, serving in that capacity from 1948 to 1968. He was the author of *A History of the Jews* (1948).

July 7, 1942
The Hebrew Union College[1]
Office of the President
Cincinnati, Ohio

My dear Max:

I was happy indeed to learn that, at last, the Army has acted favorably upon your application for appointment as a Chaplain, and that you are to report for service on July 18. I congratulate you heartily upon this and wish you all success and happiness in this work. The inestimable value of the work I know from the unanimous testimony of quite a number of Chaplains who are already in the service. I want to tell you sincerely that I am proud of you because of the spirit you have manifested in this undertaking. My blessing goes with you, and my fervent prayers for your protection and eventual safe return to your family and to your congregation.

I note the content of your telegram to Lorge. He and his wife have accepted the appointment at a Jewish Camp for service during the entire summer. But I am sure that, under the circumstances, he will have no difficulty in obtaining his release, so that he will come to you immediately, as you have instructed him. You will find him a splendid man in every way and worthy of your confidence and cooperation.

With warm regards and all good wishes, I am ever,
Faithfully,
Julian Morgenstern, President[2]

[1]Hebrew Union College was founded in 1875 and is the nation's oldest institution of higher Jewish education, described in its web site as "the academic, spiritual, and professional leadership development center of Reform Judaism." In 1950, the college merged with the Jewish Institute of Religion, founded in 1922 by Rabbi Stephen S. Wise, a colleague of Rabbi Eichhorn.

After receiving his A.B. from the University of Cincinnati in 1928, Eichhorn attended Hebrew Union, was ordained in 1931, received a doctor of divinity in 1938, and was awarded an honorary doctor of Hebrew letters in 1956. His rabbinical thesis concerned *Seger Hanitsachon*, an anti-Christian polemic written in the fifteenth century by Yom Tov Lipman Muehlhausen of Prague. His 1938 doctoral dissertation was titled *A History of Christian Attempts to Convert the Jews of the United States and Canada.*

[2]Julian Morgenstern (1881–1976) was the first native-born American and Hebrew Union College graduate to become president of the college (1921). Morgenstern received his Ph.D. in Semitic languages in 1904 from the University of Heidelberg. During his tenure as president, Hebrew Union grew dramatically. His books include *The Doctrine of Sin in the Babylonian Religion* (1905) and *As a Mighty Stream* (1949).

After waiting seven months for the birth of Judy, the youngest of his four children, David Max Eichhorn reported for duty on July 18, 1942, to the Camp Croft Army Infantry Replacement Training Center, a 19,000-acre site five miles southeast of Spartanburg, South Carolina. A quarter of a million soldiers trained at Camp Croft before it was declared surplus in November 1946. The site is now a popular state park.

Except for a month at the Army Chaplain School at Harvard University in December 1942, Rabbi Eichhorn (accompanied by his family) was stationed at Camp Croft for almost two years, where he participated in both training and traditional chaplain duties. He was occasionally invited to speak over the camp's radio station, WORD.

September 28, 1943
Camp Croft
Spartanburg, South Carolina

RADIO MESSAGE FOR JEWISH NEW YEAR

I am very glad that Station WORD and the Jewish Welfare Board[1] have made it possible for the Jewish men at Camp Croft to bring this Jewish New Year program into the homes of the good people in this area. I am delighted to have an opportunity to speak to you on this occasion, and to express the hope and the prayer that the coming year will bring victory and peace to our beloved country and success to the cause which we seek to serve.

This Jewish New Year period is not a time for rejoicing. It is, rather, a time for spiritual stock-taking, a time in which we must seek to plan for the future by evaluating that which has happened in the past.

As we search our ancient tradition in an attempt to read the riddle of the future, as we seek to learn from Holy Writ some worth-while lesson which may help us in the months that lie ahead, our attention becomes fixed on the year 721 before the Christian era. In that year, the empire of Assyria was attempting to conquer the world and, in that year, the Assyrians overran the little kingdom of Israel in northern Palestine. When it became apparent that the southern kingdom of Judah was next on the conqueror's list, the Judeans made an alliance with Egypt, hoping that, with the aid of the Egyptian army, they would be able to repel the invaders.

Then it was that the word of the Lord came to the great prophet Isaiah and he warned his people, saying: "The kingdom of Assyria will lead the army of Egypt away captive. Men will be dismayed and ashamed because of their trust in Egypt. And the inhabitants of Judah will say, 'See, this is the fate of those on whom we set our hope, and to whom we fled for help to save us from the king of Assyria; how, then, can we escape?'"

The people of Judah, who had much faith in the wisdom of their prophet, were stricken with terror and they asked, "What shall we do? How shall we save ourselves?" To this, Isaiah replied, "You have looked to the weapons of war for your armory. You have counted the houses of Jerusalem and broken some of them down to fortify the walls, you have built a special reservoir so that you may withstand a long siege. But you have not looked to Him who brought this about. You have paid no heed to Him who planned this long ago."

Then the people, fearing that their doom was sealed, cried out to the prophet, "O watchman of our spiritual destiny, what hour of the night is it? Shall God's light never shine upon us again? Are we to be utterly destroyed, we and our children and our children's children?"

And Isaiah answered them, saying, "The night is not yet finished but morning will come. If you diligently seek the path of righteousness, morning will come."

Tonight, as the old year draws to a close and a new year approaches, the descendants of Judah again stand before their spiritual watchmen with trembling hearts and troubled minds. Again they ask, "O guardians of our spiritual heritage, what hour of the night is it? Will this age of dismal calamity never come to an end?"

One-fifth of our number lie in martyr's graves. The lights of freedom and happiness and mercy have completely extinguished for millions of Jews in Germany and Poland, in France and Roumania. Even in the countries of the United Nations, in Russia and Great Britain and Palestine, the pall of the black-out hangs like a gloomy veil over the lives and thoughts of men. It is only here, here in these blessed United States of America, that five millions of Jews out of a former world-population of seventeen millions, live tonight with no fear of pogrom or Gestapo or Iron Guard or Messerschmidt. It is only here that the lights of freedom and brotherhood burn fiercely and brightly in a world torn by blood-shed and hate.

Small wonder, then, that the advent of this new year finds us in no holiday mood. We Jews are filled with grief and with fear. We mourn for those who have already been stricken and we dread to think of that which may yet happen to the millions upon millions of enslaved, helpless men, women and children of many faiths and many nations who are being beaten and starved to death in that vast concentration-camp known as the "Festung Europa," the Fortress of Europe. We are in dire need of a word of comfort and a word of faith.

For that word, let us turn again to the year 721 B.C.E. and to the prophet Isaiah. The sublime faith of the prophet in the eventual triumph of goodness was richly rewarded. The people of Judah, led by their noble king Hezekiah, strove mightily to follow the path of righteousness. And then, a number of years later, when the army of Sennacherib the Assyrian[2] appeared before the walls of Jerusalem, one of the most miraculous events in all world history occurred. A mysterious pestilence swept through the camp of the Assyrians and wiped out that mighty army. Never again did the Assyrians attempt to conquer Jerusalem.

I do not ask you to believe that Adolph Hitler and Premier Tojo and their devilish crews will meet a similar fate, though stranger things than this have happened. But I do ask you to believe, you who bear within yourselves the seeds of Jewish and Christian faith, you who are determined to seek the path of righteousness, you who acknowledge and serve only one Dictator, the King of Kings, the Holy One, blessed be He, that God will make the right to triumph now and in the future as it has always been triumphed in the past. Even though the present is extremely dark, let us not despair for the future. This advent of the New Year may find us full of grim foreboding but there will be many new years in the centuries to come when men will be happier because we have struggled and men will be nobler because we have refused to retreat.

> Though the heel of the strong oppressor
> May grind the weak to dust
> And the voices of fame with one acclaim
> May call him great and just,
> Let those who applaud take warning
> And keep this motto in sight:
> No question is ever settled
> Until it is settled right.
>
> Let those who have failed take courage;
> Though the enemy seems to have won
> Though his ranks are strong, if he be in the wrong
> The battle is not yet done;
> For as sure as the morning follows
> The darkest hour of night,
> No question is ever settled
> Until it is settled right.[3]

Amen.

[1]Among many other activities, the Jewish Welfare Board (JWB), based in New York City, oversaw the work of Jewish chaplains during the war through an organization it created: the Committee on Army and Navy Religious Activities (CANRA).

[2]Rabbi Eichhorn appears to reference Sennacherib a few years out of place. Sennacherib was the king of the Assyrian empire from 705 to 681 B.C. Although his reign saw several revolts, each was defeated. In 701 B.C. the Egyptian-backed rebellion led by King Hezekiah, which is mentioned in the radio message, broke out in Judah. Sennacherib was never successful in his quest to take the capital of Judah — Jerusalem.

[3]The last two stanzas of "The Inspiration" by Ella Wheeler Wilcox (1850–1919). The omitted first stanza reads: "However the battle is ended / Though proudly the victor comes / With fluttering flags and prancing nags / And echoing of drums / Still truth proclaims this motto, / In letters of living light — / No question is ever settled, / Until it is settled right."

January 3, 1944
Camp Croft
Spartanburg, South Carolina

RADIO ADDRESS

I am indeed happy to have this opportunity to represent the Jewish soldiers of Camp Croft on this special New Year program. I am glad, too, to join my brother-chaplains in expressing the hope that the coming year will bring victory and peace to our beloved country and to all the United Nations.

Last Friday evening most Americans celebrated the advent of the New Year with much less gayety than usual. With the thought of the war uppermost in our minds and with so many of our loved ones scattered all over the world and engaged in mortal combat with the enemy, we were in no mood for parties or festive celebrations. In every military camp here and abroad and in every community, soldiers and civilians alike carried out President Roosevelt's proclamation making January first a day of prayer and a day of re-consecration to the ideals for which we are fighting.

On that day, we thought about many people and many things. We thought of man's inhumanity to man that has brought this horrible nightmare upon us. We thought of the arrogance, the avarice, and the apathy that have been displayed by so many of the nations of the world, the hideous doctrine of race supremacy, the overwhelming desire for political power and material wealth, and the refusal of the healthy and the strong to recognize their responsibility and their duty with regard to the poor and the weak.

We thought of the millions upon millions of homeless and starving men, women and children who wander about aimlessly in lands of darkness and realms of evil. Yes, we thought especially about the little children, Chinese children, Polish children, Belgian children, Russian children, Dutch children, Norwegian children, lifting their tiny, withered arms and turning their piteous, tear-filled faces toward us and silently pleading with us to end their misery and their despair.

We thought of our soldiers, sailors, and marines, of our valiant brothers in the Merchant Marine, of our fine young women in all branches of the service, spending the New Year Day away from their dear ones, many of them in foreign lands, enduring every manner of suffering and sacrifice that war's destructiveness might be kept away from our shores and that the precious freedom which we enjoy might endure in our life-times and for generations to come.

We prayed that God would strengthen the bodies and harden the wills of all His sons and daughters who had dedicated themselves to the cause of the United Nations. We prayed that God would watch over those who were placed in positions of peril, that he would make them fully conscious of the nobility of their mission, that He would support them in trial and in danger, and that He would restore them, triumphant and unharmed, to their families and friends. We prayed for our leaders that they might be endowed with wisdom and with courage and that they might ever seek that Divine guidance which sustains and supports the righteous. We prayed, too, that our people at home might realize how much they can do to hasten the final victory by fostering national unity and individual unselfishness.

Such was New Year's Day, 1944, a somber day, a day of thoughtful-ness, a day of prayer, and a day of hope, May its spirit linger with us throughout this entire year! May each one of us do his utmost so that God willing, New Year's Day, 1945, will be a day of gladness, a day of rejoicing, and a day of triumph!

January 22, 1944
Office of the Chaplain
26th Infantry Training Battalion
Camp Croft, South Carolina

Dear Mrs. [Catherine] Maas:

I have just had a long talk with your husband, Private Monte Maas, who is a member of the battalion of which I am chaplain. Monte has explained to me the situation which has arisen in your marital life and has expressed a keen desire to have your marriage continue. He tells me that, despite your suspicions to the contrary, he loves you very much and has so stated to you in his letters and he is very much upset because you apparently refuse to believe him.

Listening to Monte's words, it seems that the following is the situation: Monte's grandmother supported him for many years until Monte was 17 years of age. In return, Monte's grandmother, now in need, desires Monte to help her. In accordance with this desire, what has Monte done? He has signed over $5 of his monthly pay to his grandmother, to which the government will add an additional amount for her support. Does this, in any way, decrease the amount which Monte and the government have been paying you each month for your support? No, it does not. Will you suffer any financial hardship whatsoever by reason of Monte's action? No, you will not. Who will suffer such hardship? Monte will, because he will have to get along on $5 less each month. Was Monte duty-bound to do what he did for his grandmother? Any religious and ethical person will say that he most certainly was.

Because of what Monte has done, what have you done? You have broken up housekeeping, stored the furniture which Monte and yourself worked so hard to get, joined the WACs [Women's Army Corps], and threaten a divorce unless Monte assures you in clear, unmistakable language that he loves you! And you seem to be entirely oblivious of the responsibility that a wife has toward a husband who is in the Army, of the obligation which you have to cause Monte as little worry as possible so that he can be a good soldier, of writing him cheerful, helpful letters instead of letters that cause him no end of mental discomfort, of trying to help him through this trying period of his life instead of causing him worry and pain.

I believe that you should discuss this entire matter with an unbiased person whom you know to be interested in your welfare, preferably your family minister who married Monte and yourself. And, if the minister tells you that you are wrong, you should have the goodness and the courage to write to Monte immediately and admit that you are wrong and ask him to go on loving you despite your error, which I am sure he will do. You may be doing Monte and yourself a grave injustice, which, once accomplished, could never be righted.

Trusting that you will give this suggestion earnest and prayerful consideration, I am,

Very sincerely yours,
David M. Eichhorn, chaplain

January 30, 1944

Dear Chaplin [*sic*],

Received your letter and want you to know what happened wasn't all my fault. First I'll tell you I said nothing about a divorce in my letters to my husband. I do remember telling my brother-in-law that I don't think Monte loves me any more and that he might ask me for a divorce. You see Chaplin I asked my husband as a matter of fact I begged him to write and tell me if he still loves me. But he never answered my letters. I also tried to tell him I would sign up in the WAACs [Women's Army Auxiliary Corps] if he didn't love me thinking he'd write to me. But I didn't. I have a swell home and I have the best husband a girl could ever want. I really wouldn't want anything to come between us. I love my husband very much and if we ever did split up it would break my heart.

As I read through your letter I realize I've done wrong by telling Monte to have his grandmother's Allotment stopped. What puzzled me was why did she wait so long for support from Monte. I know that wouldn't decrease my Allotment, but it does make my husband's pay short. Right now he needs the money, so he can come home in Feb. I'm working now but don't make enough to send my husband money unless I work until 9 o'clock for 5 days. You see Chaplin I'm not well myself and its really hard for me to work if I don't feel good. Chaplin please don't let my husband know that I'm not in good health. I really don't want him to worry over nothing.

If my husband doesn't come home next month, I'll feel very bad because I promised him I'd send him enough money to come home. Starting Monday 1/31/44 I'm going to work until 9 o'clock up until Friday.

The overtime money I do get I'll send it to Monte so he can put it away for his furlow [*sic*] which I do hope they give him. Chaplin would you tell my husband that I think a lot of him and I can't wait till he comes home to prove to him that I can be a true wife and keep my respect as a serviceman's wife should.

I've already written to my husband asking him to forgive me which I received my answer.

Believe me I am grateful for receiving a letter from you concerning my husband.

Well I find that there isn't anything else to write, except that my husband knows by now that I really love him and that I really didn't mean anything by these letters. I realize I've done wrong by writing Monte such letters. The next time I'll think twice before I write such letters as those I wrote to my husband.

I will thank you again before I close as I appreciate it very much.

> God bless you
> Very truly yours,
> Mrs. Maas

April 24, 1944
Camp Reynolds[1]

Dear Zelda, Jonny, Mike, Jerry, and Judy,[2]

I suppose that, by now, you have arrived in Tulsa and are probably engaged in a keen search for living quarters. I hope that you had a not-too-unpleasant trip and that the old Olds got you there safely and, beyond doubt, weary of traveling.

The seventeen days which have passed since I left have been busy and exciting. In Washington, I was told at the War Department that I might go to England by plane but, from the looks of things, it seems that I shall go by boat. From Washington, I went on to N.Y.C., conferred with the JWB, met some old friends, and mixed business and pleasure. I saw Paul Robeson in "Othello." It was very good. I spent two days in Columbia with dad and Henny.[3] Dad looked much better than I had anticipated. He looks older but is still full of life and opinions. I also spent a half-day with Helene and had lunch with Eli and Norman Corwin.[4] Eli and Helene and Bobby all look wonderful.[5] Eli and Helene continue to be the same conservative, kindly, well-meaning, self-satisfied people they have been for so long. Norman is the same wonderful person he has always been, only more so. He took several hours out of a very busy day to talk with me of many things. He took me to the BBC to listen in on a wonderful 45-minute hill-billy broadcast to England and then we went back to CBS where I listened to a transcription of his Tel Aviv broadcast. It was very good as a whole but rough in spots. I was rather critical in my comment. He jotted down my remarks for use in a re-broadcast that he intends to do of the program soon. I also arranged for him to get material to do a national broadcast on the "Struma" incident.[6]

I left for this camp on Friday April 14th and, with the exception of spending a day in Pittsburgh — 70 miles away — I have been busy getting ready to go overseas. There are, as you know, 9 other Jewish chaplains going with me. We are leaving this afternoon for a port of embarkation and it will probably be some time before you will hear from me again. My address for the present will be A.P.O. 7782, c/o Postmaster, New York City. So far as I know, my ultimate destination remains England.

As you can guess, my typewriter was shipped with my luggage, and so, for the present, I am forced to scribble. I am returning to you, by express collect (the only means of shipment available) the hand bag and foot-locker. The government furnished me with a stronger one than that purchased for me by the good people of Spartanburg. I am enclosing keys for same.

Jerry, be sure to write me a long letter as soon as you can. Mike, have a lot of fun this summer because when the fall season comes you will be going to school with Jonny. And you, Jerry and daddy's little angel Judy, be a good boy and girl and help mama all you can.

>Please remember me kindly to Lily and Hymie and Ronnie.[7]
>With love and kisses for all, I am,
>Affectionately yours,
>Max

[1]Camp Reynolds, in Greenville, Pennsylvania, was an overseas training and replacement depot.

[2]David Max Eichhorn and Zelda Socol were married by Rabbi Ira Sanders on June 23, 1935, in Texarkana, Texas, where Zelda's father, Jacob, owned a women's clothing store and Rabbi Eichhorn was with Mount Sinai synagogue. They had four children: Jonathan (Jonny) born in 1936, Michael in 1938, Jerry in 1941, and Judy in 1942.

[3]Rabbi Eichhorn's father, Joseph (1878–1964), lived in Columbia, Pennsylvania, with his second wife, Henny, a Viennese refugee. Joseph Eichhorn owned a men's clothing business in Columbia for fifty-five years and retired at age eighty in 1958.

[4]For more information about Norman Corwin, see the following entries.

[5]Helene Eichhorn Tash (1907–1999) was Rabbi Eichhorn's only sibling, nearly two years his junior. She was married to Eichhorn's former roommate at Hebrew Union College, Eli Tash, who became a vice president of Macy's Department Store, based in Milwaukee, where they lived with their son, Bobby.

[6]On December 12, 1941, the *Struma*, an old, barely seaworthy cargo barge commissioned by the New Zionist Organization and the Irgun (a Jewish military group), sailed from Constanza in Rumania with 769 immigrants aboard, including 103 children — the last such ship to leave Europe during the war. It was bound for Palestine via Turkey, but the Turks refused to let the passengers leave the ship, and the British denied them permission to enter Palestine. On February 23 the *Struma* was forced to leave port. The next day, on the Black Sea, a Russian submarine torpedoed the ship. All but one were lost.

[7]Lily Socol Viner, Zelda Eichhorn's sister, lived in Tulsa, Oklahoma, with her husband Hymie and son Ronnie. Initially, Zelda and her children stayed with the Viners after Rabbi Eichhorn went overseas. Eventually, they rented a three-room apartment of their own in Tulsa.

Norman Corwin, mentioned in the previous letter, first met Rabbi Eichhorn in the fall of 1932 in Springfield, Massachusetts, where Eichhorn had accepted his first permanent position, as rabbi of Sinai Temple. (His previous rabbinical experience, while still a student at Hebrew Union College, included Temple B'nai Sholom in Huntsville, Alabama; Temple Ohev Sholom in Harrisburg, Pennsylvania; and Temple B'nai El in Logan, West Virginia.) The following is from Eichhorn's 1969 autobiography.

Shortly after arriving in Springfield, I made the acquaintance and came to share an apartment on Maple Street with a brilliant young writer, newspaper reporter and radio newscaster, Norman Corwin. At that time Norman had been greatly attracted to extremely leftist and anti-religious ideologies. I think that I was partly responsible for convincing him that Judaism has more genuine concern for humanity than has Communism. I have derived much pride and satisfaction from my long friendship with this gifted American Jewish writer. Because of my close association with Norman and his connection with the Springfield papers, most of my sermons were printed in extenso in the newspapers. Our little Reform group, which met in the local Masonic Temple, got more publicity than the six much larger "shules" in the city.

It was in a letter to Corwin that Rabbi Eichhorn elaborated on the origin of his name.

Eichhorn is not a Jewish name. It is predominantly a Bavarian Catholic name, meaning "squirrel." The English words "oak" and "acorn" are derived from the same Anglo-Saxon root. The few Jewish families named Eichhorn give various reasons for the origin of their surname. The most generally accepted is that some medieval Jew was a tax collector of some Bavarian landowner and, as was much the custom in those times when Jews had no last names, the Jew took the last name of his protector and boss.

Norman Corwin became a legendary writer and producer in radio's Golden Age, as well as being the author of seventeen books, five stage plays, and the screenplays for The Story of Ruth, Lust for Life, *and other films. Now in his nineties, he teaches at the University of Southern California and in 2001 created a series of dramatic specials for public radio.*

Although Rabbi Eichhorn was told that because of "defective vision" he would not be allowed to serve outside the United States, he received notice from the War Department in March 1944 that he was being sent overseas, and he eventually learned that he would be stationed with a combat unit in Europe. According to his autobiography, when he reminded Rabbi Aryeh Lev in the Chief of Chaplains Office of the stateside restriction, Lev laughed and replied that the restriction had been removed, "because intensive investigation has convinced the military that bullets, properly aimed, make no distinction between the normally sighted and the half-blind."

Eichhorn reported to Fort Hamilton, New York, his port of embarkation for Europe, on April 24, 1944.

Dear Daddy and all,

We miss you very much and think of you all the time. I hope you had a good trip. I hope you will come home soon. Tell granddaddy and Henny that I would like to see them. I got a letter from granddaddy in

Texas. He said that he would come to see us in Tulsa. We are all well. Mother cut Judy's hair and it curls so pretty. We kiss your picture every night but I would rather kiss you in person. Daddy please write to me. Mike loves you, Jerry loves you, Judy loves you, mother loves you and I love you.

Your love son Jonny

May 9, 1944
Somewhere on the East Coast[1]

Dear Zelda, Jonny, Mike, Judy and Jerry,

It will be two weeks tomorrow since I arrived at this Port of Embarkation[2] from the staging area. If I had had any idea that we would hang around here this long, I should most certainly have written you sooner. There was every indication when we arrived here that our stay would be very brief but, as happens so often, the Army's thoughts were not our thoughts and we are still waiting, not knowing from one day to the next what may happen. I figured up to now that it was no use writing because you wouldn't get the letter until I had gotten safely across the pond but I've finally decided that this letter will probably reach you before then since, so far as I can now learn, the letters are not held up until safe arrival is reported. What can be written is very much restricted as there is a strict censorship here and anything which smacks of military information is either taken out of the letter or, sometimes, the entire letter is returned to the author for re-writing. I shall try to word this, my first attempt under censorship, as carefully as possible, so that it does not meet any untoward fate.

I was so glad to get your letters — especially the wonderful news from you, Jonny. You certainly write like a real man and I showed your letters very proudly to the other chaplains. They were amazed to learn that the letters were written unassisted by one so young and they think you are a very smart boy, which opinion, of course, is shared by your daddy. I hope that, as part of your share in the war effort, you will keep writing as often as you can, so that you will help to keep your daddy in good spirits, no matter where he may be. The letters which you wrote to me at Columbia were forwarded to me by Henny only a few days ago — after your letters came from Tulsa — so that is the reason why I have not written to you about them before.

I am so sorry that the trip to Tulsa was so unpleasant — and am deeply grateful to Hymie for having been of invaluable aid. I was surprised to read that the children were ill. All of you have always been such good travelers that this was very unexpected news, indeed. While I didn't expect the car to behave like a brand-new vehicle, I did not anticipate the serious difficulties which you encountered. As far as the garage mechanics had assured me, both the wheel-bearings and radiator were O.K. but the inefficiency of present-day mechanics is well-known and selling the car will probably save many head-aches that an old car and careless fixing will inevitably bring.

The arrangement with Lily is almost too good to be true. It is certainly very generous and kind of her to take you all in to live with her and I sincerely hope that all of you children will behave in such a way that Aunt Lily will never regret having invited you in. I am not too concerned on this score — because I honestly believe that you are much better behaved children than the average and I think that you will confine your running around to the out-of-doors and will treat Aunt Lily's home with the proper consideration. I am very pleased to know that you are all well and happy. It is, indeed, one of life's greatest joys to live in an atmosphere where contentment and love prevails and I am happy that you have found such an atmosphere in Tulsa. Please give my warm greetings to Ely Pilchik when you next see him — and tell him that I was pleased to learn that he is coming into the service — a step which should have been taken long ago by many of our younger rabbis.

As for myself — there isn't too much I can say. I am well and happy. According to my friends and colleagues, I look much more rested and at peace with the world than I did when I first arrived from Spartanburg. I had a cold which has now departed and I also did some damage to my left-hand sliding down a rope during some more severe physical exercises than those to which I have been accustomed. One thing that I discovered very quickly was that I was very much out of condition physically but I think the past month's rest and relaxation has helped a great deal. Since arriving here, my diversions have consisted mainly of sleeping all day and going out at night. We are allowed to leave here at 5 p.m. in order to wend our way to a nearby metropolis and do not have to return until 7:30 the next morning. After the very restricted life of the past few years, this unaccustomed freedom has served as quite a morale-booster and I've taken full advantage of it. However, one can have too much of anything and I'm beginning to feel bored and to look forward to the next step of the adventure. Today, as a fairly typical example, I came back to camp at 2 a.m., slept until 10:30, shot pool until 12:30, ate lunch, and then played gin runny until 4 p.m. It is now close to 5 p.m., when we shall again be free to leave camp. A tough life! But a month of such stuff is more than enough — and I am now anxious to get on with the serious business at hand.

This is the only letter I've written to anybody since I last wrote to you — but I think I'll turn over a new leaf tomorrow and write to Columbia and to Chaplains Gregory and Colden and some of the other folks who are probably beginning to regard my silence with some degree of anxiety or resentment.

I wish I could write more that would be of interest to all of you but many things which I should like to write about are in the realm of the forbidden and so I must content myself and you with vague generalities.

I miss you all and, whenever I see some especially attractive little boys or some adorable little girl, I think of you right away and wish that I could see you. But I am afraid that that will not be for a long, long time and we must all be brave and live life as best we can and have confidence that, in time, everything will work out all right. I am not one of the many foolish optimists who believe that the war will end soon or that the millions of American men now scattered all over the world will be marching back to their home-towns this year or next. Perhaps some of them will come back sooner than others. There are those who will never come back and there are many who will not return for a long, long time. If it be, children, that I am to be numbered among the late-returners, you must make the best of that, too, and be good and kind and helpful to each other and to your mother and all those with whom you come in contact. I try not to look upon either the bright or dark side of things too much but to look at both of them honestly and to meet each situation as it arises without speculating overly much on the future.

Please remember me in fondness to Lil, Hymie, and Ronny — and tell them that I am deeply grateful for their generosity and kindness.

With a warm kiss and a hearty embrace for each of you and hoping to hear from you soon (V-mail will be the speediest method),[3] I am

Your loving husband and father, Max

[1] In this and many subsequent letters, Rabbi Eichhorn was not allowed to identify his location because of military censorship.

[2] Fort Hamilton is located in Kings County, Brooklyn, New York, now at the eastern side of the Verrazano Narrows Bridge.

[3] V-mail was allegedly the quickest and definitely the safest way to get letters to and from soldiers during the war. The original letter was photographed, and only the film was sent overseas, where it was printed as a letter again and delivered. With the government's encouragement, more than a billion pieces of V-mail were sent during the war.

[Blacked out]
[June 6–13] 1944
Somewhere in the Atlantic

Dear Zelda, Jonny, Mike, Jerry, and Judy,

Well, here I am right out on the great big Atlantic Ocean, feeling fine, and bound for the United Kingdom and the battlefront of the greatest war of all time. From now on, I'm going to keep a sort of a diary of various and sundry interesting events that transpire and, from time to time, I shall send it to you. I want you to know of some of the things which military intelligence allows me to tell you and I also want you to send these letters on a sort of round-robin to granddads Eichhorn and Socol and to the Tashes or anyone else that you think might be interested in reading them. Much as I should like to keep in touch with everyone individually, this will hardly be possible under existing time limitations. I should have to write the same things over and over again.

I am sorry that I shall not be with you for the anniversaries which occur this month. However, before leaving New York, I arranged for Jonny to get two religious books which I trust he will read and use with much enjoyment and profit. I also enclose the 4th Service Command insignia which were taken from my uniforms. These you kids can sew on your clothes so that you can look and act like real soldiers.

I suppose that you all think I'm a bad boy for not writing for such a long time. The simple truth is that I just was not in the mood to write. The long delay, first at Camp Reynolds and then at the Port of Embarkation, practically killed any desire that I might have had to do anything remotely resembling physical or mental effort. From April 25th until yesterday, I led the life of O'Reilly, definitely no work and all play, at the P of E. About the only really constructive thing that I did was to organize and lead a Bible class among the Jewish chaplains who were and are still with me. Every morning, for about one and a half hours, we studied the book of Ecclesiastes, an effort which was greatly enjoyed by all. We are continuing our study on the boat.

Day by day, our routine is the same. Ecclesiastes class from 9 a.m. to 10:30, gin rummy until noon, eat, bridge, gin rummy, or a pool game until 5 p.m. At 5 p.m., we left camp to go to a city whose name I cannot tell you but if I say it is the biggest city in the world you may be able to guess its name. There I did plenty of singing and dancing and spent plenty of money — and, according to my friends, looked and acted like the Eichhorn who once was but has not been for some time. Returning to camp in the wee small hours, I hit the hay — and so it continued both day and night. Occasionally I did some work. I mended torn clothes, sewed on buttons, and once immediately prior to our starting on this journey, I did a whole wash by myself, including two shirts, ten pair of hose, handkerchiefs, underwear, etc., etc., and it didn't look bad at all.

I never did get to see Helene but I spoke to her on the phone and I visited Eli at Macy's. I also preached one Saturday morning for Bill Rosenblum on a Jewish Welfare Board Sabbath.[1] There were about 300 people present and they were very complimentary in their reactions. It certainly felt funny to preach to a bunch of civilians and I felt somewhat nervous — preaching thru a mike, and all that.

I was very much touched by the Father's Day greeting which you all sent to me and thank you very much for it. I am very happy to know that you are all feeling well and that you children are getting along so nicely. I hope that will continue to be your contribution to the war effort during my absence. I show your pictures every chance I get and I want all of you, "scholar" Jonny, "jolly" Mike, "butch" Jerry, and "Queen" Judy, to always live up to the good things I tell people about you.

I certainly treasure the last letter you wrote me, Jerry. I trust that you will live up to your promise to always be a good boy and help mother all you can. As I think I told you once before, it may be a long, long time before I can come back and you must be prepared to take my place for as long as that may be necessary. You, in your whole make-up, are so much like me that I do not doubt that you will do and act exactly as I should have done and acted. I hope that mother will write to me that you are a very big help to her. Thank you for your blessings and good wishes, Jonny. They are heartily reciprocated and I hope, too, that God will watch over you and mother and Mike and Jerry and Judy throughout the years to come. And it begins to look as though you may be the second Eichhorn to enter the Hebrew Union College ten or so years from now.[2] If that should be your ambition, it would please me very much. And I like to know that you and your brothers and sisters kiss my picture and think of me each night before you go to bed — but I don't want you or anyone else to cry whenever you think of me. I miss you just as much as you miss me but, for all the money in the world, I wouldn't want to be anywhere else than where I am, working with the finest bunch of men I ever knew for the greatest country and the greatest cause in the world and, no matter what happens, I hope that you will always be brave and keep your chin up and never cry and feel proud that your dad is part and parcel of a great crusade to keep this country a good place for you to live in — and neither I nor any of the rest of those who are with me will come back in one piece until that crusade has been at least partially won. The rest of the crusade will be fought after we get back with certain narrow-minded bigots and certain folks who should be in uniform instead of sleeping in comfortable beds and eating good food and seeing how many rooms they can paper with bonds purchased with money made from this bloody mess.

SOMEWHERE IN ENGLAND

Here I am. Don't have time to write now but, in my next, I'll try to tell you as much as I am permitted about the trip over and my first days here — during which I have already seen much of both Scotland and England.

Love, Max

[1]Bill Rosenblum (d. 1968) was the rabbi of Temple Israel in New York City before the war and for many years thereafter.

[2]Jonathan Eichhorn graduated from Hebrew Union College in 1962; his father preached the sermon at the Consecration Service at his ordination. After three years as a military chaplain stationed in Germany, the younger Eichhorn became rabbi of Temple Emanuel in Kingston, New York, where he served for thirty-five years until his retirement.

When he was deployed to Europe, Rabbi Eichhorn lived much of the time out of a jeep or near headquarters that moved frequently. So it is understandable that he rarely saved the letters he received from home. He simply did not have the room. Although his wife, Zelda, wrote frequently, only one undated, handwritten page of a letter from her survives, placed here at the approximate time it was sent.

Have you seen Yetta yet? Have you seen any more mutual friends? What do Londoners do for amusement — when they find time for it? Is London a pretty city — in spite of the many bombings? Have you seen Churchill or the King — his family? Silly questions but I want to know so much — and you can tell one so little. Are the soldiers (ours) happy — Do they complain as much overseas as they do at home?

Please take care of yourself. Don't lose any weight. Do you get enough to eat? Are you sure there isn't something you'd like for me to send you?

Tell me about some of your men — And do write often. The Children send you loads of love and kisses — And we want to know if you miss us.

Love and kisses from your loving Wife Zelda

June 21, 1944
Somewhere in England

Dear Zelda, Jonny, Mike, Jerry, Judy, and all:

In my last letter to you I carried the account of my peregrinations up to the time we got on the boat. In this letter, I shall tell you what I can of the trip across and perhaps something of our early days in the United Kingdom.

We were very, very fortunate in that we came across on a big, fast, and beautiful liner — the most gorgeous hunk of metal that I have ever seen.[1] Even though the steamer had been stripped of its pre-war fineries in order to accommodate as many soldiers as possible, it still was a grand looking sight, inside and out. Eight of us, all chaplains, occupied a state-room on the Main Deck, normally meant to accommodate two people, but there was still plenty of room to move around. We had an English steward who made our beds and brought us hot water and drinking water, both of which were strictly rationed, whenever we needed them. Our journey across was quite without danger and quite smooth, except for about 1½ days of rough weather during which two of us took to bed. Not me, however. Thank the Good Lord and knock on wood and all that — my tummy took everything in fine shape and I didn't miss a meal. Because of the large number of men on the boat, we were only served twice a day and supplemented our diet with Hershey almond bars and sandwiches furnished in advance by the JWB. The meals on the boat were extremely good and we ate in real style. We carried our life-belts with us wherever we went and had life-boat drill every day but, fortunately, did not need to make use of this knowledge.

(It is now two days later. I have just returned from a 24-hour pass and have been working since noon today censoring mail. But I'll tell you about these things when I reach them in due time in the narrative.)

One of the earliest thrills on the boat-ride was when the steward told us that our state-room had been used by the Right Honorable Winston Churchill on one of his trans-Atlantic crossings.[2] He used it as a living room. Another similar thrill came a little time later while I was luxuriating in the very lovely bath-tub which Winston had also used. A tall, fine-looking blond was shaving in the same bath-room in which I was luxuriating. In walks another officer and addresses said blond as "Lieutenant Eisenhower." After the other officer left, yours truly, just to keep our previous conversation going, asked the blond if, perchance, he was related to "the" General Eisenhower. Casually the officer replied, "He's my daddy." Whereupon Eichhorn discovered, quite by accident, that this modest, quiet, skinny, but muscular blond in the stateroom next to his with whom he had been very friendly without ever being interested enough to ask for his name, was none other than the son of General Ike, just graduated from West Point, and on his way over to join his daddy!

I met others of interest on the boat — a Major Safer, nephew of Rev. Safer, the Jacksonville circumciser — and at least a half-dozen Jewish boys from Croft.

There was a very lovely room on the boat fitted out as a synagogue and we conducted services there every morning at 8 and every night at the same time. In addition, we assisted the ship chaplain in every way that we could — visiting the men all over the ship, distributing magazines, games, and prayer books. The rest of the time we played cards, saw movies and stage shows, and really had a very enjoyable time. No dances though — the only women on board were a few nurses and English soldieresses and they were not much in evidence.

After this pleasant ride across the Atlantic, we arrived in good spirits and ready to go to work in the United Kingdom at the job of chaplain-izing which was so rudely interrupted on April 7th. But such was and is not yet to be. Weeks have passed and my orders have not yet come. Of the original crew, [Hirsch] Freund, Al Goldstein, [Arthur] Brodey, and [Lewis] Milgrom have gone on to their allotted tasks but the rest of us are still awaiting our assignments. We are situated in a so-called Replace-ment Depot[3] until the Army decides where we shall go and what we shall do. We have been expecting these orders for the last few days and shall be very happy when they arrive. Our present routine is as follows: Reveille at 6; breakfast at 7; then to work as a mail censor from 9 to 12; dinner; more mail censoring and some gin rummy until 4; get dressed for formal retreat which is at 5; supper; and then either a movie or more rummy or a six-hour-pass (the usual thing) to a near-by small town. The officers are taken in on a special truck. In town, we walk or play minia-ture golf or go to a dance (held 3 nights a week) or sit in a pub and drink English un-iced beer. The truck goes back at 11. By 12 we must be in bed. What a well-regulated existence. Every ten days or so, we are eligi-ble for a 24-hour pass to a big city about 20 miles away [London] where civilization goes on at a slightly accelerated pace. I've been on one such binge thus far, as previously mentioned. That week happened to be the "Salute The Soldier Week" (the English equivalent of our War Bond Drive) and this particular day was American Day. There was a fine parade of American soldiers in the afternoon which was witnessed by large crowds. The greatest amount of applause was reserved for the WACs and the Negro soldiers (especially the latter), a none-too-subtle reflection of what the average British thinks of the manner in which certain Americans regard certain other Americans. I then saw a fine show called "Salute the Soldier," an historical portrayal of the development of the British Army. Then went to a dance, then back to the hotel where I was staying where I met a Mr. Max Green, an English Jew who has charge of RKO movies in the British Isles and he treated me to a Scotch and other delicacies which helped enliven the conversation until the wee small hours. Then to bed, most wonderfully soft and downy bed I'd slept in since leaving the States. (On the boat, we slept on cots and at the Replacement Depot we are sleeping on straw mattresses.) The next morning—back to the Depot and the usual routine. So it continues both day and night.

A number of other items of interest—The Jewish chaplain at this depot is Max Sandhaus,[4] brother of Mr. (Captain) Grantz of Croft. . . . I followed my usual bent while here and organized a refresher-school during the last ten days here for my fellow-chaplains. I supervised courses in map and compass reading, first aid, graves registration, and duties of a combat chaplain. It was very enjoyable and I think that both the students and myself learned a great deal. . . . I met one of my former Croft cantors here, John Mognus by name, and also Dorothy Charles' husband (Dotty is the girl you liked who used to help me with the Friday refreshments).

June 28th

My orders to move have come at last. I am to join the headquarters staff of an Army Corps "somewhere in England." I'll let you know my new address and my exact duties when I get set there. I leave here early tomorrow morning. At last, at last, it seems that I'm really going to get a chance to go to work. I have a hunch (only a hunch—no positive information) that I may get a chance to ride across the Channel before many weeks have passed. Limited service, eh? Ho, ho!

I was quite pleased to learn that my talk was used at the Tulsa confirmation. I don't believe I ever told you that it was also published in a Baptist ministerial journal a few months ago. I haven't done any more on the "Rachel" article.[5] Haven't been in a very literary mood. I'm a little too close to more serious business at present. My thoughts have been concentrated as much as possible on the grim work that lies just ahead and also on having as good a time as I can while I can. I have an idea that, for some time to come, there won't be many more good times.

I haven't heard from anybody — which is not surprising — since, aside from letters to Chaplain Gregory (while I was still in the U.S.) and Judge Josephs[6] and the few letters I've written to you, I have not written to anybody. I never was much at this correspondence business, especially when I have to write by hand. Maybe when I settle down to a more regular routine, I'll be in the mood to write hither and yon. As I suggested in my last letter, please circulate this communication around the family as I am sure the opportunity to maintain an extensive correspondence with many people will be entirely lacking. I shall be happy to hear what's doing in the "auld country" from any who may have the time and inclination to write. I am not going to mail this letter until I reach my new post so that the outside of the envelope will bear a new APO address to be used in future communications.

I got a big kick out of that announcement that I addressed a Spartanburg WCTU [Women's Christian Temperance Union] meeting after leaving Camp Croft. Must have been two other people.

In my next I'll tell you all I can about my new assignment.

Love to all the family and more especially to all of you. Stay good, kiddies, and don't give mama any trouble so that you can be doing your bit to help with the war on the home-front. Here's a big kiss for each one of you — X X X X X X.

> Your hubby and papa,
> Max

P.S. I haven't told you anything about England or the English because that would be a book in itself. I've learned quite a bit about the people and the country in the short time I've been here and I'll try to answer any questions. I may say that in general, I like the country and the people much more than I had expected to like either.

[1]In his autobiography, Rabbi Eichhorn reports sailing to England on the *Queen Mary*, along with 10,000 officers (many destined to replace those lost on D-Day) and 7,000 officers and men of the Seventh Armored Division. The *Queen Mary* was requisitioned from Cunard Lines in 1940 by the British government. Stripped of everything but the essentials, the 2,300-passenger luxury liner became a troop ship that, at maximum capacity, could carry 15,988 troops. Because Rabbi Eichhorn reports being one of 17,000 on his voyage, it is likely that he overestimated the number of his fellow passengers.

[2]Because of their size and speed — the ability to outrun German submarines — Churchill credited the *Queen Mary* and *Queen Elizabeth* with shortening the war by a year.

[3]Replacement depots, called repo depos, were universally hated by GIs. They were bureaucratic morasses where there was almost nothing for troops to do but wait. Rabbi Eichhorn's was the 10th Replacement Depot in Litchfield, England.

[4]After the war, Morris "Max" Sandhaus became the first rabbi at Mishkan Torah Synagogue in Greenbelt, Maryland, a part-time position he held while serving as the Jewish representative of the Veterans Administration Chaplain Service.

[5]In his correspondence soon after leaving Camp Croft, Rabbi Eichhorn makes a number of references to "the Rachel article." No evidence of this work, in either draft or published form, has been found. We suspect that as his chaplain duties increased dramatically, he abandoned the article.

[6]Judge Louis Josephs of Texarkana was a key figure in a 1939 racial episode involving Rabbi Eichhorn. See page 87.

July 2, 1944
Headquarters, XV Corps
Somewhere in England

Dear [Rabbi] Phil [Bernstein][1]:

Here comes the first of those narrative reports which we were requested to send to JWB from overseas.

At long last, the 10 fugitive Jewish chaplains who had languished so long at the POE "somewhere in the East" embarked for England early last month and arrived in the United Kingdom in due time, safe, sound, and without untoward incident (except for two of our number who were slightly sea-sick). On board the boat, we held services morning and evening, studied the book of Koheles on two occasions, and assisted the transport chaplain with personal conferences and the distribution of games and religious literature. We also attended daily chaplains' conferences.

Upon arrival in the United Kingdom, we were sent to Replacement Depot #10 where we languished some more. We were assigned to duty in the mail censorship department, a very interesting assignment.[2] I organized and conducted a chaplains' refresher course for my colleagues. A 24-hour course was conducted in first aid, map and compass reading, graves registration, and practical problems. The instructors were First Aid: Freund, Milgrom, Eichhorn, and the Lt. Colonel who was in charge of the Depot Dispensary; Map and Compass: Lt. Taylor (an engineering officer) and Eichhorn; Graves Registration: Lefkowitz; and Practical Problems: Sandhaus. It worked out very well. We also had a couple more sessions on Koheles (when we disbanded we had reached the end of Chapter Six — we had some swell arguments but all in fun, especially Al Goldstein and myself — Al insisted on regarding Koheles as an adolescent while I took the more traditional stand). We had a conference with Chaplain Nadich and Mr. Sills.[3] I preached at 2 Sabbath evening services and attended 2 held in the morning. (Riddle: Guess how long we were at the Replacement Depot?) I also attended a very interesting mid-week Protestant service in a near-by town and heard an address by the Episcopal bishop of Japan. His description of the Japanese, based on 40 years' residence in Japan, did not correspond to the generally accepted notions. He said that, intrinsically, they were good people but that they were helpless tools of a military clique. Where have I heard that before?

On June 29, I was assigned to the Headquarters of the Fifteenth Army Corps for duty. As you probably know, this assignment is a direct outgrowth of Rabbi Brickner's visit to these parts.[4] The nature of the assignment can be judged from a short letter which the corps commander will send to all unit commanders and chaplains. The letter follows:

"1. A Jewish chaplain has been assigned to this headquarters for the purpose of setting up facilities to meet the religious needs of all Jewish personnel within this Corps.

"2. As soon as practically possible, this chaplain will make the necessary personal contact with each unit in order to assist the unit commander and unit chaplain to establish such facilities.

"3. It is desired that all unit commanders and unit chaplains give this undertaking their full support."

I am to serve as advisor to the Corps commander on Jewish religious matters and also to serve personally those units which have no Jewish chaplains. There are two Jewish chaplains in the XV Corps, Manny Schenk and [Herman] Dicker,[5] but there is quite a handful of men who have had no chaplain and they become my special care. This will involve almost continual traveling on my part and, while I will be part of the Corps staff and will maintain my office at Corps headquarters, I won't be in the office very often. However, a Warrant Officer, Mr. Felix Miller, will be in the office at all times and he will open all business correspondence and handle as much of it as he can in my absence. I shall try to get back here at least once a month for a few days and even oftener if practicable.

The Corps chaplain is Colonel Gustave Schellhase (American Lutheran),[6] a really swell guy, and the assistant Corps chaplain is Lt. Col. Dan A. Laning, formerly a very popular professor at Chaplain School at Harvard. I am #3 on the staff. Under us is Warrant Officer Miller, and also a staff sergeant, a buck sergeant, and two corporals. "Like a mighty army moves the church of God." (Just noticed that I forgot to note that Chaplain Laning is a Roman Catholic.) Incidentally, I am a "surplus" or non-TO officer which means that, in all likelihood, I shall never be promoted, although the scope of the job definitely calls for a major's leaf.

I have been placed on DS tomorrow to go see Chaplain Nadich and Mr. Sills to explain to them the nature and scope of my new job so that we may make whatever plans are necessary.

There is a colonel on the corps staff who holds a very responsible position who is definitely Jewish but seems to take no interest in Jewish activities and a Lieutenant Colonel Goldstein, a highly respected officer, who is definitely Jewish "an dam proud of it," if you know what I mean. Also 2 captains, 3 lieutenants, 1 warrant officer, about 20 non-commissioned officers (including a master sergeant), and about 15 privates, of our faith.

This morning I conducted a general service for the troops of a Quartermaster Company near here. Among those present was a Lieutenant Leiter, whose wife, Bee Leiter, works in Rabbi Toubin's office.[7] Please convey to the young lady my assurance that her husband is in the best of health and spirits. The lieutenant seemed somewhat startled when I showed up to conduct a service for his company of Goyim. However, they survived the experience none the worse for the "ordeal."

> With all good wishes, I am, Cordially yours,
> David M. Eichhorn

P.S. The balance of the revolving fund in my possession stands, on July 1, 1944, at $263.10.[8]

[1]Rabbi Philip S. Bernstein (1901–1985) was the executive director of CANRA, the JWB agency that recruited, evaluated, supplied, and coordinated the work of all Jewish chaplains during the war. Before and after the war, Bernstein was rabbi at Temple B'rith Kodesh in Rochester, New York. His books included *What Jews Believe* (1950) and *Rabbis at War: The CANRA Story* (1971).

[2]Censoring the mail of enlisted personnel was a common assignment for lower-ranking officers, especially chaplains. Letters were checked for information that the enemy might find useful, but also for morale issues, especially a "weakening of desire" among the troops. Letters in foreign languages (from an immigrant son to his parents, for instance) were always suspect, and if the censoring officer did not speak the language, the letter usually was not delivered. This was especially true of letters written in German, Polish, and Italian. Officers generally censored themselves, with sporadic checks from their superiors.

[3]Rabbi Judah Nadich (b. 1912), the first Jewish chaplain in the European theater, was General Dwight Eisenhower's special adviser on Jewish affairs. In that capacity, he was instrumental in getting aid to Jewish refugees and camp survivors during and after the war. The author of *Legends of the Rabbis* (1994) and *Rabbi Akiba and His Contemporaries* (1998), Nadich became rabbi of Park Avenue Synagogue in New York City in 1957 and, as of this writing, is rabbi emeritus there. John Sills was an official with CANRA and the JWB.

[4]Rabbi Barnett R. Brickner (1892–1958) was the administrative chairman of CANRA. Accompanied by Rabbi Aryeh Lev, Rabbi Brickner toured American military facilities in the fall of 1943, interviewing commanding officers, chaplains, and others to determine how Jewish chaplains might be most effective during the remainder of the war. The result was a series of recommendations to the JWB and the War Department, including the suggestion that rabbis be assigned to headquarters at the corps level.

[5]Rabbi Herman Dicker (b. 1914) was a German immigrant to the United States, which made him ineligible to be a chaplain. He enlisted in the army as a private and became a chaplain shortly after becoming a naturalized American citizen. After the war, he was a noted author, with a specialty in East Asian Jewish populations.

⁶Colonel Gustave Schellhase (1897–1961), one of eight brothers from Willowdell, Ohio, was a graduate of Capital Academy and the founder of Truth Lutheran Church in Detroit. He served as pastor there until entering the service in his forties and returned to Truth Lutheran at the war's end.

⁷Rabbi Isaac Toubin (1915–1986) would eventually become director of the JWB European office. After the war, he served as assistant executive director of the American Jewish Congress and was a noted sculptor.

⁸CANRA issued each Jewish chaplain going overseas a "suitcase Ark, with Torah," as well as funds (on average, $50 a month in 1944). CANRA assumed that, unlike their more numerous Christian comrades, rabbi-chaplains would have greater out-of-pocket expenses for such things as transportation to contact Jewish troops, kosher meals for themselves and Jewish GIs, and books needed to prepare sermons and study courses. The chaplains were required, in their monthly reports, to account for their expenditures.

In his autobiography, Rabbi Eichhorn further elaborated on his wartime assignment and the nature of the XV Corps.

On June 28th I received my orders. I was to be the Jewish chaplain on the staff of the Commanding General of the XV Army Corps,[1] the first Jewish chaplain in the history of the American Army to receive such an assignment. This was to be an experiment to determine whether a Jewish chaplain could function effectively at the corps level. An Army corps, in WW2, was a tactical unit, with assigned heavy artillery, motorized reconnaissance and anti-aircraft battalions, and engineer and ordnance groups, plus an attached force of minimally three combat divisions, two infantry and one armor, and of as many more such divisions as the assigned mission seemed to require . . . including our own assigned units, the corps strength varied from as few as 75,000 to as many as 150,000 men. At no time during our 9½ months of combat did we have more than two Jewish chaplains in these attached divisions; most of the time there was only one and sometimes none. My job was to serve those assigned and attached units which had no chaplain.

[1]The commanding general of the XV Corps at the time of Rabbi Eichhorn's assignment was General Wade H. "Ham" Haislip (1889–1971), who in 1914 introduced Mamie Dowd to his good friend (and her future husband) Dwight Eisenhower. After the war, Haislip commanded the Seventh Army and eventually became vice chief of staff of the army. He retired from active duty in 1951 and spent the next fifteen years as governor of the Soldiers Home.

At the end of the war, Rabbi Eichhorn wrote a report, presumably for the Jewish Welfare Board, titled "Contacts with the Great and Near Great." It concerned those occasions during the war when he had crossed paths with famous people. His June 1944 conversation with John Eisenhower aboard the Queen Mary *was part of this report, as was the following account.*

It was sometime during the first half of August, 1944. The XV Corps, to which I was assigned (first Jewish chaplain, incidentally, in U.S. military history to be directly assigned to a Corps HQ — the other fellows who claim this distinction were assigned to a Corps subsidiary unit and then *attached for duty* to their Corps HQ, which is an important technical distinction, in that I was an organic part of the HQ and they were not), was serving as the leading element of George Patton's Third Army in a mighty effort to bottle up the main Panzer strength of the German army at the so-called Falaise Gap. Our force formed one side of the pincers movement which was to accomplish this objective. The other side of the pincers was to be formed by the British Army moving out of Caen under Field Marshall Montgomery. The trouble was that the British side of the pincers did not move far or fast enough and so many of the German Panzer divisions slipped through the hole created by the inability of the British to seal off their part of the line. If the maneuver had been completely successful, the European phase of the war might have ended long before it did.

While this life-and-death struggle was going on, the following incident occurred:

General George Patton[1] was an outstanding military tactician but there are quite a number of indications that his attitude toward Jews was not the most friendly. One of these indications is that, throughout all of World War II, he had no Jewish chaplain assigned to his Headquarters, although there was a vital need for such a chaplain at the Army HQ level. The result was that, in Normandy and in France, from July to September of 1944, whenever Patton's HQ needed a Jewish chaplain, which was quite often, it would call in the nearest Jewish chaplain, who frequently was yours truly.

Even under the most intensive combat conditions, Patton ran his headquarters with a "spit-and-polish" generally reserved for more peaceful surroundings. His officers had to wear neckties, keep their shoes shined, and so forth. One of Patton's most rigidly observed prohibitions was that against officers driving their own vehicles. This task was to be performed only by the driver regularly assigned to the vehicle. Any officer caught violating this prohibition was to be fined fifty dollars.

So here it was, early in August, and, for one reason or another, I had been summoned to Patton's HQ by his Army Chaplain, Jimmy O'Neill. My assistant, Irving Levine, was a grand person but quite nervous, almost as nervous as I was. I just did not trust him at the wheel of our jeep as much as I trusted myself, especially in this particular period when it might be necessary to get out of the jeep tout suite and hit the ditch a couple of times a day, by reason of the rapid approach of a German Messerschmidt, which had the unpleasant habit of strafing every Allied vehicle along its route. So I was in the habit of driving the jeep myself most of the time, including this particular trip to Patton's HQ. My "old man," General Wade Haislip, was an able administrator who demanded only that the members of his staff perform their assigned duties satisfactorily and who did not harass them with petty tyrannical nonsense. General Haislip had no objection to his officers driving their jeeps, if they so desired.

As I approached Patton's HQ, I was stopped by an MP [military police], taken to an MP officer and informed that, since I had been caught driving a vehicle in Third Army HQ territory, I would have fifty dollars taken out of my next pay check. When I returned to XV Corps HQ, I reported the matter to my beloved boss, the Corps Chaplain, Gustav Schellhase of Detroit. He reported the matter to the G-1 who reported it to the Chief of Staff who reported it to the Corps CO.

The next day I was informed by Chaplain Schellhase that General Haislip wished to see us right away. After General Haislip queried me about the facts of the occurrence, he called General Patton on the field telephone. "George, you old basket," he bellowed into the telephone, "bad enough that you refuse to have a Jewish chaplain in your headquarters and bad enough that you keep borrowing ours so often that you are interfering with his work here, but now, instead of appreciating the help which our headquarters is giving you through him, you harass him by trying to impose the regulations of your headquarters on him. I have no objection to his driving his jeep to your HQ or anywhere else. So, you old son of a birch, you either have this fine revoked and instruct your MPs to lay off my officers or I will give a direct order to this Jewish chaplain that he is to ignore any future request for assistance that may come from your headquarters." Since I did not hear General Patton's response, I cannot quote it verbatim. However, I am certain that it was equally forthright and uninhibited. The fine was revoked and I was subjected to no further annoyance by the Third Army MPs.

This is what happens sometimes in the work-a-day lives of top military commanders in the midst of life-and-death struggles.

[1]George Smith Patton Jr. (1885–1945) was one of the best, and one of the most controversial, military leaders of the war. California-born and a 1909 graduate of West Point, Patton was a member of the 1912 U.S. Olympic team, competing (and placing fifth) in the modern pentathlon. His military career began as an aide to General Pershing, chasing Pancho Villa in Mexico. His first action in World War II was leading the First Armored Corps in the 1942 invasion of North Africa. After the American defeat at Kasserine Pass, Patton was put in command of the Second Corps and promoted to lieutenant general. In April 1943, he was given command of the new U.S. Seventh Army, soon to spearhead the successful invasion of Sicily. Though victorious, Patton was sharply criticized for slapping a soldier he thought was malingering. In January 1944, Patton took command of the Third Army in England, but in an attempt to confuse the Nazis, it was not part of the D-Day invasion. Patton's Third Army arrived in Europe on July 28, 1944, and began sweeping across northern France, covering at one point 600 miles in two weeks, with many subsequent triumphs. By V-E Day, the Third Army had liberated or conquered 81,522 square miles of territory. During the occupation of Bavaria, Patton tried to justify the use of ex-Nazis in important administrative positions and suggested publicly that the United States and Britain should rearm the Germans and fight the Russians. For these remarks, which were embarrassing to the Truman administration, he was relieved of command. On December 9, 1945, his car collided with a truck near Mannheim, Germany. Patton died of his injuries twelve days later and was buried in the military cemetery near Hamm in Luxembourg.

July 24, 1944
HQ XV Corps
V-mail

Dear Zelda,

I have not been assigned an assistant as yet but hope I shall get one very soon. I run hither, thither and yon conducting services. I conducted 1

Thursday, 2 Friday, 1 Saturday, and 5 yesterday with the size of the groups ranging from 14 to 101 for a total of 229 in attendance including 1 Jewish female Red Cross worker. I have met a number of men who were at Croft when I was there. Yesterday I met an officer from New Hampshire who is a cousin of Max Wexler. He told me that Yetta Wexler is in the WAC and is in England.[1] He promised to send me her address.

I can tell you now that both times I was in London I was there while the buzz-bombs were in the air.[2] The Londoners, like the English people in general, have a lot of guts and they carry on business as usual. I slept through one of the worst raids without even knowing it was in progress. When I came down stairs next morning, the lady at the desk asked me if I had spent a comfortable night in the shelter. "What shelter?" queried I. "You mean to say that you stayed in your room during all that excitement and noise?" asked she. "What excitement and noise?" returned I. "You certainly are a brick," says she. I understand that, from an Englishman, that is quite a compliment, but I certainly didn't deserve it. I hadn't the least idea what was going on or I probably would have been one of the first to hightail it to the nearest air-raid shelter.

The London subways are marvelous. They are three times as far underground as the subways in New York. They make very good shelters and whole families bring their bedding down to the subway every night and sleep there. It makes rather uncomfortable sleeping but it is much safer than sleeping on top of the ground. It is the most effective fox-hole I've seen anywhere.[3]

Love and kisses to all, and especially yourself and the kids.

Max

[1]Max and Yetta Wexler were Russian immigrant siblings who settled in Texarkana in the 1930s and were members of Rabbi Eichhorn's congregation there. Yetta was a noted pianist.

[2]"Buzz bomb" was the British nickname for the Germans' V1 rocket, which began falling on Britain a few days after D-Day in 1944. Of more than 9,000 V1s launched during the war, 2,500 were successful in reaching their targets. The faster, bigger, and more deadly V2s, or "doodlebugs," began supplementing V1s in September 1944.

[3]During the Battle of Britain and subsequent rocket attacks on London, thousands of people sought shelter in the subterranean stations of the London Underground system.

July 28, 1944
Hq XV Corps

Dear Jonny,

I have just received your letter of June 15th and I was very happy to hear from you. It took a long time for this letter to get to me because you did not send it by air-mail and because you sent it to my old address. So when you write again, please send the letter by air-mail and I shall probably get it much faster.

I can not tell you where I am at the present time and when-ever Uncle Sam allows me to tell you I shall do so. Yesterday I sent you some English copper and silver money. The English names for these coins and their value in American money are: half-penny (copper, 1¢); penny (copper, 2¢); three-pence (brass, 6¢); six-pence (silver 12¢). I also sent a typical English newspaper, a theatre program, a history of an English cathedral, my mess ticket from the steamer on which I crossed the ocean, and one or two other pieces of printed matter. Please save these things for me. English boys and girls are very much like those in the United States except that there are more blondes. They love chewing gum and stop the soldiers as we walk along the streets and ask "Any gum, chum?" Because of the war, many young boys are working on all sorts of jobs. They have grown up very quickly and have not had much time for play.

I am glad to know that you are feeling O.K. I feel fine. I shaved my moustache off before I left the USA and so many people who knew me failed to recognize me that I have let it grow back again. Now it looks about the same as ever. However, now I have a GI hair-cut, that is, my hair is cut off to within a quarter-inch of my head so that it does make me look very funny, especially with the V-for-victory bald spot which I have in the front part of my head. I miss you very much but, as I told you in an earlier letter, we must all realize that it will probably be a very long time before we shall see each other. Even if everything goes well until the end of the war, it will probably be some time after the war ends before I shall return to the US. Please take care of my little doll Judy and of Mike, Jerry and mama. Act like a big man and do not cause your mama or Uncle Hyman or Aunt Lil any trouble. Love and kisses to you and to everybody.

> Your daddy,
> Max

Dear Daddy,

Why haven't you been writeing to us? Daddy we found a house. I hope you received my letter Daddy. I hope you are well Daddy. We are well and happy. I hope the war will be over soon. I hope you enjoyed Father Day. Daddy please tell me where you are when you get my letter. Do you miss us. We miss you very much. We had to move twice in one week. I was going to camp school. Since we are going to move it is to far to go. I hope all the chaplain are well. Daddy why did you shave off your mustache. Its been so long since we have seen you. I wish I could see you right now. Tulsa is a beautiful city. I wish you could come and stay with us. Everyone that sees Judy loves her and loves Jerry too. Ed [unreadable] came to see us for a day. We were surely glad to see him. I went to the station with Aunt Lil to meet him. Keep well and please write to us. Love and kisses from Mother, Jerry, Judy, Mike and me.

> Your loveing
> Son, Jonny

August 6, 1944
V-mail

Dear Zelda, Jonny, Mike, Jerry, Judy, and all,

It was a great pleasure to get your cheerful letter of July 8 and to learn that, for the time at least, everything is going more smoothly. Your new place sounds as though it has certain advantages that cover up whatever disadvantages there may be and I hope that you will be very happy living in it. Ice cream and Hebrew schools are so remote from me at present that it is good to be assured that they still exist. I am happy that you are contemplating sending the boys to Hebrew school. I am sure that they will be very grateful to you in later years if you send them now and I am all for it. (I am once more under the handicap of writing this in near-darkness — so if I happen to make many typing errors you will know why.) Mr. and Mrs. Shackman sound like very lovely people. Please tell them that I am deeply grateful to them for the splendid help they have been to you. It is in situations like these that one learns the true nature of people and discovers which are willing to lend a real helping hand to those who need help. It is wonderful to read all the fine things about our beautiful and lovely Judy. Please give her a fond kiss for me and tell her that daddy is so proud of her and so happy that she, so early in life, has learned the art of making other people happy. It is a gift that I pray she may keep with her all the years of her life. I certainly agree that none of our children is inherently bad — nor is any child, for that matter, bad by nature. They are whatever their elders make them. Although we may not have done the most perfect jobs along this line, I am quite sure that our kids can stand comparison with any similar group of kids of their own age and station. When you write to Mary Jane and Louise, please extend hearty congratulations and good wishes from me and also if you write to any of the people in Spartanburg. I have delayed writing to the Wrubels and the Weinsteins until we are granted permission to give fuller details of our present activities. I am well and doing whatever it lies in my power to do. I am happy to know that my children are proud of their daddy and I hope that I shall never do anything to make them ashamed. I want them to know and to feel that I am doing as much as my limited abilities allow to be a good soldier and a good rabbi. And they must know that, in their limited ways, they must all be good soldiers too. I may meet Arthur somewhere along the line. I shall write him when the occasion seems propitious. Sam Rappoport has not yet let me know just where he is located. If you find out, please let me know. Glad you enjoyed the war-show. The reality is even more exciting. Love and kisses to all.

Max

Tulsa
August 11, 1944

Dear Daddy,

We received both of your letters. Mother got sick and I fixed her sup-
per and cleaned the house. And bathed Judy, and Jerry, and Mike.
Aunt Lil cooked and cleaned for us during the day. Mother is Feeling
Fine now.

Tomorrow we are going to see the show to see *Snow White and the
seven Dwarfs*. We four children play together every day. Ronnie comes
to see us almost every day. I will be glad when Sunday school and
Hebrew classes start. Oh yes, I'll even be glad when school starts.

Take good care of yourself daddy dear and may you return safely
home to us real soon. Love and kisses from all of us.

Your loving son Jonny

August 14, 1944
Somewhere in France
V-mail

Dear Zelda, Jonny, Mike, Jerry, Judy, and all,

At last we are allowed to mention what you probably have guessed
long ago — that, Lafayette, we are here again. Just when we got here
is still unmentionable but it was far enough back that I think that I
may call myself, without exaggeration, a bit of a veteran. I have not
been able to write for a while because I have been just too busy and
too tired to write. I am writing you after an all-day jaunt of about 125
miles over various and sundry parts of the territory that you read
about in the papers. I have not been in my "office" since last Tuesday
nor do I know how long it will be before I am able to visit it. I suppose
that there will be quite a bit of mail waiting for me when I get back
there eventually as, in addition to our other duties, my assistant and
myself have been writing hundreds of letters to the families of the

men we have met. Since last Tuesday, we have visited quite a number of hospitals in this area, trying to comfort the Jewish patients and holding services. I am now (beginning today) visiting the various units of one of our divisions and have just now (9:15 p.m.) finished holding a service for one of them. I do not think I shall ever have a more attentive or a more appreciative congregation. This is a rugged life but a very satisfying one which is full of ever-new complications, thrills, surprises, and enjoyment. One gets so much pleasure out of simple little things and one learns to thrill to such common-place matter as a spring onion or a clean sheet or a piece of real white bread. One learns, too, I think, what it really means to share and what a real friend really is and one learns, too, I regret to say, how selfish a really selfish person may be and how big a fool a fool can really be. I feel fine and am taking quite good care of myself and not running any more risks than are absolutely necessary. I have written up a number of interesting little anecdotes for the Jewish press and, in due time, you may see them printed somewhere or other. Many others I can not tell at the present time and they will have to wait for a more opportune occasion. I shall write you what I can and when I can. I hope that you are well and happy and that you are doing your part in this great struggle. I heard President Roosevelt on the radio yesterday. It is truly wonderful to think that people in all circumstances all over the world were able to listen to his message. He spoke very sensibly and I hope that his warning against over-optimism is heeded by people at home. There is no doubt that we are winning but anyone who ventures to predict how long or how short the war will be does so from the safety of an easy-chair thousands of miles away from the actual conflict. Those who are doing the actual fighting know that only relentless activity and sober realistic thinking will hasten the day of victory.

> Love and kisses to all,
> Your daddy and hubby,
> Max

August 14, 1944
France
[Report to the Jewish Welfare Board]

Today I have come to the end of a search, a search which lasted five weeks and covered many a blood-bathed mile. Because of the military censorship I cannot tell you the exact name of the village where I am at the time writing this. Let it suffice to state that it is not too far from the French village of Le Mans and that it is a little rural town which only days ago was filled with the sounds of war and now is quiet in that strange sort of way in which all towns and countrysides are quiet after the sights and noises of warfare have proceeded on their fearsome way. A beautiful sunset fills the evening sky as I sit on a bench in the middle of a grassy pasture, balance my typewriter on two sawhorses and recall a period of my search — my search for French Jews who have escaped the keen eye of the Gestapo and the crazy wrath of Hitler.

Ever since landing on Omaha Beach July 10, I have been asking people in the various cities and villages through which we have passed, "Are there any Jewish people here?" Invariably, the reply has been a sad shaking of the head and a "Non, messieur, there are no Jews left here." Once, when I inquired at a Norman farmhouse near Perriers, a grave peasant woman (after giving me a welcome gift of two precious chicken's eggs) told me a gruesome tale. The Jews of that part of Normandy had been gathered together last April, with a number of Christian hostages, and had been transported to Germany. There the Jews had been placed in specially prepared vans and had been literally boiled to death by being exposed to jets of live steam that spurted at them from the inside of these vehicles of destruction.[1] The Christian hostages had been forced to bury the bodies of their Jewish friends. The hostages had been told that they were to return to Normandy and tell their neighbors what they had witnessed. They were to tell their neighbors that they would meet a similar fate if they aided the Allied troops if and when these troops invaded their country. This tale had been told my informant by a woman who had been one of the hostages.

Today I had come to visit an evacuation hospital, to contact its Jewish personnel and to seek to comfort its wounded patients. Later I visited the 647th Medical Clearing Company which was nearby. When I returned to the hospital, I was met by my assistant, Corporal Irving Levine of Chicago, beaming as only Irving can beam. "Chaplain," he cried excitedly, "while you were gone the most astounding thing happened. A lady and two children came into the area with a basket filled with eggs and pears to give to the wounded (the French have been wonderfully generous in sharing their pitifully small possessions with their American liberators, especially in their gifts to the wounded and their flowers showered upon the heads of the living and the graves of the dead). When this lady passed our jeep and saw the Magen David on it, she became very excited and ran up and asked in the purest Yiddish, 'Bist du a Yid?' Chaplain, you could have knocked me over with a feather. I told her I sure was and we've been chewing the fat in her French Yiddish and my best Chicago Yiddish ever since. She is waiting for you at the jeep."

Yes, there she was, standing by the jeep, holding in her hands a Jewish Welfare Board Siddur which Irving had given her. She was trying to read the first Hebrew book she had seen in five years. She was about 35 years old, prematurely gray (as were all the other adult refugees I was yet to meet, save one), but very alert looking and supremely happy. Her children, a boy of twelve ("I hope now he will be able to become Bar Mitsva," she said) and a darling girl of nine, looked quite typically French. She had been born in Poland but had come to France when she was four years old and she regarded herself as almost native-born French. Her husband, a Polish citizen, had been in a concentration camp in East Prussia for two years. She had not heard from him in seven months. She had left Paris when her husband was arrested and had come with her mother and children to a village eight kilometers from the hospital. Her family had been protected by the mayor and the villagers, all of whom knew that they were Jewish. Only once had she been in danger. An English warplane had bombed the village by accident. A woman, whose home had been destroyed and whose child had been killed by a bomb from this plane, threatened in retaliation to turn the helpless Jewish family over to the Vichyites.[2] The villagers told the grief-crazed mother that, if any harm were to come to the Jewish strangers in their midst, her own life would be forfeit — and that ended that. Later we met our refugee's mama, a haggard old woman of 69, very poorly dressed, who cried when we talked to her and, in very fluent Yiddish, assured us that not one day, during all her troubles, had she neglected to say "Krishma" — and now God had answered her prayers.

I went back to the 647th to tell the good news to one of the grand-est persons I have met in the American Army, Captain Haim Agus of Brooklyn, who, for more than a year, has been acting as "rabbi" of this medical unit. "You have nothing on me," said Haim, "I've just found my first Jewish family, too. A dapper French gentleman walked in here a while ago and wanted to know if there were any Jews he might talk to and the CO sent him to me. We will visit him this evening and I promise you that you will meet the bravest and most intelligent Jew you have met in a long time."

Captain Agus did not exaggerate. He introduced me to Ben Zion Frydman, frontline fighter in World War I, founder in 1937 and general secretary of the Ligue Internationale des Anciens Combattants Juifs, frequent contributor to the *Pariser Heint*,[3] and editor in 1940 of *Der Yid-dishe Kempfer, The Jewish Combatant,* which the Nazis suppressed after three months. The Nazis have not aged him. He is every inch a man and every inch a fighter. He has been attacking the Nazis by word of mouth and by pen ever since Hitler came to power. Things got too hot for him in Paris a year ago and he escaped with his wife and two daughters to a village about three kilometers from where we are. With him also were his wife's two sisters (one a war-widow and the other with a six-year-old son whose daddy had been taken to the dread prison at Drancy, eleven kilometers from Paris, and then deported).[4] The Frydmans learned for the first time from us that there was another Jewish family so close to them, so well had each village guarded its precious secret. The Frydmans, too, had been protected by the good mayor and the people of their little community of 700 blessed souls.

Mr. Frydman has kept a diary in Yiddish of all that has happened to French Jewry since the Nazis conquered France. He also has written a novel in Yiddish based on his own experiences. I hope that some enter-prising publisher will be interested in these manuscripts. Mr. Frydman was full of valuable bits of information. I asked him about André Mau-rois.[5] He said the charge that Mr. Maurois had been friendly with the Vichy group was baseless. He said that he knew of no Jew in France who had betrayed our people, that the few Jews who had worked in factories and shops for the Vichyites and the Nazis did so very un-willingly and because of threats made against themselves and their families. He expressed great admiration for Leon Blum as Jew and Frenchman.[6] He described to us in bitter tones how certain wealthy "sha sha" Jews had tried to dissuade Blum from accepting the French premiership and how Blum told them in no uncertain fashion that, as one who loved the Law and the Prophets, he held their cowardly advice in utter contempt. It was thrilling to listen to Ben Zion Frydman. I was reminded of his good friend, the late Sholom Schwartzbard, with whom I had talked when the latter visited America about ten or eleven years ago.[7] These men, small in physical stature but with the hearts of lions, make one so proud of our people and its heroic past and present.

In one sense, my search had ended; in another, it has only begun. For now I know there are Jews, fine loyal Jews left in France; and as we drive the Nazis back and back, I shall seek ever more eagerly for this French "she'erit" to let them know that American Jewry respects their courage and their fidelity and will do all within its power to restore to them their long-denied security and happiness and peace.

(Note — In looking back over my chaplain's report for August 1944, I found the following paragraph relating to this and other events in the Le Mans area: "I discovered two Jewish refugee families hidden in villages approximately 40 kilos north of Le Mans. With the help of the Civil Affairs detachment in Le Mans, I located 65 Jewish children and 75 adult refugees in 6 villages in the neighborhood of the town of Bonnétable. At a religious service in Le Mans the Jewish men raised 5,000 francs ($100) to help care for these people and this money was entrusted to Captain Leon Applebaum of the local ECA [European Civil Affairs] contingent. The Civil Affairs men gathered clothing and shoes for these people, which I distributed to them. The men in the ASCZ (Advance Section Communications Zone) barracks at Le Mans collected two boxes full of food and candy for the refugees, which I distributed. A platoon of Negro soldiers in this barracks contributed its entire week's ration of candy to this collection.")

[1]Yad Vashem, the Holocaust memorial, museum, and research center in Jerusalem, estimates that as many as 700,000 people may have died in gas vans during the Nazi regime.

[2]Vichyites were French collaborators with the Germans. The name came from the city of Vichy, where Marshal Henri Philippe Pétain established the French government under German control.

[3]*Pariser Heint* (Paris Today) was one of two Yiddish newspapers published in Paris before the war.

[4]Drancy — named for the northeastern Paris suburb where it was located — was a "relocation" camp, originally for foreign Jews in France. Between establishment by the Germans in August 1941 and liberation by the Americans in August 1944, 70,000 people — all but 5,000 of them Jews — passed through Drancy on their way to extermination camps in Poland, especially Auschwitz. Fewer than 2,000 of these people survived the Holocaust.

[5]André Maurois (1885–1967) was the nom de plume of Émile Herzog, an Alsatian Jew who served as a French liaison officer with the British Army in World War I. At the start of World War II, though outspoken against Hitler, he allegedly supported the Vichy government. When Hitler took France, Maurois escaped to the United States, returning to France in 1943 to fight with Allied forces in North Africa. As a writer, he is best known for "novelistic" biographies of Shelley, Proust, Disraeli, Voltaire, and others.

[6]Leon Blum (1872–1950) formed the French Socialist Party in 1925 and became prime minister of France in 1936 — the first Socialist prime minister since 1870, and the first Jewish prime minister ever. Arrested in 1940 by the Vichy government, he was imprisoned in Buchenwald and then Dachau. At war's end, he led the provisional government of France until elections were held.

[7]In May 1926 in Paris, Sholom Schwartzbard (1886–1938) assassinated Simon Petlura, leader of the Ukraine, whose soldiers had slaughtered thousands of Jews. Schwartzbard was acquitted of the crime after a three-week trial. He was the author of *At War with Myself* and *Over the Years,* both published in 1933.

David Max Eichhorn was no stranger to helping the victims of persecution and prejudice. The following is from his autobiography, describing an incident in Texarkana in 1937.

Just after one of my Sunday afternoon radio lectures, the editor of the *Texarkana Gazette,* which owned the radio station, got hold of me to tell me that, a few minutes before, a Negro bank porter had shot and killed Bryce Williams, a prominent white realtor of Texarkana, and that, unless prompt action was taken, there would be a lynching.

The facts about the killing were these: Williams went to the bank and demanded that the porter pay him a week's rent which was due. The porter refused because he claimed that Williams had not had a roof leak repaired, as Williams had promised to do, and he would not pay the rent until the leak was fixed. Williams drew a revolver from his pocket, pointed it at the Negro, and said, "You black s.o.b., pay me the money you owe me or I'll kill you." The frightened Negro, who was five feet four inches tall and weighed 140 pounds, lunged for the gun, which went off and wounded him in the side. He grappled with Williams, who was over six feet tall and weighed more than 200 pounds, and they fell to the floor. When they fell, Williams' head hit the bank's tile floor, he was knocked unconscious, and the gun flew out of his hand. The Negro porter reached for the gun and shot Williams through the head. He then left the bank, got a taxi and went to the Negro hospital to have his wound treated. After this he turned himself in to the police. This entire story was fully authenticated by white eye-witnesses.

I telephoned Dr. Kominsky (who was a very prominent member of the American Legion and who was to be, in 1941–42, national commander of the Legion's honor society, the 40 & 8),[1] who had organized within the local Legion post a group of volunteers pledged to help maintain law and order in just this kind of situation. Within an hour, these Legionnaires gathered, were sworn in as deputy sheriffs, given guns and placed around the jail. To our great surprise, no Texarkana lynch mob appeared. Two nights later, a caravan of cars loaded with hillbillies from nearby rural communities surrounded the jail and demanded that the prisoner be handed over to them. By this time, he had been spirited away to another county jail and so the mob's thirst for blood was not satisfied. On Friday evening, in my sermon, I praised the people of Texarkana for their restraint and condemned those who had come into the community for the purpose of taking the law into their own hands. The gist of my sermon was printed in Saturday's *Texarkana Gazette.*

When the case came to trial, the Negro was defended without fee by municipal Judge Louis Josephs, a past president of my congregation (born in Koenigsberg, East Prussia; reared in Dublin, Ireland; spoke with a decided Irish brogue). Judge Josephs asked me to help him conduct the defense, which I gladly consented to do. I was sworn in as an "amicus curiae" [friend of the court] and, during the two days of the trial, sat with Josephs and gave him what help I could. There were two lawyers on the other side, the district attorney and a raucous, racist lawyer retained by the Williams family. The district attorney conducted himself in a gentlemanly manner but the family lawyer ranted and raved like a typical white-supremacy maniac. Both lawyers demanded that the Negro be given the death penalty. In summing up the defense's position before the all-white jury, Josephs made an eloquent plea, liberally filled with quotations from the Jewish and Christian Bibles, stating that the Negro's actions were fully justified on the basis of self-defense. "If this man were white and not black," Josephs declared, "he would have been declared innocent without being brought to trial. The conscience of the white man is on trial here and not this defendant."

Late in the afternoon of the second day of the trial, the jury retired to begin its deliberations. That night, Josephs and I agreed that, if the Negro received the death sentence (which was what we both expected would happen), we would try to interest the American Civil Liberties Union in the case; but, if he got off with a jail sentence, we would be content. The next morning the jury came into the courtroom and rendered its verdict: Not guilty! This was the first time in the history of Arkansas that a Negro had been acquitted for killing a white man. Judge Josephs was so overcome with emotion that he fainted. From that day until he died, the Negroes of Texarkana would not go to any other lawyer for legal help if Judge Josephs was available. They were convinced that God had helped Judge Josephs and me "pass a miracle."

[1]La Societe des Quarante Hommes et Huit Chevaux, commonly called the 40 & 8, is an invitation-only veterans organization started by the American Legion in 1920. The name refers to the capacity of French boxcars in World War I — they could carry forty men or eight horses.

Dear Dad,

We received the English money and papers. Thank you very much. I am very proud of everything you sent. I am very proud of you, Daddy, I sure miss you and that is the truth. Be sure to take good care of yourself. Write us lots of letters. We are saving your letters. We are well, I hope you are well.

Love and kisses from Mother, Mike, Jerry, Judy,
And your loving son, Jonny

August 19, 1944
Somewhere in France

Dear Zelda, Jonny, Mike, Jerry, Judy and all,

I have just returned from an 11-day trip, six days spent in evacuation hospitals visiting the wounded and five days at the front conducting services for the fellows who are out there in the thick of it. I am now back in the comparative safety of corps headquarters, i.e., I can measure the distance from me to the nearest German in miles instead of yards.

There was a lot of mail waiting for me when I got back, including a letter from Zelda (July 23) and 2 V-mails from Helene (July 26 and August 3). I was happy to read that everyone seems to be getting along O.K. and to be as happy as is possible under present circumstances. I am in excellent health and in much better shape physically than I've been in many a moon. My little paunch is about gone. The parts of me which have been exposed to the wind and sun are a deep tan and quite rough and hard and I have undoubtedly lost weight, if one can call the getting rid of lazy fatty substance losing weight.

I'm so glad that my family is now living by itself and am sure that this procedure is proving most satisfactory to all concerned. All the kids' doings are of great interest to me and especially the cleverness and cuteness of my littlest sweetheart, Judy. I am glad that all the Socols were able to get together. I'm sure it was a very joyful reunion. I'm afraid that, under existing conditions, I shall not have much opportunity to visit Mrs. Jablon's English relatives. Perhaps, if I return to England at some future date, I shall have an opportunity to do it. You might be interested to know that, of all the chaplains who came over with me, I landed right in the thick of things first, limited service and all. This seems to have been the result of the reputation that I built up at Croft. My stay in England was quite brief and I had little opportunity to do much running around, although I did get some idea of living conditions in England and of the ways of the English.

I hope that you have taken steps to collect compensation from the railroad for the household goods that were lost and broken. This can be done very easily unless you signed a statement that all came in perfect condition, which I hope you did not.

You ask me to write, Zelda, about what I see and about my work. My work can be described very simply; it is to hold religious services for and to give religious comfort to Jewish soldiers wherever and whenever I find them. In that it does not differ in the slightest from the work I did in the States. The only thing which is different is the surrounding circumstances. I travel around in a jeep and trailer, live in a pup-tent, sleep on the ground, eat sometimes quite well and sometimes not so well. I've become quite adept at doing a high-dive out of the jeep (from either the front or back seats) whenever a bullet-spitting plane with a swastika painted on it swoops down on the highway whereon I am riding. I've been shot at, bombed, and strafed so often that it has ceased to be a novelty — and it really is not as bad as the movies make it. Thus far, the Germans have done little damage to the groups among whom I was while I was there. Everybody over here is going through the same thing, to a greater or less degree, and there seems to be little point in dwelling on these things continually or even often. I don't take the vitamins any more. It is rather unnecessary to do so when one lives out-doors 24 hours a day and seven days a week.

I am glad you are making out O.K. financially. I came overseas in debt because of the money I spent during the 5 weeks in and around New York but I have paid back what I owed and am once again in the clear. As I wrote before, my only regret now is that I didn't let myself go even more than I did. I knew that, once I got here, my recreational opportunities would be very limited — how limited even I did not realize. I've played cards twice since I got here — period. That has been the sum-total of my relaxation. All towns are off-limits to us and I wouldn't have time for sight seeing even if they weren't. Days off just aren't. One lives in an atmosphere of work and tension. Being with a corps headquarters, I naturally get a broader picture of the situation and the needs than those with smaller units and the more I see and hear, the less anxious I am to do anything but work until the job is done. To give my mind an occasional rest, I work on my "Rachel" article in the rare moments when I have a little time to spare.

Well, my assistant has finally finished and I can finish on the typewriter, thank goodness. I certainly do hate to write long-hand. The soldier over here isn't interested too much in politics. It is a subject that is not often discussed. For one silly reason or another, many of the officers seem to be anti-Roosevelt although they certainly are not pro-

Dewey.[1] Their attitude is: we'll vote for anybody but Roosevelt if we get the chance. The attitude of most of the soldiers seems to be: a. A deep resentment that many of the states have put so much red tape in the way of their voting in the presidential election. b. A definite belief that no man should be president of the USA for four terms. They like Roosevelt. They do not think that Dewey is a big enough man to be president. They like Willkie much more than Dewey and think that Willkie would make a good president.[2] They think that the middle of a war is no time to change political administrations. I believe that most of the soldiers who are given a chance to vote will vote for Roosevelt for the last mentioned reason. If the war was over before the election and if the Republicans had put up a man of more experience and ability, most of the soldiers would not vote for Roosevelt.[3]

Here are a couple squibs that I am sending on to the JWB:

"While I was riding along a road in Normandy, my attention was attracted to a German grave surmounted by a Maltese cross ornamented with a star and crescent. Closer examination revealed that the first name of the deceased was Chaium, that he was a Turkish volunteer, and that he was feasting with the houris[4] in Paradise as a result of an American Fourth of July celebration, 1944 style. All of which indicates that there may be some hope for the wicked after all — if even the Nazi dead have Chaium!"

"Even the grimmest hour may have its thrilling moments. There we were seated in the farm-house whose inhabitants had fled to a cave in the woods because of a number of Nazi planes overhead who, together with our own ack-ack guns, were furnishing a musical background for our feast. On the table before us there was some real white bread and butter and raspberry jam (courtesy of U.S. Army), "vin ordinaire" and, wonder of wonders, a baked goose, purchased by our chief forager, Warrant Officer Felix Miller of Memphis, and prepared by my assistant, Irving Levine of Chicago, former mess sergeant, who took a bust from a staff sergeant to a T-5 because he wanted to work with a Jewish chaplain.

"As we sat down to eat, someone (Aside to the family: I was the 'someone') suggested that we give thanks to God for his goodness to us. In the semi-darkness of the blacked-out room, with the sounds of war periodically lending an unusual note to the proceedings, we bowed our heads and each of the four officers of our section blessed

the food in the manner of his fathers: Chaplain Gustav Schellhase of
Detroit intoning the 'Komm, Herr Jesu' of his German Lutheran ances-
tors; then myself, repeating our traditional 'Motsi'; and, finally, Mr.
Miller, concluding in the language common to all of us with a fervent
English 'May God bless this food and this fellowship. Amen.'

"We shall long remember the well-blessed goose and the moment
of inspiration that preceded its annihilation."

When I returned from the front last evening, the folks seemed glad
to see me here at headquarters and this morning Chaplain Schellhase,
as a reward for my "valor," went through a very funny mock decorat-
ing ceremony, in which he presented me with 3 German medals,
including a brand-new "Eisernes Kreuz, Erste Klasse" [Iron Cross, First
Class]. If I can, I'll send them to you. Many of the men here go in for
collecting souvenirs in a big way but, so far, I haven't had much of an
urge in that direction.

I had one very amusing experience on my way to the front. At one
town, our convoy had to stop for two hours to allow another convoy to
pass and, as luck would have it, my jeep stopped right in front of the
mayor's house. The old boy, his wife, and quite attractive daughter
came out, and, surrounded by a group of neighbors, the mayor proceeded to deliver a quite flowery speech to me, of which I understood
none. Perceiving that I was not getting the drift of his remarks, hizzoner started all over again and in a mixture of French, English, and
appropriate gestures, proceeded to tell me the following tale: He had
been the leader of the underground in this area. He had been hiding
until the Germans left 3 days previously. He and his people were very
grateful to the Americans for having liberated them. He and his people were thoroughly democratic and hoped that the Boches would be
amply punished for the manner in which they have treated the Jews.
He had served in the last war in the same regiment with a Jew (Zadoc
Kahn)[5] who later became Chief Rabbi of Paris and he and his wife
came out of the house with a bottle of cognac and gave Levine and
myself each a glass of cognac. After we had drunk this, the wife went
in and came out with a bottle of very excellent liqueur, which we also
drank, after which the mayor handed the empty glasses to his daughter. "Now," said hizzoner, "comes the 'cidre.'" "No, no," said I, "too
much is enough." I pointed toward the glasses which the young lady
was holding and, in my best French, tried to tell hizzoner that the

drinks were making me sleepy and that, if I drank any more, I should get too sleepy for the long journey ahead. My best French must have been none too good because hizzoner took his daughter by the arm and, pulling her toward me, with her blushing like a rose meanwhile, told me, in his best French, that nothing was too good for the valiant Americans. Whereupon, according to Levine, I started to blush, which may or may not have been so, and I hastily went into an act complete with gestures of driving and of pretending to be drunk and weaving and swaying, etc., and then the light dawned for his honor and he began to laugh and to say, "Oui, oui, je compree, je compree; zigzag, zigzag," and he joined me in the drunk-act. All the folks standing around had a good laugh and we departed amidst cheers and the throwing of flowers (beautiful dahlias and daisies for the most part). The story is going the rounds and I am getting quite a bit of kidding as a result. Most of the officers say that, if they had been in my boots, they would have put on a different kind of act. "C'est la guerre."

The weather here has been very pleasant and quite warm. It has rained only twice since we have been here. I understand that the real rainy season lies ahead of us. I can't say that I anticipate its coming with much pleasure.

You ask, Helene, whether the soldiers and myself think of civilians as people "who walk the even ways of life"? Most assuredly. Too many letters from back home reflect an unwarranted optimism over the course and possible length of the war and an unwarranted self-pity over the enduring discomforts that, from this particular neck of the woods, seem quite bearable. There is also a feeling that things would be better if home folks spent less time worrying and more time doing. Most of these soldiers would testify that the more time one spends doing, the less time he has in which to worry.

> Love and kisses to all.
> Your husband, daddy, son and brother, Max

[1]Thomas E. Dewey (1902–1971) was governor of New York and the Republican Party presidential nominee in 1944.

[2]Wendell Willkie (1892–1944) was the Republican candidate against Roosevelt in 1940 and lost badly. He then became a Roosevelt ally, traveling the world as a government representative. His 1943 book, *One World*, called for international peacekeeping after the war.

³Of the 48 million votes cast in the presidential election of 1944, Roosevelt received 25.6 million to Dewey's 22 million — Roosevelt's smallest margin of victory in all his presidential campaigns.

⁴Houris are beautiful black-eyed virgins that some Muslims believe are waiting in heaven to amuse the faithful, especially martyrs.

⁵Besides being chief rabbi of France, Zadoc Kahn was honorary president of the Alliance Israelite Universelle, an officer of the Legion of Honor of Paris, and author of *Etudes sur le livre de Joseph le Zelateur* (The Book of Joseph the Zealot).

August 30, 1944
Somewhere in France

Dear Zelda, Jonny, Mike, Jerry, Judy and all,

I have been gone on a nine-day visit to the rear and have just now returned to the outfit. Just prior to leaving, I was handed Zelda's letter of Aug. 7 and Jonny's of Aug 11 (both sent air mail) and when I returned there was quite a bit of mail waiting for me. I was very glad to hear from you and sorry that I have been too busy to answer your previous letters up to now.

The trip was quite in contrast to its predecessor, which ended with a 5-day stay at the front. This time, when my outfit moved forward I moved the other way, in order to visit our unit's hospitals and cemetery. It was a very peaceful journey. Jerry is moving so fast in the other direction at the present time, thank goodness, that he has no time to pay any attention to me. So, all during this particular voyage, I saw not one German plane nor heard one shot fired. After visiting a number of hospitals, I had the following experience, already written up elsewhere but here copied for your information and for placing among the scraps: [The August 14 report to the Jewish Welfare Board beginning "Today I have come to the end of a search" is inserted here.]

That is the end of the article. After leaving the hospital, I journeyed to a large city forty kilos away [Le Mans] and stayed there for five days, conducting services, visiting hospitals, and, above all, seeking for and helping Jews who had been in hiding for from one to three years. I found many of them. In one town alone, I found a French farmer playing god-father to 65 children and 75 adults whom he had placed in homes in six different villages. All these Jewish people had been sent to him from Paris by a French priest. He protected them at the risk of his own and his family's lives. At the service which I held in this city, 81 Jewish soldiers (many of whom had not been paid for as long as four months) emptied their pockets and contributed more than 5,000 francs (more than $100) to help me in this work. The soldiers went through the barracks and collected food and cigarettes and candy for these people. One company of Negroes contributed its entire week's candy ration to the cause (and let me tell you, candy is quite a scarce commodity here). The local Civil Affairs unit gave me three boxes full of clothing and shoes. It was an experience I shall not soon forget. Jewish aged and Jewish children and all types and sizes in between, hugged me and kissed me and told me that I was their "Mawshiach. . . ." After I left this city, I spent 2 more days visiting hospitals and then journeyed back a long distance to rejoin this headquarters. You may get some notion from this recital just why I did not have time to write until now. This is the first time I have had to myself since I left nine days ago.

And now to re-read your letters and make some comments. (But, before doing that, I want to mention that, during the trip I visited our cemetery and said Kaddish at the grave of each Jewish soldier buried there. It was not exactly a pleasant experience but a very satisfying one.)

I am very glad that Jonny and Mike are learning to swim. It is well to start them when they are that young and I hope both of them will do much better at this than their daddy did. They had to throw me in to make me learn — and to this day I don't like water. I don't think anybody minds less than I the fact that we have to go weeks over here sometimes before we are able to take any kind of bath. . . .

I am very happy that all you children got a chance to see your grand-daddy Socol and your uncle Harry and aunt Mickey and I am greatly pleased that you loved them so much and that they love you too. . . . I've met many boys who trained at Croft while I was there. Just read that one of my old students, Sandy Swedlin of Tampa, a captain in the Air Force, has just been decorated for bravery. And so it goes. I've met all sorts of old friends and acquaintances all along the line. The commander of the outfit at the cemetery was from Springfield, Mass., and the brother of a girl who took a prominent part in a play I directed there [*Nathan the Wise*, by Gotthold Lessing]. It is good to meet people one knows over here. . . .

Sometime ago, I sent Eli a list of a number of things that I should like to have and asked him to send them to me. I had a fine letter from Major (Dr.) Sam Greenberg today. He organizes services at his hospital, conducts them and preaches. Can you imagine that! He is good enough to say that, under my influence, he became a Jew again and wanted me to know about it. As you may remember, he always was a favorite of mine. He is Chief of Medicine at a general hospital in England. . . . Just got an announcement from Edythe (Handman) Caine that she had a little baby girl. Named it, of all things, Allison Donna Caine. It beats me where they find these names. . . .

Jonny, I was very, very happy to get your two letters and I think that you are a very smart and kind son. You certainly were a good boy to be able, when mama was not feeling well, to fix her supper and clean the house and bathe our darling Judy and little Jerry and bigger Mike. Mike is a big boy now, too, and he should be able to bathe himself. Shouldn't you, Mike? I hope you all liked the picture of *Snow White and the seven dwarfs* and I'll bet you were glad when the wicked fairy got what she deserved. I am glad to know that you, Jonny, and you, Mike, are going to start Hebrew school soon and I hope that, when I return, you will both be able to speak to me in Hebrew. I certainly don't mind your going to Orthodox school instead of to the Temple. I doubt if the Temple has a five-day school and the more Hebrew you can learn the better I shall like it. I think you will like it, too. I've always been sorry that I did not have the chance to begin studying Hebrew when I was your age. But the town in which I lived was too small and there was no one to teach me. . . .

I hope my dad took that trip to Atlantic City that he wrote about to you. I haven't heard from him but once since I've been across. I guess that he doesn't have any more time for writing than I do. I refer, of course, to personal letters. All because I write too many of the business variety. . . .

The soldiers here, in answer to your question, do little complaining and the worse they hurt, the less they moan. That is what makes me so angry at civilian jerks who think they have it tough. . . . It is so dark now that I can't see to either read or write so I shall have to quit.

> Love and kisses to all and a special hug for each one
>   of you kids.
> Your husband and daddy,
> Max

September 14, 1944
Somewhere in France

Dear Zelda, Jonny, Mike, Jerry, Judy and all:

Sorry I have not had a chance to write for a while but sometimes I am kept so busy that I do not have a chance to write and this is one of those times. I am enclosing 4 little French flags, one for each of you kids, and also some French money. I bought some stuff for you on a recent trip to Paris. I had it all wrapped up in the best box I could find and using the best rope I had and I mailed it but the best was not good enough and the post office sent it back as being unsuitably wrapped for its long journey. Now I do not know when I shall get to send it as, where I am now, there is not much chance of getting hold of a better box or of better rope but, maybe in time, I'll find some means of sending these things. Don't expect too much. These toys don't look like much when compared to American toys but they are the best the French have and the French haven't very much that is very good. And they cost just about five times as much as the same sort of toy would have cost in an American store. And I also have some Parisian perfume for mama which is good and which would probably cost more in the States than it cost here. But the transportation problem here is really something when it comes to sending home things so you all will have to be patient and wait for the proper opportunity to present itself.

This Parisian trip of mine was quite a jaunt. I went into Paris to meet one of the boss-chaplains [Rabbi Judah Nadich] to see what arrangements were under foot for the High Holydays [Rosh Hashanah and Yom Kippur].

And, before I go any further, may I wish you one and all the happiest possible New Year's. I suppose that you will receive this around Yom Kippur and, as we severally observe these days, we all will be hoping that, please God, the next High Holydays will not find us separated by such a long distance. When I got to Paris, the chaplain I wanted to see was not there and I was told to stay in the city until he should arrive in a day or two. The next morning I hunted for and found the ghetto in which the Nazis had kept the Jews of Paris. My arrival there created a sensation and in less than no time, I was mobbed by crowds of Jews who came to greet me from everywhere. I was escorted first to a soup kitchen and lodging house which the Jews had set up for their poverty-stricken brethren, of whom there are about 10,000 in Paris. Before the war there were about 200,000 Jews in Paris. About 75,000 of them escaped from Paris to unoccupied France or are hidden all over the country. About 85,000 were killed or deported by the Nazis and most of these may be presumed to be dead. About 40,000 remained in Paris, of whom most either went into hiding and fought with the French underground or took out forged papers and passed themselves off as Christians. It is a long story and I can't at this time give you all the details. The Jews had their own militia who fought with the courage of demons. They killed many German soldiers in Paris and 200 of their number were caught and shot by the Gestapo. A Parisian journalist has written an article for me in Yiddish which I had translated by a Jewish medic and, after a foreword of my own and some linguistic embellishments of my own, I have sent the article through the censorship to Rabbi Philip Bernstein of the NY JWB and hope that, in due time, the article will appear in print. It will tell in brief the sad tale of how Parisian Jews fared under Hitler.

I was conducted by the Jews in the ghetto to the headquarters of the Jewish underground and had a number of conferences with the leaders of this band of heroes. They told me that the Jewish organization which had been set up by the Nazis via Vichy and which had worked hand in hand with the Gestapo was still functioning in Paris. I relayed this news to our military intelligence who acted with proper speed with the result that these renegade Jews were soon under lock and key and telling many a pretty story that I am sure has been of great value to our own Secret Service. For this I received the thanks of our intelligence who called it a very helpful bit of work. The chaplain whom I awaited as well as a representative of the Jewish Welfare Board arrived on the scene that evening and we went to work to try to be of some assistance to the Jews of Paris. Aided and abetted by Captain Eddy Warburg,[1] one swell guy, vice president of the JDC [Joint Distribution Committee] and son of the late Felix Warburg, we pitched in and soon had things rolling with the American Red Cross, the French Red Cross, the French Secour Nationale, the American Army, and all the various appendages thereof. One afternoon, we sat down with the leaders of the Paris community (what was left of them) and indeed it was an inspiring session. They made speeches welcoming us, we replied, everybody had a good cry, and it was something to remember. The JWB feller will be back in America somewhere between Oct. 15 and Nov. 1 and, if any of you happen to be around the JWB offices in NY when he arrives, he can tell you all about it. He is bringing back messages and stories and reports from the Jews of Paris to the Jews of America and maybe if some of it gets into print somewhere maybe somebody will be good enough to mention my name. Late that afternoon we went to the biggest synagogue in Paris [Rothschild Synagogue] and there, together with the Chief Rabbi of Paris, we participated in the first service held in the synagogue since the city's liberation. About 3,500 to 4,000 Jews crowded the place, including about 200 American soldiers. I had been designated tentatively to represent General Eisenhower at the service but after the Jewish boss-chaplain [Rabbi Nadich] arrived, he took my place and did a swell job. He preached a sermon in French and in English and brought down the house. However, I was up on the altar with the big shots and it was all very thrilling. The next afternoon I was in the official party surrounding the tomb of the Unknown Soldier at the Arc d'Triomphe which gathered to watch General Eisenhower present a plaque to the people of the city of Paris for their heroism — and, believe you me, they deserved it. They, the overwhelming majority of them, fought like hell against the Germans while they were in the city in every conceivable way and I think most of the German soldiers garrisoned in the city were glad to get out. We were warned against snipers but I never heard of any. There was more danger of getting hit by cars driven by the FFI [Free French] who drove like mad around Paris looking for snipers. I could write much about Paris and the French and my opinions thereon but time is of the essence and this will have to wait.

I finally returned to this headquarters having had a hectic and pro-
fessionally pleasing time in Paris but knowing about as much about
the High Holyday situation as I did before I went.

Since returning to my unit, we have journeyed about 125 miles
closer to Germany than we were before and we are not a considerable
distance away from that benighted land. However, the Germans still
do not want to understand that the war is lost for them and they are
fighting our fellows for every inch of ground. Some of those fellers
back in the States who had the war all tucked away in a bag by this
time and back to "business as usual" and all that stuff ought to be over
here in this grand-stand seat and maybe they would tuck in their tail-
feathers a little bit.

> Love and kisses to all you kiddies big and small from
> Your husband and daddy,
> Max

[1]Edward M. "Eddy" Warburg (1909–1992) came from the most prominent
Jewish banking family in Hamburg. They were initially tolerated by the Nazis
for their financial abilities but were finally forced out in 1938. Warburg went
to Harvard, where he became lifelong friends with Lincoln Kirstein. Together
they championed the cause of contemporary art, organizing the first New England showings of works by Picasso, Matisse, Braque, and others. Eventually
the two men founded the New York City Ballet and recruited George Balan-
chine to run it. An army volunteer in charge of refugees, Warburg landed in
Normandy the day after D-Day. His mother, Mrs. Felix Warburg, was on the
board of the JWB.

*In his 1969 autobiography, Rabbi Eichhorn provided more details of his
visit to Paris shortly after that city was liberated on August 25, 1944.*

I came into Paris on September 4, when the fighting inside the city was
just about over except for some sporadic sniper fire. I was taken to the
headquarters of the Jewish "milice," the Jewish underground, located,
in the Nazi-created ghetto, in what had been a rabbi's home in the Rue
des Rosiers. I was warmly greeted by a large crowd of Jews who gathered from all parts of the ghetto area to welcome me. I was told that
the UGIF (Union Generale Israelite d'France), the so-called Jewish relief
organization set up in Paris by the Vichy government, had collaborated

with the Gestapo and was still functioning. I reported this to the French and American military authorities. Soon thereafter, all connected with the organization were rounded up and arrested. Two of those arrested, one German Jew and one Polish Jew, were found to be actual members of the Gestapo and were shot. The Polish Jew had been planted by the Gestapo in the Paris Jewish "milice," who trusted him so much that they replanted him in the UGIF. At first the Jewish leaders refused to believe that this man was a double agent and they asked for his release; but, after they were shown the man's Gestapo ID card which had been found sewn into the bottom of his shoes and a copy of his confession, they offered no further objection to his execution.

I assisted Captain Edward M. Warburg of the Civil Affairs Section to set up soup kitchens for the Jews of Paris, after Warburg had gotten the funds needed to do this by personally endorsing a loan of $60,000 from the Bank of France for the American Jewish Joint Distribution Committee. Also I was present on September 7 at the service of thanksgiving attended by about 3,500 Jews in the Rothschild Synagogue on the Rue de la Victoire. Originally I had been designated to speak on behalf of the American Army at this service but, on September 6, Chaplain Judah Nadich, the Jewish chaplain on General Eisenhower's staff, arrived and the next day he delivered an eloquent message at the service in faultless French. On September 8 I was a member of the official party which was with General Eisenhower when he presented a plaque at the Arc de Triomphe to the people of Paris in gratitude for their heroic resistance to Nazism.

September 20, 1944
V-mail: Somewhere in France

Dear Zelda, Jonny, Mike, Jerry, Judy and all:

I have just returned from seeing Bing Crosby (himself in person) and a group of entertainers put on a very fine show for a large bunch of soldiers. Good old Bing. From where we are to the front lines isn't very far and it does one's heart good to see these show-people leave their comfortable habitats and travel thousands of miles to risk their lives to bring a smile into lives which are almost completely devoid of humor most of the time. Dinah Shore visited our headquarters some time ago and got a very warm reception. I was working at the time and missed the show.[1]

I haven't very much time at present and so I can not write at great length but I thought you would like to know that I spent a very thrilling Rosh Hashanah. I was sent to a city [Verdun] which was very famous in World War I to conduct services. When I got there I learned that the Nazis had completely destroyed the Jewish community of this city and had converted its synagogue into a soup-kitchen. A recent bombing had partially wrecked the building and it was in a sad state. The sanctuary was heaped with fertilizer, put there deliberately, of course, by the Nazis. I went to work on the synagogue, aided by ten German prisoners of war (poetic justice, eh what?). The Germans did a good job. Without urging, they scrubbed the walls and floors thoroughly and when they got through the place did not look too bad, although the roof was quite completely demolished and, during our services on Erev Rosh Hashanah, the congregation got a good drenching from the downpour that went on without interruption day and night. Despite the miserable weather, more than 500 American Jewish soldiers jammed into the place for the evening service and the next morning we had over 600. The second night we had 250 and then I had to leave in order to come back to this headquarters to hold two more services in this area on the second day which were attended by 70 and 80 men respectively.

The first service in the synagogue was very dramatic. We opened with singers singing the "Marsellaise" [the French national anthem]. After that, Chaplain (Colonel) Schellhase of our Corps, who had driven a long way especially for the occasion, gave a beautiful opening prayer. Then the city architect spoke and, in the name of the mayor and citizens of the city, promised that the city would express its feelings with regard to its lost Jewish friends by restoring the synagogue to its original condition as quickly as possible. The next morning, since we had no Shofar, an Army bugler played the traditional notes on the bugle and, though we had no Torah, we opened the Ark and went through the entire Torah service just as though we had a Torah. Everyone was profoundly moved. The Army Pictorial Service took pictures and it is possible that you may see them in the newspapers.

Love, Max

¹Although all branches of the service had entertainment groups, by far the biggest troop entertainer during the war was the United Service Organizations (USO), which ran thousands of servicemen's clubs and presented nearly half a million camp shows, for audiences from 25 to 15,000. (The British equivalents were Stars in Battledress and ENSA, which officially stood for Entertainments National Service Association but was known universally by British troops as Every Night Something Awful.) For every Bing Crosby and Dinah Shore performing in huge halls, there were dozens of small-time performers (many of them vaudevillians who had not worked in a decade) juggling, tap dancing, and doing magic tricks in sometimes wretched and dangerous locations.

October 2, 1944
Somewhere in France

Dear Friends of JWB,

Here is the manner in which one Jewish chaplain in France spent the Yamim Noraim, as well as that chaplain is able to remember the rapid-fire sequence of events during these (for him) hectic days:

Since there were only about 15 Jewish chaplains in France for the High Holy Days, I felt that I should be placed somewhere for this period where I would be in a position to serve other men besides those of my own organization. With this in mind, I requested and received permission to hold Rosh Hashana services in the historic city of Verdun, which was situated at some distance from my headquarters.

I arrived in Verdun three days before Rosh Hashana and found the people of the community still celebrating the departure of the Germans and the arrival of the Americans and busily engaged in clearing up the debris of the conflict. I found the synagogue in a rather run-down condition to say the least. The Nazis had gutted it completely of all its religious fixtures and had used it as a soup-kitchen to feed starving Frenchmen. The Aron Ha-kodesh was piled high with ill-smelling fertilizer and the place was quite a mess. The roof of the edifice had been hit by bombs and the whole interior was quite exposed to the winds and the rain. I advertised my presence as best I could in the short time that was available and went to work to clean up the synagogue and prepare for the service. At first I sought to procure civilian labor for the clean-up job but, because it seemed that this would require the unwinding of a little red tape plus transportation and food problems, I found a speedier and more satisfactory solution of the problem through the co-operation of the commander of a nearby prisoner-of-war camp, who loaned me ten prisoners for a day for the job. These erstwhile "super-men" really did a super job. They cleaned out the synagogue in a jiffy, scrubbed the floors and the walls, and turned the desecrated sanctuary into a place of worship with an efficiency and a speed that defies description. During the operation, one of the prisoners, a man well over fifty, turned to me and said: "Rabbi, helping with this task is giving me much inner spiritual satisfaction. While the great wrongs that have been committed can never be righted, this day's work is, for me, an act of penance for being a part of that people which has done such terrible things to the Jews and to the world."

While I was attempting to get word of the Rosh Hashana service to the troops in the area, a very amusing incident occurred. I was seeking the Adjutant of the Verdun headquarters in order to get him to send out High Holyday notices to all units of the command. His office was in a tented area around the Grand Hotel. As I was searching among the tents for the one which held the Adjutant, I spied an officer wearing a field-cap. I presumed him to be a French liaison officer, because they are the only ones hereabouts who wear such caps. The rest of us wear helmets. I walked over to him to inquire the location of the Adjutant's tent. When I got within a few feet of the "French" officer, I noticed, with amazement and chagrin, that his cap and collar-band were studded with stars. The "Frenchman" was four-star General Omar Bradley,[1] second only to General Eisenhower in rank and importance! Wow! I wanted to turn and run. General Bradley noticed my discomfiture and grinned. "What's the matter, chaplain?" he asked. "I am sorry to have troubled you, sir," I replied. "I was trying to find the Adjutant. From your cap, I thought you were a French officer and I was just about to ask you the location of the Adjutant's tent."

"Your mistake was a natural one," said General Bradley. "Generals are the only American soldiers permitted to wear field caps in this combat area. The Adjutant's office is right over there. And the next time you bump into a general unexpectedly, chaplain, don't feel badly about it. Deep down, chaplain, most generals are plain, humble human beings trying to do their job just as you are trying to do yours." I saluted and made what I hope was a dignified exit in the direction indicated to me by the General.

The day before Rosh Hashana it rained cats and dogs and my hopes for a large congregation went glimmering. We had to move the benches to the sides of the synagogue because the rain was pouring down through the roof right into the middle of the synagogue. When Erev Rosh Hashana approached, much to my surprise, Jewish men and women in uniform began to pour into town from all over. Some traveled 75 miles to get to the service. Somehow, the news had spread throughout that territory and in came the Jewish soldiers, nearly 500 of them, right through the mud and the water. And most of them stood up in the damp and the rain for an hour and a half through the entire service — and they loved it. We opened the service with our National Anthem and then a fine baritone from the local opera company sang the "Marsellaise." The opening prayer was given by my wonderful boss, Colonel Gustav Schellhase, chaplain of the XV Corps and, in civilian life, pastor of the Truth Lutheran Church on Woodward Avenue in Detroit. He had come more than a hundred miles to be present at the service. Then the city architect of Verdun made a speech in halting English in which he promised, in the name of the mayor and citizens of the stricken city, that, at the earliest possible moment, the city would restore the synagogue to its original condition as a tribute to the Jewish community of Verdun which had been completely annihilated by the Nazis. It was a thrilling moment. The congregation cheered. (I hope that a way will be found for the Jewish people of America to give financial assistance to the brave citizens of Verdun to aid them in their endeavor to restore the synagogue.)[2] Next morning we were blessed with a little better weather. Over 600 soldiers crowded into the synagogue. We had no Shofar so an Army bugler blew the traditional blasts on a good old GI bugle. We had no Sefer Torah but only a Hebrew Bible; but we opened the Ark and went through the entire Torah service just as though the Torah had been there. The Army Pictorial Service came in and took some pictures of the proceedings. (If you want to obtain copies of these pictures, get in contact with the Signal Corps in Washington and tell them that you want the pictures taken in the Verdun synagogue by photographer Joseph Brignolo of Detachment D, 162nd Signal Photo Company, APO 113, on September 17, 1944.) The evening of the second day, 250 soldiers attended the service. On the morning of the third day, I returned to my own outfit and held two more services in the afternoon which were attended by 70 and 65 persons respectively.

Between Rosh Hashanah and Yom Kippur, I visited what had been a German concentration camp for American and British citizens in the resort-town of Vittel[3] and I found about 300 Jews among the 2,000 people there. Among these Jews were Dr. Angelo Rappaport, former professor at London University (who wishes to send warm greetings to Rabbi Stephen Wise), Mr. George Shapiro, former head of the Paris Ort, Mr. Eisenzweig, former secretary to the Jewish deputies in the Polish Sejm[4] in Warsaw, Mr. Homsky, brother-in-law of the late Hebraist, A. D. Friedland of Cleveland, and the daughter and three grandchildren of Rabbi Schorr, former chief rabbi of Warsaw. Last spring, a number of Jews, including the wife of Rabbi Schorr, committed suicide at this camp in protest against the deportation to Poland of 240 Polish Jews at the camp who had Central and South American passports.

Also at this camp I found 28 Sifre Torah, together with many other synagogal appurtenances which came from the Alsatian Jewish communities of Hagenau and Saargemuenes and which these internees had guarded at the risk of their lives. In fact, one Jew by the name of Dreyfuss had given his life al kiddush ha-Shem rather than reveal to the Nazis where these holy objects were. A Christian in the neighboring community had aided the Jews by hiding in his house a box full of silver synagogal adornments. I promised the faithful sh'eris Yisrael [remaining Jews] at the camp that I would return after Yom Kippur and take these precious books and adornments to a place of safe keeping.

I wanted to hold my Yom Kippur service in Nancy. I went to that city and located the synagogue, a huge, beautiful structure, capable of seating at least 2,000 persons. It had been used by the Germans as a medical supply dump. Cots and stretchers were piled up in it to a height of ten to twelve feet.

But the Commanding General of my Corps, Gen. Wade H. Haislip, decided that, since I could hold Yom Kippur services in only one place, that place must be conveniently located for the troops of our Corps. He asked me which city in our Corps area had a synagogue. A careful examination of all available data revealed that there was only one synagogue in the area. It was the city of Lunéville. However, there was one slight hitch: the city of Lunéville was three miles ahead of our lines and was firmly in the hands of the German Army. When I reported this to General Haislip, he said to me, "Chaplain, you will hold your Yom Kippur service in the synagogue in Lunéville."

As you know, Yom Kippur was on Tuesday evening and Wednesday. The preceding Friday, an order was issued by Headquarters XV Corps: "All personnel of the Jewish faith will be excused from duty next Tuesday and Wednesday in order that they may attend Day of Atonement services in the synagogue in Lunéville." Quelle chutspa! Never was a military order more widely discussed by Jew and Gentile alike. Lunéville and its synagogue were still in the hands of the Germans, two miles ahead of our most forward positions. You can imagine with what interest I read the daily battle-situation reports. Monday morning's report stated: "Street-fighting continues in the city of Lunéville." Monday afternoon, my assistant and I packed my jeep and trailer with prayer books and headed for Lunéville. To reach it, we journeyed past our artillery, our tanks, and most of our infantry. At one point, the MPs had to remove a road-block to let us pass. About a half-mile in front of the city, there was a river. The engineers were putting up a pontoon-bridge across the river when we arrived. When the bridge was completed, my assistant and I chugged across it and into Lunéville. The city was completely deserted. Not a person was on the streets. Our hearts were in our mouths. Just as we reached the main street, we saw a big American flag being put out of a building about three blocks ahead. Never was there a more welcome sight. When we reached the building, which was the city's town hall, we found inside an American MII (military intelligence) team of an officer and two men. They looked at us in amazement. "What in h— are you doing here, chaplain?" "I'm here because I've been instructed to hold a Yom Kippur service in this city tomorrow evening." "Well, if you can hold a Yom Kippur service with two Jews and three Gentiles, that will be it, for there will be no more American soldiers in this town by tomorrow night. This town is still in No Man's Land. It is not yet officially taken."

We learned that early Monday morning the Germans had retreated from the city to the Forest of Parroy, about a mile west of the city. The citizens of the city gradually came out of the cellars where they had been hiding. They greeted us joyously. In an atmosphere permeated with snipers, artillery shells whining around and overhead, of bombs and strafing, I began to prepare to celebrate Yom Kippur. I've been in some pretty tough spots the last few months but I believe that, up to now, this one takes first prize.

There was a synagogue in the town. It was sealed up. With the aid of the French, we unsealed it. The external structure of the synagogue was practically untouched, except for some broken stained glass windows, but, inside, it was a worse mess than the one in Verdun. The Nazis had broken up and torn down everything that they could, ripped the prayer books and other s'farim in bits and piled the remains in heaps on the floor. We got down on our hands and knees and spent about two hours gathering the bits of Hebrew printing that remained. I placed the broken fragments upon the altar and there they stayed, in a place of honor, during the entire Yom Kippur service. These bits of paper, together with a shofar which was found in the debris and which we used to conclude our observance, were the only tangible remnants of a community of 200 Jewish families. Two Jews had been publicly flogged to death by the Nazis as a warning to the non-Jewish populace. Some were locked inside the synagogue and allowed to starve to death as an example of "Schrecklichkeit."[5] A few managed to escape to unoccupied France. The rest were deported to Poland. None remains.

The rabbi's house next to the synagogue had been used by the Germans as a lying-in home for French girls impregnated by German soldiers. When we arrived, about a half-dozen of these girls got up from their straw mats and scattered like a bunch of frightened chicks. I later learned that these girls now have not only swollen bellies but also bald heads, as a result of their having had their hair shaved off by unsympathetic fellow-townsmen.

The MII team, my assistant, and I requisitioned rooms at the Hotel Central. That night we sat in the blacked-out barroom of the hotel, drank vin rouge, and tried to forget the war which was going on outside. My assistant, who was by profession a Chicago piano teacher, brought in our field-organ from the trailer, and accompanied us as we sang solos, duets, trios, quartets, and quintets in English, Hebrew, Yiddish, Italian, and even a couple of songs in German. We were joined by the hotel owner, his wife, and daughter who sang for us in French. All the while this was going on the building was shaking from the concussion of exploding shells and our nerves were being shaken further by the roar of shells overhead, both outbound and inbound. After we had imbibed enough vin rouge to dull our senses sufficiently, we went to bed and, despite the noise, slept soundly until day-break.

The local people were really wonderful. They cleaned all the dirt from the synagogue. Eleven donkey-cart loads of debris were carried away. The place was strung with electric lights. It was decorated with French and American flags, all by order of and with the personal help of the Mayor and citizens of the city of Lunéville, aided and abetted by three Gentile Americans, the MII lieutenant and his two GI assistants. So far as I was concerned, all this was being done because General Haislip had so ordered. I did not expect any Yom Kippur service to be held in Lunéville. I did not think that anyone would get out of his foxhole and walk toward the enemy to go to synagogue, even on Yom Kippur. Enough is enough.

But General Haislip's hunch was right and mine wrong. At sundown on Tuesday the men came into Luneville from all along the line, mostly from the 44th and 79th Divisions, on foot, by jeep and by truck. 350 battle-grimed Jewish fighters came to the synagogue for Kol Nidre. Their places in the line were taken by Gentile comrades so that they might have an opportunity to worship. In they came, their faces coated with dirt — grim, brave, fighting sons of Judah. I tell you unashamedly that, for the first time since I have been in France, I broke down and cried. No matter what I had seen before of the wounded, the dying and the dead, I had managed to steel myself against tears, but this was too much. The noises of war raged around us as together we intoned our traditional prayers. The men kept on their full battle-dress and their guns were at the ready. Together we prayed that mankind might be spared another such Yom Kippur.

I had brought along a Torah and a Peroches from the Vittel concentration camp. So the next day we were able to have a real Torah reading, complete with aliyahs and Mesheberachs. A local photographer took pictures of the proceedings and we took down the names of the men and the addresses for their folks at home. I hope to send these photos and the list of names of these men. The Army Pictorial Service again came in and took pictures. The Army photographer said that the caption under the published pictures would state his belief that no group of American soldiers had ever held a service in a religious edifice closer to the actual line of battle.

Many of the men were not able to remain for the entire service. They had to resume their place in the line. It was, for many of them, the last religious service they would ever attend. A bitter fire-fight broke out almost immediately to drive the Germans from the Forest of Parroy.[6] Among the earliest victims of this engagement was Jochanan Tartakower, son of Dr. Aryeh Tartakower of the World Jewish Congress.[7] Jochanan had assisted me to conduct the Yom Kippur service.[8]

The service concluded at about 4 p.m. in order to give the men time to get back to their units by sundown. After the service, a high-ranking officer who was known to be Jewish but who had tried to conceal his Jewishness and who had made a poor showing in combat, came up to me and swore that, from here on out, he would be a faithful Jew and a good soldier. I can not reveal his rank because to do so might lead to an uncovering of his identity. For ten minutes I forgot that I was a lowly captain and he was "high brass" and I spoke to him as rabbi to congregant. He told me that his open profession of Judaism by attending the service and his admission of guilt before God had taken a great load off his mind and heart. He would be a better man because of this day's worship. I pray that this will be so and I believe that it will be so.

When I returned to my billet, the MII lieutenant thanked me for the great contribution I had made to military intelligence. "I do not understand," said I. The lieutenant explained. "The Germans could not fail to observe the movement of American vehicles and men through the streets to the synagogue. If they had artillery at the edge of the forest, they would have been able to drop some shells right through the roof of the synagogue. Since they did not do so, we now know that they have withdrawn their artillery to the middle of the forest. Simple, isn't it?" "Yes," said I, "but why did you not tell me this before the service?" "Duty before friendship," said he. "Besides, chaplain, if perchance you had refused to hold the service, I would not have found out what I wanted to know. And if I had told you and you still would have held the service, you might not have been able to concentrate sufficiently on your sermons and other rabbinical duties." "Thanks for your kindly consideration of my spiritual welfare," said I.

The day after Yom Kippur, I started for Paris with the Hebrew fragments from the battle-front synagogue and the Sifre Torah from the concentration camp. The Torahs and the ornaments were placed in the custody of Julian Weill, chief rabbi of Paris, to be returned, if possible, after the war, to the Jews of Hagenau and Saargemuenes. The broken Hebrew fragments were deposited reverently in the Geniza of the Rothschild Synagogue on the Rue de la Victoire.

> David Max Eichhorn
> Chaplain Captain
> Hq XV Corps

[1]Omar Nelson Bradley (1893–1981), dubbed "the soldier's general" by correspondent Ernie Pyle, led troops in Sicily before joining his former West Point classmate Dwight Eisenhower in London to plan the Normandy invasions. After the breakout from France, Bradley assumed command of the Twelfth Army Group and was an extremely effective leader. (Eisenhower called him "the master tactician of our forces.") At war's end, President Truman made Bradley the director of the Veterans Administration, and three years later, he succeeded Eisenhower as army chief of staff and then chairman of the Joint Chiefs of Staff. Bradley retired from the military as a five-star general in 1953.

[2]As of this writing, we have been unable to determine when and to what extent the synagogue in Verdun was restored or whether it is currently in operation. Barbara Holstein, a historian specializing in the Verdun battlefield, recently visited the synagogue and wrote, "The synagogue appears to be entirely closed up. There are two parts to the building, one of them looks as if it's been shut for a while but the main section has had new railings added to the front of it, closing off the steps that lead to the entrance. At the side of the entrance is a plaque with historical information, but it is impossible to get to it as things are . . . the three or four houses (in the street leading to the synagogue) were all apparently closed." As a result of three letters to the Verdun city government, we have received three brochures about touring the World War I battlefield but no information about the synagogue, other than that it exists.

[3]Vittel was, beginning in 1940, an internment and transfer camp in northeastern France, near Nancy.

[4]Sejm is the lower house of the Polish Parliament.

[5]*Schrecklichkeit*, or "terror," was the German high command's tactic to disarm or destroy resistance through the intentional perpetration of atrocities against civilian populations.

[6]The Forest of Parroy (Foret de Parroy) near Lunéville was one of the places the Germans decided to make a last stand. In deep mud, clinging underbrush, and what one soldier called "a nightmare of tree bursts," GIs fought for sixty days before securing a costly victory.

[7]The World Jewish Congress (WJC) is an international federation of Jewish communities and organizations. It represents the entire political spectrum and

serves as Jews' diplomatic arm in dealing with governments and international organizations. In August 1942, Dr. Gerhart Reigner of the WJC was one of the first to alert the world to the Nazis' murderous plans for the Jews.

[8]In his autobiography, Rabbi Eichhorn reports that thirty-eight of the men who attended the Lunéville service died within the next few days and were buried in the military cemetery at Antilly.

Further information about Vittel, the first concentration camp he visited, comes from Rabbi Eichhorn's 1969 autobiography.

This was one of two such prisons which the Germans permitted representatives of the International Red Cross to visit and inspect occasionally. The other was at Theresienstadt in Czechoslovakia. The Vittel prisoners were housed in hotels occupied at normal times by tourists who come to take mineral baths. The Vittel prison was intended primarily for British and North and South American internees. . . . Most of the 300 Jews saved their lives by getting hold of forged passports, which the Germans thought were genuine, from various countries in the Western hemisphere.

Also from the autobiography is this postscript to the story of the services held in the Lunéville synagogue:

In November, at a dinner given for General George Marshall by the "brass" in Lunéville, General Jacob Devers told General Marshall that he was having dinner in a town in which a Jewish chaplain held a synagogue service before the town was officially taken. General Marshall and the diners laughed heartily. At the time the happening was happening, those of us who were directly involved did not find it quite so funny.

October 8, 1944
Somewhere in France

Dear Zelda, Jonny, Mike, Jerry, Judy and all:

I am sorry that I have had to wait so long before writing to you but it has been simply impossible for me to do so under the pressure which has surrounded me. There is much that I could tell you but I simply have not the time to put it all in writing. I am enclosing a copy of the report on the High Holydays which I am sending to the Jewish Welfare Board and this will have to suffice as a description of how I spent those days. During this period I met two persons whom you know very well: *a.* (Now don't faint) Marty Peppercorn![1] Who is now attached with his unit to our corps. At the present time he is a few miles from us. In the same unit are a number of other men and officers from Croft, including an officer from the 27th Battalion and a Jewish medical officer, Captain Harris. You may be sure that it was a very joyful reunion. Marty looks fine. He only arrived in France recently and looks upon me as quite a veteran. I had a letter from Ruth [Marty Peppercorn's mother] some time ago which I have not had a chance to answer. *b.* First Lieutenant Dick Krause of Gainesville and West Palm Beach, husband of Genie Argintar. That, too, was a joyful reunion. Dick came to my Rosh Hashana service not knowing that I would conduct it. He, too, is attached to our Corps. And tomorrow I shall reunite, God willing, with an old friend from Tallahassee: Chaplain (Major) Earl Stone, who came to Tally to visit his cousin at Dale Mabry [now a campus of Hillsborough Community College in Tampa] back in 1941 and who went to Blanding where he wooed and wed Judy Wilensky and then went to Europe in March 1942 where he has been right in the thick of it ever since. Earl is about a 2-hour drive from here. He came over to see me last week but I was in Paris. Tomorrow, Chaplain Schellhase and I are going to see him. The day after tomorrow, he will return to the States, his tour of war duty over. He really deserves that break — after 2½ years of being right up in it. My hat is off to him and I am very happy for Judy. She is a wonderful girl and has a wonderful husband.

The package from Macy's came — but no word from Eli and no bill. Chaplain Laning got his 100 cigars — but no bill. Mr. Miller has not received his knife. I got the cigars, dictionary, knife, and Recorder — but no bill. Thanx, Eli, but we still want the bills and hope you will favor us by sending same to us at your earliest convenience. To all of you my grateful thanks for writing to me and I am only sorry that I am unable to answer these letters individually. My business correspondence has piled up beyond control and I have practically no time for personal letter writing. I shall go back through your letters to see if there are particular points in them that require comment:

Zelda — I do not take vitamins. None are available even if I needed them which I don't. The ringing in the ears has practically ceased entirely. My hemorrhoids are bothersome but not to too great a degree. At the present time, I have a cold and sore throat, nothing serious, the first illness of any kind I have had since coming over, except a mild case of diarrhea on one occasion. So far as sending things are concerned I could use a box of cigars a month. None can be gotten here. Also candy and nuts. Don't send any doo-dads or foolishness. I shall only have to throw them away. Whenever you think of sending me something, remember that I am living on a battle-field and traveling light and can not be burdened with non-essentials.

Don't expect me to guess when the war will end. I'm too busy trying to help win it to engage in foolish theorizing. The Germans nine miles from where I now sit who, at this very moment, are engaged in sending quite large cannon shells in my direction do not seem to be paying very much attention to all these predictions about the end of the war being in sight.

I have not given a moment's thought to what will happen to me when the Germans give up. If I am still alive and kicking when that happens, as I hope I shall be, I'll do one thing: whatever Uncle Sam tells me to do. And all this idle day-dreaming by shallow-minded civilians does only one thing: it delays the day of complete victory and the day when those who are left will go home. And you children, Jonny, Mike, Jerry, and my darling Judy, don't think that because daddy does not tell you about his travels and what he sees and what he does that he is not thinking of you. Your daddy loves you very much and you must all always remember that, but your daddy is not on a sight-seeing or souvenir-hunting tour. He is not playing games. He is engaged in a quite serious endeavor which deals mainly with destruction and death and in trying to keep men sane and good under such conditions. Your daddy loves to hear and to read about what you do and what you say but do not expect your daddy to engage in small-talk with you or any one else, at least not until things ease up a bit.

Helene — it was interesting to read what *Time* had to say about the exploits of our Corps. One does get a peculiar feeling out of reading about history which he, in a very small measure, has helped to make. I should say that, sooner or later, there is a good possibility of my seeing Muelheim,[2] but I know of a surety that between me and it are a helluva lot of very determined Germans who are not willing to make my getting there easy. Yes, the JWB has asked us to write up some of our experiences. I have written up a number which you have read, but, thus far, have seen none in print.

You ask me not to take chances and place certain deterrents on one side of an imaginary scale. I am sure that I do not need to remind you that a scale has two sides.

Thank you and everybody for the warm New Year Greetings. I received many touching messages from the wives and parents of my men.

As you probably know, I was in London twice but didn't stay very long. However, I have been to Paris twice for four days each time and managed to combine some pleasure with my business. The Army very obligingly billeted me in Citie Bergere (near the Folies Bergere) right on Fauberg Montmarte so I was really right in the middle of things. This is the extent of my fun since landing in France. The rest has been deadly serious business.

I have sent you, Helene, a bottle of perfume for your birthday which I hope will come in time. On my last trip to Paris I got perfume for Henny, Rae, Lil, and Micky which I am going to send to you, Zelda, to re-mail. I hope all these folks will like the perfume and will forgive me for not mailing out separate packages but it is very difficult to do from here. I sent the kids the Chanuka presents which I mentioned in a previous letter. I sent them about a week ago and in time I hope you will get them. The pocketbook and what is in it is for you, Zelda. As for the rest: For Judy: Teddy bear; For Jerry: Kaleidoscope and wagon; For Mike: Paint-book, paints, post-card puzzle; for Jonny: Boxes of puzzles; and for each one: a Pipe of Pan. As I told you before these things don't look like much but they cost plenty. I am sending along some French money and other things I want you to save for me. All for now. Love and kisses to all.

Your husband and daddy,
Max

P.S. All of us were greatly shocked here today by Mr. Willkie's sudden death.

[1]Martin Peppercorn (1915–1995) was at Camp Croft with Rabbi Eichhorn and assisted in religious services there. Other Camp Croft assistants included actor Zero Mostel and sportscaster Mel Allen. Peppercorn would become, in the 1960s, national campaign director of the United Jewish Appeal.

[2]Birthplace of Anna Zivi Eichhorn (1882–1940), Rabbi Eichhorn's mother.

The following is from Rabbi Eichhorn's report "Contacts with the Great and Near Great."

I arrived at my first duty station, Camp Croft, near Spartanburg, S.C., on July 16, 1942. In February of 1942, five months prior to my arrival, the then CG of Camp Croft, Major General Alexander M. Patch, had been relieved of this assignment in order to command the infantry assault on the Pacific island of Guadalcanal. I heard General Patch mentioned so often and in such laudatory terms by Camp Croft personnel that, although I had never met him, it seemed to me as though he was an important part of the twenty-two months I spent at this infantry training camp.

In late July, 1944, while visiting the Jewish wounded in an evacuation hospital in Normandy, I saw on the ward list the name of Captain Alexander M. Patch, Jr. I went to his bed and met a fine handsome young man in his late 20's, who had been wounded in the shoulder while leading his company in a 79th Division attack. We talked for about 45 minutes about his father and mother and his wife and his 18-month-old son, Alexander M. Patch III, whom he had scarcely gotten to know. Alex Patch, Jr. was General Patch's only son. Should I let his father know he had been hit? "No," said young Patch. "Father has just brought the Seventh Army into the Southern France invasion and I don't want to add to his worries. I'll let him know about this after I have been air-evacuated to England."

On the 28th of September, 1944, our XV Corps was transferred from the Third Army, commanded by General Patton, to the Seventh Army, commanded by General Patch. One of the first bits of news I got from Earl Stone, Jewish chaplain of Seventh Army, was that Alexander Jr. was now at his father's headquarters on recuperation leave. At this time, the 44th and 79th Divisions, under the direction of the XV Corps, was engaged in bitter combat with the Germans in the Foret de Parroy, east of Lunéville, France.

Early in October, as I was eating supper one evening in the officer's mess, the Corps Graves Registration Officer arrived, looking very tired and bedraggled. "I've just been way up front," he said, "way, way up front, into the Foret de Parroy. Special mission. Nasty job. Had to go bring back the body of young Patch. The general's only son, you know. He got it while observing artillery fire the second day after coming back to duty with his company in the 79th."

I went to my room and sat down and wrote General Patch a long letter of condolence. I told him that I was writing not as captain to general but as rabbi to mourner and as father to father and as friend to friend. I did not send the letter to him through military channels but by ordinary mail. The next morning when I told the Corps Chaplain what I had done, he chided me gently. "As well intentioned as you were," he said, "you should not have done it. He is your Commanding General and you should not have communicated with him on a personal matter of this sort outside of military channels."

Ten days later, when I returned late at night from a fatiguing tour of front-line battalions, I found a note on my desk from the Corps Chaplain: "Phone me as soon as you get in. Important." I phoned. "Should I come to see you right away?" I asked. "No," said Chaplain Schellhase, "it can wait until morning." "What's it about?" I asked. "It's about that letter you wrote to General Patch," said Chaplain Schellhase and then he hung up.

I began to think that maybe Captain Schellhase was right. Maybe I was about to be called to account for writing to General Patch outside of military channels.

Next morning Chaplain Schellhase quickly allayed my fears. "About three days ago," he said, "General Haislip called up and asked to speak to you. When I told him you were out in the field, he asked me to express to you his deep appreciation for the letter you wrote to General Patch. General Patch had called him to get your address so that he could thank you personally and had said to General Haislip that your letter had given him more solace than any other of the many kindnesses that had been shown to him in his time of great sorrow."

A few days later I received a letter from General Patch repeating these sentiments. "I have sent your letter to my wife and daughter-in-law," he wrote. "I know that it will comfort them greatly as it has comforted me."

In the months that followed, I met General Patch a number of times. Like General Omar Bradley and completely unlike the erratic, blustery, profane General Patton, Alexander M. Patch was a humble and religious man, a really great military leader in a very quiet and modest sort of way.

One story will serve to illustrate the manner of man he was: On Christmas Eve, 1944, the usual kind of drinking party was in progress in the Officers Mess at Seventh Army headquarters. General Patch did not come into the party until about 10 p.m. He walked in and, while the officers stood at attention, he said: "It seems strange and incongruous to me that we should be celebrating the birthday of the Prince of Peace on a night when our comrades are fighting and dying less than twenty miles from where we are. It seems even more strange and incongruous to me that, on such a night as this, one should want to celebrate this event by drinking intoxicating liquor. I have not taken a drink tonight and I do not intend to take any. I shall celebrate the time between now and midnight in the way which to me seems most appropriate: in my room and on my knees. How each one of you spends this night is his own private affair. But this I must say: Any officer in this headquarters who fails to be in his office tomorrow morning at the stated hour and in the appropriate physical and mental condition will not be a part of this headquarters tomorrow night." With that, he turned and walked out. Not another drink was drunk in the Officers Mess at Seventh Army headquarters during the rest of that Christmas Eve.

Within two years after the death of Captain Alexander M. Patch Jr., his father, General Alexander M. Patch, and his son, little Alexander M. Patch, III, also died. Thus the male line of General Patch's family was completely wiped out but the memory of this humble and righteous man will live on as an eternal blessing.

General Patch's letter to Rabbi Eichhorn after the death of his son:

You have written me a perfectly beautiful and thoughtful letter which I greatly appreciate. This message from you will be a very great comfort and a satisfaction to my son's wife and to his mother and sister. Noting your address, I know that I shall soon be able to thank you personally.

And he did.

October 12, 1944
Held services at these graves — U.S. Military Cemetery,
    Antilly, France

Chodrof, Sidney, R.	Chicago
Cohen, Henry	Washington, D.C.
Cohen, Irving L.	Denmore, Pa.
Cohen, Geo.	Brooklyn
Cobb, Irwin	Brooklyn
Dixel, Larry	Bronx
Dobis, Arthur	L.A.
Diamond, Marvin	Clayton, N.Y.
Fallenberg, Abe.	Brooklyn
Flomenbaum, Seymour	N.Y., N.Y.
Friend, Sidney	Bronx
Gardner, Benj.	Brooklyn
Greenberger, Marvin H.	Brooklyn
Heller, Sgt. Louis (Bronze Star)	Pittsburgh
Halperin, 1st Lt. Gabriel J.	Bronx
Heyderman, Pfc. Augustus	Brooklyn
Kerzer, Irving	N.Y., N.Y.
Korn, Irving	Dorchester, Mass.
Litman, Phillip	Newport, R.I.
Lorman, Harold	Rockaway Beach, N.Y.
Orloff, Joseph	Brooklyn
Shkolnik, Pfc. Leon	Columbus, Ohio
Tartakower, Jochanon	N.Y., N.Y.
Weiss, Stanley, J.	Philadelphia
Yankowitz, T-5 Sidney	Cleveland, Ohio
Zacharias, Nathan	Hammond, Ind.
Magill, Samuel	Philadelphia
Marcus, Sgt. Stanley	Brooklyn
Moretsky, Wilbert (Croft-Silver Star)	Pittsburgh
Matorin, Maurice	Roxbury, Mass.
Miller, David	Brooklyn
Mazie, Pfc. Joseph	Chicago
Newman, Edward H.	Boston
Weinberg, Murray	Los Angeles

Brenner, Pfc. Carl	Pittsburgh
Cravitz, Sgt. Paul P.	Fulton, N.Y.
Benn, Maurice	Lancaster, Pa.
Getz, Pfc. Barney L.	Altoona, Pa.
Isenberg, 1st Lt. Walter	Augusta, Ga.
Moritz, Sigmund	(not listed in book)
Marcus, Lt. Jerome	Kansas City
Zimberg, Pvt. Ben	Detroit, Mich.

October 16, 1944
V-mail to: Chaplain David M. Eichhorn
From: Jewish Welfare Board
145 E. 32nd Street
New York, NY

Dear Max,

You did it again. You say that you wept, well so did we. I used part of
your letter in a report to CANRA, Max. You simply have no idea what
this material means, or maybe we don't have any idea. You are the fellows who are going through it all. But when we put it all together and
get a picture of what you are doing and what has happened to the people of Europe — it leaves one unable to sleep. The nervous strain of
just reading letter after letter is enormous. How much more so must
it be for you!

John Sills returned the other day and what he had to say of the Jewish chaplains prompted us to start to work immediately on a project
we have had long in mind. On Shabbath Chanukah we shall ask all
synagogues in the country to dedicate their services to the Jewish
chaplains. JWB is also immediately assigning a staff member to col-
late all material from overseas chaplains and to prepare an appropriate booklet. If I were to write this, I would call it "Restorers of the
Breach of Jacob"[1] — because that is what you men have been.

   With best wishes and kindest regards,
   Sincerely,
   Isaac Toubin

[1]Rabbi Toubin seems to make reference to the idea that the Germans under Hitler were modern-day Esaus — a biblical embodiment of evil — and that the Jewish chaplains were responsible for the rise of good, as represented by Jacob.

October 24, 1944
HQ Com Z (Main)
APO 887 U.S. Army

Dear [Chaplain] David [Eichhorn],

I am getting a small Torah for you this week and will ship it to you. (*Sent you yesterday.) It is being loaned by the Consistoire,[1] and when you are through with it you should return it to them, at 17 Rue Saint George, Paris. They have no Perochet that they can lend out. Yesterday I sent you 300 French prayer books.

We have no JWB prayer books or Bibles on hand. I have placed your order in our file and as soon as we get our next shipment you will be the first to receive them.

You mentioned that Chaplain Schellhase stated that Corps chaplains are not getting enough various Protestant and Catholic supplies. If Chaplain Schellhase will have an order sent in to our office, it will be filled immediately to the extent of the supplies on hand. We are out of Catholic rosaries, missals, and testaments but we hope that a shipment will arrive soon and it is important to have your order on hand in our back order file so that it can be filled in order of precedence, when the supplies arrive.

I have told Mr. Jarblum of the Jewish Agency to get the Vittel sheets from Mr. Brenner.

Incidentally, in connection with your last sentence in your letter of October 19, I am fully aware that the items you requested are for "front line fighters" and you ought to know that combat troops will receive preference from our office at all times when it comes to Catholic, Protestant, and Jewish supplies.

With kindest personal regards, I am,
Cordially yours,
Judah Nadich
Chaplain (Major)
Deputy to the Theater Chaplain

[1]The Consistoire Central des Israelites is the hierarchal organization of French Jewry, established in 1808.

October 25, 1944
Somewhere in France

Dear Zelda, Jonny, Mike, Jerry, Judy, Ann and all:

First of all I want to talk to you, Jonny. I was very much distressed to learn that you have been so ill. I am very happy that you made a good recovery and I hope that by now you are feeling fine. Take good care of yourself because, after all, as I told you before, you are my biggest boy and it is up to you to do as much as you can to help take care of our family while I am away which, as I have also told you before, may be for a very long time.

I also feel quite sympathetic, Mike, with your problem at school. It does seem a shame that you should be held back at school by such a flimsy technicality but don't worry about it. You are still young enough that you will have ample opportunity later on to make up for whatever loss you are suffering now.[1]

(One of the office typewriters has just become available and so I shall continue by this more expeditious means of writing. First, I have had to administer a mild bawling out to the office force for permitting this type to get so dirty. But I'm not going to take time out to clean it. I've got too much work to do after I get through writing this letter.)

Zelda, thanks for sending me Roosevelt's speech which I read with much interest and enjoyment. He is truly a great man and I hope the American people have sufficient common sense to re-elect him, as I believe they will. Dewey is all right as an individual but he is entirely too inexperienced for the important role of the president of the USA for the next four years. If it were not that Roosevelt has already been president for twelve years, Dewey wouldn't stand a ghost of a chance. . . .

You and everybody else must be patient if I do not write as often as you think I should. I can assure you that there is a good reason therefore, i.e., I usually have so many things to do that I don't know where to turn first and if you could see what it means to my men to have me with them, I don't think you would begrudge the letter-shortage. I know how much letters mean back home and how much they mean here but it still is quite different from a situation in which one sees a soldier at a service on one day and his name on a casualty list a few days later. . . .

I enjoy so much your little dissertations on the children. Whenever I see any little cute French kids, I get lonesome for ours. I give them chewing gum and candy and get a big kick out of their sweet smiles and their polite "mercis." I am sorry that the Hebrew school plan fell through and hope that later on the boys will be able to go as I should very much like them to get this training. . . .

I note that you say it has been raining in Tulsa. They tell me that where we are now it rains about 200 days out of every year and that this is the rainiest season of all. It certainly must be because we are getting a downpour every day. We are living in buildings but I am out with the troops a large part of the time and, by this time, I am so accustomed to being wet and muddy that I am hardly aware of it any longer. Sometimes as we go barreling down a wet road on a rainy day in an open jeep at 40 miles an hour (with the wind and the rain quite literally in my hair) I have to smile as I think how very uncomfortable I should have felt to be subjected to such an experience in civilian life or even at Camp Croft. Here one takes it as a matter of course. . . .

I'm sorry to hear about Lil's poison ivy. It's no joke. That's one infirmity that I have not yet seen in France. I don't know whether or not there is any such ivy in this vicinity. Maybe Lil ought to join up and come over here to get rid of the darned stuff. Failing that, she probably will keep on using pink calomel lotion. . . .

I hope that sooner or later you will get the two packages I have sent of toys and perfumes. I also hope that I shall also get all the packages which all of you have been good enough to send to me. It seems that packages have a low priority because it certainly takes them a long while to reach us. I should like you to send my cheaper watch to me. The $4.95 wrist watch finally went out of commission after months of faithful service. It is full of dirt and I have no way to get it cleaned. Please wrap the watch very carefully (cover it with plenty layers of boxes and paper) and send it by first-class mail because packages get very rough treatment from you to us.

Helene, thanks for your offer to send me Mrs. Morris' Torah, which I must decline with thanks. The reason for our not having a Torah is very simple: In the battle-lines one doesn't have much of anything. A Torah is too much of a luxury to be lugging around in the mud. Most of my services have been held in a woods or a barn (so that lurking Jerry planes wouldn't disrupt the service by planting a few eggs on top of us) with rather meager equipment. When we have had enuf JWB prayerbooks available that two men could look on a book we have felt ourselves fortunate. I have with me a Hebrew Bible and English Bible and a book of Midrashim (Yalkut Shemoni). That is my entire library. Whenever I get hold of a Jewish magazine or tracts or any kind of Jewish reading matter (such as *The American Israelite*[2] and the like), they disappear immediately. The men are hungry for any kind of reading matter and, in their present frame of mind, they take eagerly any kind of religious literature or anything which informs them of Jewish current events. You may be interested in another recreation of theirs: The more they see and hear about what has happened to the Jewish communities of Europe, the more Zionistic they become. I believe you will find, when the men return, that the overwhelming majority of them have become convinced of the necessity for a Jewish home-land in Palestine. Of course, the majority of them were at least luke-warm Zionists before they went into the Army but their feelings along this line have been definitely intensified.[3] I don't know how long it will last but, for the time at least, our men are more intensely and proudly Jewish than I have ever known a similar group to be in the States. And they are really turning out for services. For the past few weeks, I have been fortunate enough to have the use of the same synagogue where I held my Yom Kippur services. We may be here a little while yet so I have sent to Paris for a Torah and Peroches to use while we have the shul. The Nazis completely gutted the place so there are no seats although I hope that this week the Army will provide us with same and will also repair the electrical fixtures so that we may "pretty" the place up a bit. Despite the lack of equipment and the run-down appearance of the synagogue, and also despite a shortage of prayer books and standing-room only for a service which lasts from 45 minutes to an hour, the attendance has steadily increased until, last Sunday, about 300 men and women were jam-packed into the place and some could not gain entrance. This was formerly a Jewish community of 120 families. A few of them are beginning to trickle back from hiding and from the war. And so at our services last Sunday we had as our very honored guests the vice president of the congregation (a Major in the French Army), a Captain in the French Navy, 3 members of the Maquis[4] who have been guerilla fighters for four years in South France, and a number of others who had been in hiding, from 15-year-old kids to 80-year-old grandmamas. And were they happy to be at that service! I am going to have dinner with one of them next Sunday.

There was a Zivi family here before the war.[5] Probably died in the Polish gas-chambers along with the majority of the local Jews. Which brings up a quite unusual happening. I am now holding services regularly for a large French unit which is part of the Corps. It has a large number of Jews, recruited from all over Europe and Africa. I conduct the services in Hebrew, assisted by a French captain who translates my sermons from English to French and preaches them. The Jewish Welfare Board has printed special prayer books for the use of these French Jewish soldiers. One of them is an Alsatian by the name of Lieutenant Zivy. He believes that his grandfather and [my] mother's father were brothers and that we are second cousins. He says that there were 8 brothers, and that 7 remained in Alsace or France and that the 8th moved to Freiberg, Germany, and eventually married grandmamma and lived in Muelheim. Could be. He is a fine fellow and holds a responsible position in the unit. Lives in Paris and speaks English quite well. It seems that there were quite a number of Jewish families by the name of Zivi in this part of the world.

Dad, tell Mrs. Yablonovitz that she certainly has done a wonderful piece of work as a Nurse's Aide and one which is of inestimable value to the war effort. Those of us who have worked under all conditions with the Army nurses have the very highest regard for them, their courage and their skill, and the work which they do. At the same time we know that there must be a shortage of RNs in the States and it is good to know that consecrated women like Mrs. Yablonovitz are making the heavy sacrifice of time and energy to fill this important gap in our civic life. There are a surprisingly large number of civilians who think they have made a large contribution to the war effort by simply going on with their normal routine, not realizing that those who are following normal procedures are simply contributing by not hindering and that the war is being won by those who follow a normal routine with a "something plus." And I don't consider buying War Bonds part of that something plus. An individual who loans the government money which will come back in ten years with interest, money which he will lose anyway if we lose the war, hardly deserves to be praised as highly as some have been. . . .

At the present time, we are in a situation in which there is comparatively little danger. For a while it was pretty hot around here. As I said before, I am kept quite busy. While we were galloping across France, we always had the Germans all around us and could never be quite sure if we went on a lonely stretch of road or through woods that we might not, at any moment hear a rather unpleasant sound whiz past our ears. But the rapid advance is over and the harder task of blasting the Jerries out of heavily defended and well-prepared positions has begun. It has now become somewhat although not altogether like the trench warfare of the last World War. It is a slow and bloody business. We are up against the picked soldiers of the German Army and fighting through some mighty tough terrain. But our headquarters is far enough back that I don't have to feel as though I'm sticking my neck out every time I visit some unit. . . . You might be interested to know that there are now 21 Jewish chaplains in France, of whom 10 are with rear echelons and eleven in combat zones. I'm one of the 11. I believe that only two of these have been in combat longer than I have.

So much for now. With lots of love and kisses to all of you fellers and gals, I am,

Your husband and daddy,
Max

[1]Michael Eichhorn does not remember exactly what his father was referring to, but it may have been that the Tulsa schools had a policy requiring attendance in kindergarten before one entered the first grade. Because the Eichhorns had moved so much prior to the war, Michael had not attended either nursery school or kindergarten. So while the other children his age, kindergarten graduates, went on to first grade, he had to complete his mandatory year in kindergarten.

[2]Published in Cincinnati and founded in 1854 by Isaac M. Wise, *American Israelite* is the oldest English-Jewish weekly newspaper in the United States and the second oldest in the world.

[3]The Zionist movement began in Europe in the late nineteenth century with the goal of creating a Jewish homeland in Palestine.

⁴The Maquis were guerrilla fighters during the German occupation of France. The movement began with those who fled to the forests, especially in Brittany and the south, but eventually included former French soldiers, communists, socialists, and Jews — anyone willing, to quote a Maquis recruiting leaflet, "to live badly, in precarious fashion, with food hard to find, cut off from families." Thousands joined, committing acts of sabotage and helping Allied airmen get home safely. After the war, Eisenhower said that the French resistance fighters had been worth six divisions to the Allied cause.

⁵Zivi was Rabbi Eichhorn's mother's maiden name.

November 5, 1944

To whom it may concern:

I have this day received from Chaplain (Captain) David M. Eichhorn, 0-482124, the sum of 37,393 francs to be used for the purpose of aiding the needy people of the Jewish faith in this area. This money was contributed through a collection made this date among the Jewish soldiers at a synagogue service in Luneville.

> Paul Levy
> 56 Rue Gambetta
> Luneville, France

As part of his duties as a chaplain, Rabbi Eichhorn wrote thousands of letters to soldiers' families back home. Two samples follow.

November 8, 1944
Somewhere in France

Dear Friends,

I had the pleasure of seeing your son at a service which I conducted for the Jewish men of his unit several days ago.

I feel certain that you will welcome my assurance that [he] is in good spirits and looks well. He is living for the day when victory will come and he will be able to return to you and all his loved ones.

Praying that God's choice blessings may rest upon you and yours and with Zion's greetings, I am,

Cordially yours,
David Max Eichhorn
Chaplain

Headquarters Designation
Somewhere in [France, Germany]

Dear Friend,

I have learned with deep regret that your [son, husband, brother, etc.] has died in the service of his country while fighting in [eastern France, western Germany] and has been buried in an Army cemetery in the [_____] area.

Nothing that I might try to do or say in this time of sorrow will measure adequately to the immensity of his sacrifice or of your grief. I hope that you may derive some small measure of comfort from my assurance that your [son, husband, brother, etc.] has been interred under the Star of David and in accordance with the ancient traditions of our faith.

Praying that God may bring speedy healing of mind and heart to those who mourn and may hasten the day of victory and peace, I am

Very sincerely yours,
David Max Eichhorn
Chaplain

November 10, 1944

Dear Zelda, Jonny, Mike, Jerry, Judy, and all:

First of all I wish to thank my pop for the package just received with its most welcome contents. The chocolate has already disappeared (the first which we had tasted since arriving in France save for our D-rations and our special Hershey Tropical bars, both of which were prepared for their nutritive and preservative qualities and not for their taste which, judged by Whitman Sampler standards, is no good). I was down to the last 2 cigars in the box which Eli sent me so that cigars were likewise a welcome sight. The peanuts will also disappear in jig-time.

The only family letter I have before me at the present time is a V-mail letter from Zelda, just received, dated October 26. Very cute story in it about Jerry, Judy, Jonny, and babies. Sorry to hear that Jerry has been ill and glad to know that he is OK again.

Am enclosing a story from a Chicago paper about my successor in Tallahassee and also a story of importance from a recent *Stars and Stripes*.[1] The Army has at last taken who we are, what we are, and where we are off the secret list and if you read the enclosed article carefully and take a good look at the map, you will find out a great deal more about where I have been and what we have been doing for more than a month. As you will note from the map, we are occupying a sector which runs from Nancy in the North to Le Thillot in the South and which faces the German cities of Strasbourg and Colmar. Also on our southern tip, at not too great a distance away is a little village called Muelheim am Rhein.

There isn't any news of a striking nature. Had a letter recently from Herman Snyder, who has been with the Marines for seven months and is by now probably somewhere in the South Pacific.

Here are some recent items as they occur to me: The attendance at our Sunday synagogue service increases constantly. Last Sunday we had 372 present, a larger crowd than I ever had in the Army or civilian life except on the High Holydays. Some of the men travel as far as 80 miles to make the round trip to come to the service. We are gradually making the synagogue look like something. We've brought back the pews from the place where they were hidden and installed them. We have electric lights working in the place and it is lit up beautifully, including the Ner Tamid. We have put in a wood-furnace which is not yet working. We have a Torah, Peroches, and velvet altar cloth. From the four bare walls which we found when we arrived, we have built it up to where it really looks like something. For this my assistant, Irving Levine, deserves most of the credit. He has a fine artistic sense which he delights in putting to good use. Tomorrow there will be an all-day Armistice service in the synagogue beginning at 10 a.m. and lasting until 5 p.m. Catholic chaplains will officiate from 10 to noon,

Protestant chaplains from noon to 4 p.m., and I will hold forth from 4 to 5 p.m. This was my idea. I don't know, of course, how successful it is going to be. The Christian Scientists hold a service in the synagogue every Sunday afternoon. I am trying to have the building used as much as possible.

I have been conducting a number of French military funerals. The French, wherever possible, bury their dead in civilian cemeteries with full military rites. Since I am their Jewish chaplain, I conduct the services for their slain Jewish soldiers. I read the service in Hebrew and a French officer translates it into French. I have buried both officers and enlisted men, all of them so far from North Africa, from Morocco, Tunis, or Algiers.

I have been doing quite a bit of work among refugees. In one town [Rosieres-aux-Salines], I located 22 old Jewish women, ranging in ages from 68 to 97, whose husbands and children had been deported and who had been left behind by the Germans deliberately as a burden upon the community. The 97-year-old lady, a staunch Orthodox Jewess, has died and I conducted her funeral. I have been taking care of the rest with the aid of money raised by Jewish soldiers and supplies furnished by the American Army and the French. I found these helpless beings existing in two rooms in a city hospital, dirty, lousy, and half-starved. They had to stay in bed most of the time because they had few clothes and no means of heating their rooms. The sight and smell required quite a bit of stamina to endure. The Army has given them food, wood for their stoves, woolen underwear, shoes, and heavy coats. The soldiers in the past two weeks have given me over $800 to help these and other Jewish refugees who needed help. God bless the American Army and the American Jewish soldiers. There is no other Army like it in the world. I had to plead with the men not to give me as much as they wanted to give. Many of them wanted to empty their pockets and give me all they had. I am trying to get the old ladies placed in an Old Folks Home (Jewish) at Nancy.

Two Jewish chaplains visited me recently, Harold Saperstein and Emanuel Schenk, both of JIR (Stephen Wise).[2] Schenk preached for me last Sunday. Did a very good job. Said he was inspired by the fact that I had more Jews in my congregation than he has in his whole outfit. That does not hold true for me. I don't know exactly how many I have but it must be between 2,500 and 3,000. There are 2 Jewish chaplains in the whole 7th Army. Chaplain Schellhase told me today that he has told them that he is going to fight like the dickens to have me kept here. I am quite willing to abide whatever decision is made. I only want to be wherever I am considered most useful. It tickles my vanity, or course, to know that my work has been good enough that these two outfits are both interested in having me work for them, especially having seen, on a number of occasions, how these same outfits seek to get rid of officers that they do not like.

I am busy, busy, busy and work from early morning until late at night seven days a week. Here is how a few days go by: Yesterday I traveled 35 miles to an Ordnance Battalion to hold a service. To get there I had to pass through flooded areas where the water was 1½ feet deep in some places. Spent the night there with artillery fire from both sides zooming over my head. Got back at noon today and spent the afternoon writing an Armistice Day talk. This evening I traveled through pitch-black darkness to hold a service for an anti-aircraft battalion. Tomorrow morning I shall travel 15 miles toward the front-line to hold a service at a French Division HQ. Then back 20 miles for a service at an artillery HQ. Then back to where I am now for the Armistice Day service in the afternoon. Sunday morning at 10 I shall have my usual synagogue service and then, in the afternoon, will journey to the HQs of two infantry regiments to hold services for their men. At these HQ services, the attendance runs anywhere from 15 to 75 men. On Monday, I will leave bright and early for the big general hospital 30 miles away where I shall hold a service for the wounded and spend the day talking to them and planning to write letters for them to their folks. So it goes. The fellows are so earnest and so grateful and I am so deeply content with this privilege of working with and for them. The letters I get from their folks are a great inspiration. For example, here are excerpts from two letters from mothers which were among those received this evening: "Manny wrote us about the fine work you are doing and I know it must be a source of great satisfaction to you to know that the boys appreciate your work." "I am thrilled to know that in a world so full of misery my boy could still get spiritual help and be thrilled by it. He wrote me a letter, filling 2 V-mail pages, to describe your High Holy Day services. He told me how you explained the history of the Ram's Horn and how, when the men turned toward the East to davan, the sun came out.[3] Let us hope that this was the Divine handwriting on the wall, which promises that it would not be long until there will be peace and every mother's son and daughter will come home to their loved ones."

> Love and kisses to all,
> Your husband and daddy,
> Max

[1]The *Stars & Stripes* newspaper for soldiers began during World War I, at the suggestion of General Pershing, and was revived for World War II. Unlike the other military newspaper, *Yank,* which was created in 1942 and was written entirely by enlisted personnel, *Stars & Stripes* had officers on its staff and used wire services for news from home, especially sports.

[2]The Jewish Institute of Religion (JIR) in New York was founded by Dr. Stephen Wise in 1922 and was the principal competitor of Rabbi Eichhorn's alma mater, Hebrew Union College. The two schools merged in 1950.

[3]During the course of the service, the congregation turned toward the second temple in Jerusalem to pray.

> November 17, 1944
> National Jewish Welfare Board
> New York, New York

Dear Max,

I don't know where to begin or end in writing to you. I have been out of town a great deal lately and am in the midst of hectic preparations for a trip to the Pacific at the invitation of the War Department so that there has not been the opportunity for long leisurely correspondence with you. However, I have ascertained that your letters and article have received attention.

I write you now for two purposes — first to tell you that your letter which we are using in the next issue of *The Jewish Chaplain* is one of the most moving documents I have ever read. You wept; so did we! We hope that through imprisoning such a document in print, we will help to make it part of the permanent historic record.[1]

Second, you will probably think that I am either a sentimental sissy or endowed with a sympathetic imagination, but I must speak with great fervor also of the article by Mr. Frydman. I found it of such an unusual character that with some minor editorial revisions, chiefly in the beginning, I have sent it to my friend, Frederick L. Allen, Editor of *Harpers Magazine*.[2] I hope that he will be struck, as I have been, with its unusual poignancy and significance and will find it suitable for publication in that periodical. If so, there will be a substantial fee which on the basis of my own past experience will probably be not less than $200. However, Mr. Frydman should not count on this because as you know the very best of articles can be rejected if it does not happen to strike the momentary public interest. If it should be rejected by *Harpers*, I will try to place it elsewhere. In the meantime, our Yiddish Department has written about Mr. Frydman in the Yiddish press which I trust will please him.

I leave for the Pacific around December first and will be gone two months. I do hope that I will be hearing from you before I leave.

I take it for granted that your present experiences are imposing a strain upon you that you never would have had if you had remained in civilian life. You must be a very different man from the guzzler of chopped liver with schmaltz whom I last saw at Segal's extra fancy kosher restaurant. However, I think also that in a whole lifetime of civilian experience you would not have known the satisfactions that must be yours in the present service you are rendering. My blessings on you.

As ever,
Philip S. Bernstein

[1]Rabbi Bernstein is referring to the JWB report of October 2, 1944, concerning the service in Lunéville.

[2]Frederick Lewis Allen, besides being an editor at *Harpers* (and before that, *Atlantic Monthly*), was also the author of *Only Yesterday: An Informal History of the 1920s* (1931) and other best-selling histories, including *Since Yesterday, Lords of Creation, Keeper of the Flame,* and *Great Pierpont Morgan.*

November 21, 1944

Dear Rabbi Eichhorn,

I received a most welcome V-mail letter from you today telling me that you had the pleasure of seeing my son Irving Epstein. And that you gave him your blessing. I can't express in words how glad I was to hear from you. Your Blessing sure helps my daughter-in-law back home — Irving's wife — because the same day I received the letter from you my daughter-in-law gave birth to a 6½ lb. Boy. God Bless you and all our Brave Boys. I will never forget you for sending me this wonderful letter. Irving wrote and told me he went to a shul. He said that he prayed like he never prayed before. I never stop praying for one moment that all our boys should come home soon and safe.

I hope when you see my son again [you will] send him our love. Well Dear Rabbi Eichhorn I will close now thanking you from the bottom of my hearth [sic] for taking time and sending us that wonderful V letter.

> I remain sincerely yours,
> Mr. and Mrs. Herman Epstein
> Chicago, Ill.

On the day after Thanksgiving, the staff of the 21st General Hospital presented their frequently visiting rabbi with a large cake, as a way to thank him, while also acknowledging his renowned love of sweets.

TWENTY-FIRST GENERAL HOSPITAL
APO 0-3 6 2-USA
FRANCE
Pursuant to V.O.C.O.
DETAIL FOR THE BOARD:
MAJ ABE B BOLOTIN 0253803, MAC
CAPT WILLIAM J DANN 0441488, Sn C
WOJG COLEMAN FRIEDMAN W2115428 AUS
THE BOARD Met At The 21st General Hospital 24 November 1944
All Members Present
The Board Then Proceeded With The Examination Of:
CAPT DAVID M EICHHORN 0482124, Ch C
Ass't Corps Chap, XV Corps, APO 436, U.S.A.
LENGTH OF SERVICE: Long Enough AGE: Old Enough, Too
WHO WAS ADMITTED TO THE FRIENDSHIP OF THE 21ST
GENERAL HOSPITAL
UNDER THE FOLLOWING CIRCUMSTANCE
<u>SERVICES</u>

BRIEF HISTORY OF THE CASE:
Cannot Remember How Early In Childhood Became Addicted.
Admits Father and Grandfather Had Same Condition.
AFTER A THOROUGH EXAMINATION OF THE PATIENT AND
HIS CLINICAL RECORDS THE BOARD FINDS THE DIAGNOSIS:
CAKE-IVORE, Congenital
CAKE-OPHAGY, Chronic, Moderately Severe
LD: No, EPTAD
THE BOARD RECOMMENDS THAT THE SUBJECT BE
CLASSIFIED AS HOPELESSLY INCURABLE, BUT THAT A SINGLE
MASSIVE DOSE OF CAKE BE TRIED AS PALLIATIVE THERAPY.
(signed) A.A. Bolotin, President; W.J. Dann, Member; Coleman
Friedman, Member and Recorder
Approved: Lee D. Cady, Colonel, MC, Commanding

November 26, 1944
New York, New York

Dear Chaplain [Eichhorn],

Thank you for your kind letter of the 14th. We are very gratified to learn from you that our son, Elliot Rose, is attending Hebrew services being conducted by you and that he is in good physical and mental condition.

We are thankful that, in the midst of the hardships and cruel conditions which necessarily must prevail at the front, our sons find time and desire to worship their God, in freedom and piety. Our cause must indeed be a just one and our ultimate victory assured.

You write that our son is living for the day when victory will come and he will be able to return to us and all his loved ones. Amen! And please tell him for us (although the statement would be redundant and self-evident) how fervently we and all his loved ones also await that day.

Thank you again for your helpful letter and for the kind thoughts therein contained. With assurance of our cordial esteem and with the hope that we may see you in happier days, we remain,

Sincerely yours,
Mr. and Mrs. Murray B. Rose

7 December 1944
Restricted
Headquarters, XV Army Corps United States Army
Office of the Commanding General
Subject: Jewish Services

A celebration of the Jewish festival of Chanuka (Feast of Lights) will be held in the synagogue at 11 Wildemann Street, Sarrebourg, on Sunday, 10 December 1944 at 1530. Chaplain Gustave A. Schellhase will speak. The Corps Old Hickory Choir will sing. Miss Beth Dodge, Mr. Lee Royce and Mr. Carl Tatz will entertain. The traditional candle-lighting service will be observed. By command of Major General Haislip:

> Arch A. Fall
> Colonel, AGD
> Adjutant General
> Restricted

December 10, 1944
Philadelphia

Dear Chaplain Eichhorn,

A week ago I happened to read a letter sent to a Mrs. Drucker in Philadelphia, Pennsylvania, in regard to her son (Bernard Drucker) having attended services with you. When I read your signature, I realized a most pleasant surprise. For you see, you are the Chaplain who performed my marriage ceremony in Spartanburg, South Carolina on September 5, 1942. I wonder if you recall this ceremony? At any rate, I thought it would be nice to let you know that, even after a lapse of two years, I still remember your name and still feel eternally grateful for the happiness that you have made mine.

Sgt. Jarvis has been overseas almost 23 months serving with a Quartermaster Truck company in Europe. He has served in N. Africa, Sicily, and now in S. Italy. He anxiously awaits the termination of this war so that he may return to the States.

And so, dear Chaplain, hoping that this letter has brought forth the bit of joy intended for you, and wishing you the best of luck, I am,

Gratefully yours,
Mrs. Ida B. Jarvis

December 14, 1944
Somewhere in France

Dear Zelda, Jonny, Mike, Jerry, Judy and all,

Have just taken the first bath I've been able to take for two months and I feel fine. Mail has been pretty spare lately. Have in front of me from Zelda V-mail (Nov. 13) and air mail (Nov. 25) and from Helene V-mail (Nov. 12 and 20). Have not yet received snapshots mentioned by Zelda and am awaiting arrival of same with much eagerness. Also today received lovely package of goodies from Temple ladies in Lancaster as very welcome Chanuka gift. Isn't much going on here right now. We have been in quite safe surroundings for quite a while now — very much of a contrast to our earlier experiences. Of course, this is something that can very easily change but, for the time being, we are enjoying the lull. I am being kept very busy, mostly visiting hospitals and writing to home-folks, wrote 395 letters last month and over 100 so far this month. Visited hospitals on 16 days of last month and saw 217 Jewish boys, an indication of how much this type of work is needed.

Believe that I wrote the last letter to you on a hospital tour around Thanksgiving. Or have I written since? It certainly doesn't seem like that long since I wrote. Did I tell you of the Thanksgiving service I conducted (or rather, helped conduct) at the 21st General Hospital and how they baked a big cake afterwards with my name on it in icing and "Thank You" iced underneath it — a delicious chocolate cake which was eaten with great relish by our section? Also did I tell you of my trip to the battle-lines to get hold of two little Jewish kids (boy of 4 and girl of 2) who had been separated from their parents for 19 months and had completely forgotten same? We had a tough time persuading the kids to leave their foster-parents and return to their real ones.[1]

We have moved away, after two months, from the city wherein I had the rather tempestuous Yom Kippur service and I am now permitted by censorship regulations to mention it by name, i.e., Lunéville. If you look at the map, you will see where I have been sojourning from Yom Kippur until recently. There are now two other Jewish chaplains very close to where I am and we have been conducting joint services. We had a service for Erev Chanuka last Sunday night in the local synagogue with more than 450 men in attendance. Chaplain Schellhase preached for us and spoke, as he always does, with oratorical brilliance. A choir directed by Corporal Levine sang very beautifully and, afterwards, a USO Camp Shows gang put on a very lively program including singing by one Jewish actor of "Eli Eli" which, as you may imagine, brought down the house.[2] Corporal Levine's choir (all Protestant), as a special treat, had learned what they had been told was the traditional Chanuka hymn, i.e., "Rock of Ages." Unfortunately, no one told them that this was not the same "Rock of Ages" as we use but the one which is sung in Christian churches and when they began to give out with "Rock of Ages, cleft for me, let me hide myself in Thee," I was forced to halt the choir before they shocked our Orthodox constituents by telling them of "the water and the blood, from his wounded side which flowed."[3] It was an embarrassing moment but we managed to smooth it over very quickly. I've been taking quite a kidding about it ever since from the choir members and Chaplain Schellhase and others. However, the affair as a whole was a great success. I am sending herewith an account of the affair as it was released by our XV Corps newspaper section. The other chaplains with me are Herbert Eskin[4] of Detroit and Chaplain [Louis] Engelberg[5] of Cleveland, both Orthodox and both fine fellows and easy to get along with.

I am very glad that Helene liked the birthday perfume so much but I also hope that the other bottles of perfume intended for Henny, Rae, Lil and Micky reached their proper destinations. Noticed from Zelda's letter that the bottle intended for Rae was to be sent to Helene. It may be, at this writing, that Rae has not received any perfume. If so, please let me know, and, if I get another chance to go to Paris, somewhat unlikely at the moment, I'll see that Rae's interests are well taken care of.

It is quite clear from what you write that Arthur was wounded but not seriously enough to have to leave the Army. I am glad to know that he is still alive because I was afraid, after the long silence, that he might have gone down for the count. His new assignment sounds good and I am sure he will like it. I'll write him when I can.

Jerry and Mike, I am very proud of your fine work on the paper drive. Keep up your good work! As young as you are, you can do much to help with the war.

It looks as though I'll have to ask you to send me some cigars after all. We were issued cigars twice and then it stopped. I still have about a dozen cigars left from the box my dad sent me some time ago. I don't know of anything else that you should send me at the present time. So far we've gotten plenty of cigarettes but I'm getting tired of smoking them — never did like them very much anyhow.

I get to see Marty [Peppercorn] occasionally. We are both kept very busy. Haven't seen Dick Krause since Rosh Hashana. It's chow-time now and I gotta go. Love and kisses to all.

> Your husband and daddy,
> Max

[1] The children of Mr. and Mrs. Marx of Lunéville had been hidden on a farm in Cirey, France.

[2] "Eli Eli" was written by Jacob K. Sandler for M. Hurvitch's play "Brokhe, oder der yiddisher kenig fun poyin eyf eyn nakht," first staged in New York in 1896. The song subsequently became a vaudeville favorite. With a Hebrew title but primarily in Yiddish, the first verse can be translated as follows:

> My God, my God, why hast thou forsaken me?
> With fire and flame they have burned us,
> Everywhere they have shamed and derided us,
> Yet none amongst us has dared depart
> From our Holy Scriptures, from our Law.

[3] The thirteenth-century Jewish "Rock of Ages" — "Maoz Tzur" — is traditionally sung each night after lighting the Hanukkah candles and describes various moments in history when the Jews were miraculously saved. Here is one version of the first verse:

> Rock of Ages, let our song praise Your saving power.
> You amid the raging throng were our sheltering tower.
> Furious they assailed us, but Your help availed us.
> And Your word broke their sword when our own strength failed us.

[4] Rabbi Herbert Eskin later achieved considerable renown for his efforts (legal and otherwise) on behalf of Jewish refugees around Stuttgart, including

leading a small group of Jewish soldiers on armed raids against the farmers of the region, forcing them to slaughter their cattle and prepare them for cooking. Learning that women were still being used as prostitutes at a labor camp near Heilbron, Rabbi Eskin and three soldiers closed off the rear exit to the building, and when the male patrons came out the front, the soldiers hit them with their rifle butts. The women were liberated.

[5]Louis Engelberg returned to Cleveland after the war and became rabbi of Taylor Road Synagogue. At the time of this writing, he is rabbi emeritus there.

January 7, 1945
Somewhere in France

Dear Zelda, Jonny, Mike, Jerry, Judy, Dad, Helene, Lil, and all:

I am sorry that it has been so long since I have written. I have been very busy and, in addition, we have all been under a nervous tension which has not been exactly conducive to letter writing. As you are undoubtedly well aware by now, the German counter-offensive which many of us have been expecting for some time somewhere and at some unknown time, is well under way and, at the present time, the Germans are giving ample evidence that they may be down but they are far from out.[1] I can just imagine how the complacency of some folks back home has been given a rude shake, especially those arm-chair diplomats who were sure that the war would be over by Xmas and all that stuff. Those of us who were a little closer to the realities of the situation knew how misshapen such ideas were but what is a little thing like reality to the wise-guys and the wishful thinkers? Too many of us, too, know only too well not only how little real sacrificing is being done on the so-called home-front but, from far too many of the letters that we get, we can easily discern how psychologically un-prepared too many people back home are for making real sacrifice. The complaints that we find in our letters are tragically laughable. This has been, for those who are making the main effort, a tough war and it is going to get tougher not only for those who are doing the fighting but also for those at home. It is going to be a long war and, when it is over, everybody is going to be much poorer than they are now. And those who think in terms of their own comfort and welfare and ambitions, instead of giving unstintingly of themselves in every

possible way and enduring every manner of discomfort uncomplain-
ingly in order that the war may be completely won are unconscious
saboteurs and are helping Germany to obtain the compromise peace
which she is so zealously seeking through the current offensive. I repeat what I believe I have written before: It is difficult to reconcile the
uncomplaining manner in which American soldiers accept the most
horrible suffering and the most rigorous living conditions with the letters which I read from civilians containing the most inane comments
and attitudes and complaining about social and economic conditions
that, from this end of the line, look mighty good. The American public's mind and body have not yet been toughened and, until this happens, the war will go on and on.

I have before me Zelda's letters of Nov. 6, 18, and Dec. 1, 6 and 10.
Also dad's letter of Nov. 28, Helene's of Nov. 30, and Lil's of Dec. 2.
(To show you how balled up the mail situation is sometimes, I
received Zelda's air-mail letter of Dec. 6 before I received Zelda's air-
mail letter of Nov. 6.) I also received the packages sent by Zelda and
Lil which were devoured not only by me but especially by the men in
the section and those I meet in the hospitals and in the lines. For all
of this I am very thankful.

It is not possible for me to comment on everything in these letters
but I shall re-read them and sort of comment as I go along. I can
hardly see what I'm doing and am writing under somewhat adverse
conditions. I am writing this with an old-fashioned kerosene lamp on
one side of me and 3 little candles on the other as my total illumina-
tion in the blacked-out room not too far from where there's a lot of
good old-fashioned fun a-goin' on in the form of bombing and strafing
and artillery and small arms fire and such. A couple of hundred yards
from me the ack-ack boys are standing by their guns in snow about
six inches deep with a pretty good gale a-blowin' and about a quarter
mile beyond them brave but nervous American kids are standing
guard in fox-holes which are a grand mixture of mud and ice. I'm
operating from a division forward HQ and going around conducting
services for Jewish front-line fighters at their battalion CPs [command
posts] — and do those fellows appreciate it. Practically none of them
has seen a Jewish chaplain since he's been in combat. On this particular mission, I am the guest of a very lovable Baptist chaplain from
Columbia, S.C. (Chaplain Kinlow) and he as well as all the other

officers and men around here are simply grand to me. It's what one might call a pretty rugged life but as nothing compared to what those kids out in front of me are enduring to protect my life — and yours.

I enjoy very much reading about the kids and what they do and say and I hope that you will continue to write me about them. I was glad to get the pictures but they are not very clear. I should greatly appreciate your taking the children to a photographer every few months and having small inexpensive pictures taken of them instead of depending on amateur photography. In this way I could keep in touch with their physical progress. . . .

I have had another letter from Major Greenberg. He is still the rabbi of the hospital in England. Said some very flattering things about me being his favorite preacher. Didn't mention a word about his girl friend in either the last letter or this. I was glad to learn that Art is still alive. I haven't had a chance to write him yet but will do soon when I can. Goodness knows when that will be. My unanswered mail is piling higher and higher. I'm slipping on the mail business. Last month I only wrote, aided and abetted by Levine, 185 letters to relatives of soldiers, not including uncounted letters to personal friends and relatives. . . .

The other day I bumped into a Captain Corti who commanded a company in the 26th Battalion at Camp Croft. He remembered my family very well and, like so many others whom I continue to meet, looks on Camp Croft as the happiest days he spent in the Army. He's been through some quite rough encounters and so far has been very lucky.

I got a big kick out of seeing the kids holding the Paris toys in the pictures you sent. . . . Time out while I drink a pot of cocoa prepared by my good friend, Chaplain Kinlow of Columbia, S.C. . . . I have just received a letter from Rabbi Phil Bernstein of the JWB in which he tells me that the letter I wrote him describing my experiences during the last High Holydays "is one of the most moving documents I have ever read. It is being used in the next issue of the *Jewish Chaplain*. We hope that through imprisoning such a document in print, we will help make it part of the permanent historic record."[2] He also says this of an article which I sent him, written in Yiddish by Bernard Frydman, a Parisian journalist and under-ground fighter, translated by a Jewish doctor (captain in the U.S. Army) and re-written by me (with a foreword written by me). . . . [Rabbi Eichhorn then quotes the letter from Rabbi Bernstein concerning possible submission of the Frydman article to *Harpers*.] So maybe one of these days you will see my name somewhere in print. . . . One candle has just gone out. 2 more to go. . . . Sorry about the mix-up on the cigars and the perfume. Next time you buy cigars I would suggest that you send them right on, whether you think I need them or not. Even if they become plentiful again, which I very much doubt, I will be saved spending money for them. We are issued cigarettes and chewing gum. All else that is available we do not receive gratis. We pay for them, including cigars. I am sending herewith a number of requests which you, dad and Zelda, can use as you see fit. None of these requests is to be placed in the hands of the Tash family until said family fulfills my original request and sends me a statement of what the items they sent me some time ago cost. . . . I am very glad that you, dad, are feeling better and I certainly hope that this continues. I have received the ointment which I shall use if the trouble recurs. I haven't been bothered much the last few weeks and for the present I'm going to let well enough alone. I certainly hope that an opportunity will present itself for you to visit Zelda and the kids. I have mentioned before that you are missing a wonderful opportunity in not becoming acquainted with your grandchildren, especially your very adorable grand-daughter. . . . I wrote my first letter to a Tulsa family of a Jewish boy recently. I don't remember his name just now. Just found it. His name is Pfc Jerome C. Feenberg, Troop A, 106 Cavalry Squadron. His mother is Mrs. J. A. Feenberg, 26th St, Tulsa. . . .[3]

I'm afraid I won't be able to send anybody any presents for a while. I'm a long way from Paris and where I am there is nothing worth buying or sending. The main problem the civilians have around here is to find enough to eat and wear to stay alive. And they are very much worried about the Germans coming back — which we all hope they won't. . . .

I don't think the American girls need worry very much about the GIs marrying European girls. It is practically impossible for them to do so. Very few of the GIs that I know are interested in marrying their French girl friends. As one sage GI philosopher has said, "French girls haven't got anything that the American girls haven't got. The important thing at the moment is that the French girls have it *here*." The WAC recruiting campaign and the failure thereof seemed to indicate that American girls were not willing to transport what they have outside the continental limits of the USA.[4] Incidentally, I hope that Jonny and Mike are making out OK with their girl friend (or is it "friends"?).

Dad, I fully expected by this time to see some of the towns that you mention but the Germans don't seem to be very willing at present to let me go on a sight-seeing tour. . . .

Am enclosing a number of items which I want you to save for me. They include a curriculum of the school for Jewish chaplains which I conducted in England, a copy of the program of liberation of the Roth-schild Synagogue in Paris last September in which I participated, a picture of the Lunéville synagogue which I redeemed from decay, a thank-you letter from General Patch of the 7th Army answering a let-ter I wrote him about his son whom I knew and who was killed at the end of October. (General Patch is not only a great military leader but a great Christian and I value his friendship very highly); also a few letters which I have saved for souvenirs from the hundreds I have received from soldiers' relatives; also a New Year greeting from a Jew-ish chaplain whom I am very fond of. You will also find two sacred pictures given me, one for Zelda and the other for Judy, by a French priest with whom I lived for a few days while visiting one of our divi-sions. He had lived in Canada for 40 years and spoke English fluently. I had a grand time with him. In case you can't interpret his writing, he lives in the French Alsatian city of Cirey. In Canada, he lived in Lil-looet, British Columbia.

That's about all for now. It's after 11 p.m. and I've got to get ready for bed. Tomorrow will come very soon, another day of sloshing through the snow with Levine, jeep, and Co. to try to be some spiri-tual comfort to Jewish boys from Brooklyn, Detroit, and Los Angeles who have icicles on their beards and guns in their hands.

Love and kisses to all — and a big hug and kiss especially for every member of the East Fifth St. Tulsa branch of the Eichhorn clan.

Your husband and daddy, Max

[1]Rabbi Eichhorn is referring to the Battle of the Bulge, which began on Decem-ber 16, 1944, with a massive German counterattack in Belgium's Ardennes for-est. This ferocious conflict, which occurred under horrendous conditions, would become the biggest battle of the war, and the most deadly: 110,000 Germans were killed, wounded, or captured, and there were 80,000 American casualties, with an estimated 17,000 killed — a death toll unequaled in American military his-tory.

[2]Besides being published in *The Jewish Chaplain* during the war, Rabbi Eichhorn's report was reprinted in Rabbi Bernstein's 1971 book *Rabbis at War: The CANRA Story.*

[3]In honor of Private Jerome C. "Jerry" Feenberg, who was killed in the Battle of the Bulge, the Tulsa chapter of the B'nai B'rith Youth Organization AZA (Aleph Zadik Aleph) — a high school fraternity — is named the Feenberg Rubin AZA.

[4]The Women's Army Auxiliary Corps (WAAC), created in May 1941, initially recruited single American women between the ages of twenty-one and forty-five to perform noncombat, stateside-only jobs and thus "Release a man for combat." In terms of the range of jobs they did, and the way they did them, the WAAC was a huge success — too successful, in one sense, because many soldiers who held safe clerical jobs at home did not want to go into combat, and their loved ones agreed. For this and other reasons, WAAC women were subjected to vicious slander, including the false allegation that they were routinely issued condoms, and needed a lot of them. Because some soldiers believed that the WAAC's duties included boosting morale by "keeping the men happy," the recruiting slogan had to be changed from "*Release* a man . . . " to "*Replace* a man for combat." As the war progressed, the need for women in noncombat jobs, especially overseas, increased greatly. But the WAAC, as an auxiliary to the army, did not get the pay, privileges, and protection of regular troops. So in July 1943, President Roosevelt signed into law a bill subsuming the WAAC into the Women's Army Corps (WAC). All WAACs were given the choice of joining the army — with the opportunity of going overseas — or returning to civilian life. Seventy-five percent joined, but the WAAC "image" controversy of 1943 and the conversion to regular soldiers led to recruiting difficulties. WAC enlistments never reached the high levels of WAAC recruitment earlier in the war, although eventually 150,000 women served in the WAC — the first women other than nurses to serve in the U.S. Army.

One American loss as a result of the Battle of the Bulge was intentional. The following is from Rabbi Eichhorn's 1969 autobiography.

No American soldier had been executed for desertion in the face of the enemy since the American Civil War. During the Battle of the Bulge, December 16 to 30 (during which I was with a forward unit, the 103rd Infantry Division, that was completely isolated for almost a week), thousands of green American troops, who had been placed in what was thought would be a quiet sector, fled to the rear. To prevent a future re-occurrence of this kind of debacle, General Eisenhower's staff persuaded him that one deserter must be shot to convince would-be deserters what might possibly happen to them. The military prisons were combed to find condemned deserters who had thrown down their arms and fled from the enemy on two or more occasions. Six such were found. By some method, one was selected. He was a Jewish soldier from Philadelphia, the only Jew among the six. Preparations were begun for his execution. I was notified that I was to be his spiritual comforter during his last hours on earth and was also to be present at his execution.

General Eisenhower ordered that all six should be given intensive psychiatric examination. A number of the six, including the Jewish soldier, were declared to be mentally unbalanced. So the Jewish lad was not executed; but one of those who were given psychiatric "clearance," a Private Slovik, was shot. William Bradford Huie tells much of the story in his brilliant book, *The Execution of Private Slovik* [1954]. What I have just written he does not tell. I do not think he knew. If he had known, I believe he would have told. It should not be difficult to imagine my feeling of relief at not having to be part of this gruesome ordeal. A number of years later, I heard that the condemned Jewish soldier had ultimately been released from military custody, placed in a mental institution and remained there until he died.

Although 21,049 service personnel were charged with desertion during World War II, Private Eddie Slovik was the only one executed.

February 5, 1945
Somewhere in France

Dear Zelda, Jonny, Mike, Jerry, Judy, and all,

I have before me Jonny's letter of December 28, Helene's of Jan. 1, and Zelda's V-mail letters of Jan. 1 and 9 and air-mail of Jan. 6. There are probably more letters which you have written since these dates awaiting me back at the Corps HQ but I've been gone from there for the last 8 days and will not be back for 5 more. I've been up in the lines holding services and have been into Germany twice. Things up our way are going very slowly but, at the present date, the Russians are making wonderful progress and all of us are praying that they will continue to do so.[1]

First of all, I want to thank Helene for the package, the race-horses and the *SatEvePost* article. All were thankfully received. The things in the package were shared with soldiers and civilians, the race-horses raise the morale of the soldiers wherever they run, and the *SatEvePost* article ["Are the Chaplains Doing a Job?" *Saturday Evening Post*, December 16, 1944] was read with great approbation. It is one of the very few articles which I have seen which gives a fairly true picture of the work of the chaplains without laying on the goo an inch thick. The chaplains are doing a grand job but so are all the other fellers. It's one Army and one fight and most everybody is doing as much as he can to get the enemy down and keep him there.

Thanks, Jonny, for your very sweet letter. I hope that you will continue to write me. I hope, too, that you are doing a good job of acting as head-man of the family in my absence. I am sure that you are a big help to mama and do everything that you can to be of assistance. I hope you all, Jonny, Mike, Jerry, and Judy are being just fine children and trying to help your mama all you can. I wanted to send a money-order for you birthday-people to buy something for yourselves but it is not very easy to get a money-order here. One must be at least two days in the same place to do so and, unfortunately for me, my duties at the present time are such that I don't stay two days in the same place. As soon as I get the chance, I shall send this money.

I can understand how anxious you get when you don't hear from me for a while but try not to worry too much. I keep going from morning to night and, when I am on these trips (which is practically all the time now), I have very little opportunity to write. I'm usually too busy arranging for services, holding services, and trying to keep warm. Last month I held 27 services which is quite a bunch of services. If this month continues the way it has started, the number this month will be even greater. . . . I am glad you have gotten to know the Feenbergs. I am sure that you will be a great source of comfort and strength to them. . . . That certainly must have been a lovely birthday party you had for me and I wish I could have been there. I appreciate the gift very much and especially the children's giving up their Chanuka money to buy a bond. That will not only help to win the war but it will come in mighty handy during the, I hope, years of peace that lie ahead. I wish I could be with all of you, Jerry, Mike, Judy, Zelda, and dad on your respective birthdays from January through March but present circumstances do not seem to permit me to do so. . . . Levine isn't with me on this trip. Couldn't take the constant rugged conditions under which I've been doing my work so they had to send a younger fellow, Sergeant Milo Ryan, with me this time. Levine claimed he was too old for this sort of thing. He is 37. That kinda gave me a laugh for a reason not too hard to guess.[2] The spiel the office gave me when the boss replaced Levine (temporarily) with Ryan was quite flattering. I was told that Levine looks and acts ten years older than me. Sounds good anyway.

Thanks for the extra copies of the snapshots. As you now know, I have already received the others. I hope, as I suggested, that you will periodically visit the photographer instead of depending on these amateur things. In the end, the amateur pictures cost just as much and are not nearly as good.

Sure glad that you were all so good to each other on Chanuka. And also that I am going to get some cigars. My wants continue to be cigars, nosherei, and chocolate candy. All are non-existent here. And the sameness of the food, good as it is, does get annoying once in a while.

My German has come in very handy lately. I've made many friends among the folks of Alsace and Lorraine and they certainly are fine people. Their culture is German but their spirit is French. After we get into Germany, all conversation except on strictly business matters will cease so far as we and the Germans are concerned. That day may not be too far off. I understand that the Russians, God bless 'em, are about 35 miles from Berlin and still going.

Am enclosing two letters which I should like to have preserved.

> Love and kisses to all from,
> Your husband and Daddy,
> Max

P.S. If you can find a cheap fountain pen around somewhere, please send it to me. I've lost the two I had.

¹In the weeks before this letter was written, the Russians had reached the Oder, fifty miles from Berlin, and taken Warsaw.

²Rabbi Eichhorn had just turned thirty-nine when he wrote this letter.

February 14, 1945
Minneapolis, Minnesota

Dear Captain Eichhorn,

My parents received your letter yesterday, February 13, 1945, along with 3 of Bob's letters. I'm Eugene, Bob's 16 year old brother. I'm a Junior at West High in Mpls. Since this is Valentine's Day I'll send you my greetings. I just finished my homework, Physics, Latin, American History. My friend is going to get his dad's car one of these nights, and so I'll have to go over to his house tonight & give him my greetings.

I just got a job in a defense plant sort of. They make pup tents, sleeping bags, & waterproof things out of canvas. Well I have to go now, but say hello to Bob for me and if you get this letter please answer. P.S. I'm 5'9" tall, 145 lbs.

As ever,
Eugene Epstein

February 24, 1945
Somewhere in France

Dear Zelda, Jonny, Mike, Jerry, Judy, dad, Helene, and all,

I have before me all manner of correspondence which you all have been good enough to send me and I am sorry that it has not been possible for me to write sooner. I was in the lines until Feb. 10, then went to a Jewish chaplain's conference at Dijon to plan for the Passover holidays, then went on a tour of 7 general hospitals to visit the Jewish wounded of the XV Corps and finally returned here 3 days ago and have since been bogged down with so many administrative details that this is my first chance to write. In the absence of a Jewish chaplain at 7th Army HQ, I have been given the job of planning Passover celebration for the whole 7th Army and that is a fair-sized job. It involves the providing of wine and Matsos and such for well over 10,000 Yiddlach. In addition, Chaplain Schellhase went to the hospital four weeks ago with bursitis. Whether he will return here or go back to the States is at present indefinite. All of us here are hoping and praying that he will come back. He is among the finest men I have ever known. We have worked very well together and have become close friends. His going away has thrown an extra burden on the three officers (Chaplain Laning, Mr. Miller, and myself) who are now carrying on the Corps Chaplains office work and it is now necessary for me to stay closer to the office than has been the case for several months past.

So much for the immediate past. . . . Now to write of many matters as they come to mind. . . . I was very sorry to learn of dad's motor accident and am very happy that he was spared any serious hurt. . . . I am enclosing a money order (which I was finally able to get) for $40. It is to be considered a birthday present for you four boys and girls that have had or are about to have birthdays. $5 apiece for Jerry, Mike and Judy, and $25 for mama for each of you to buy yourselves something that you want. And the happiest of birthdays to Zelda and Judy. Sorry I can't be present personally at the celebration. . . .

(It is now 11 a.m. I have just been instructed to leave at 1 p.m. for our Corps Rest Center 35 miles away to arrange for Purim services for the men there. So it goes.) . . .

I have received a box of 50 cigars from Zelda. Thanks very much for them. They are one of the few things that I like which are rather difficult to obtain over here. Since everyone is so insistent on this point, I shall try to remember to include some sort of request at the end of every letter. . . .

I understand that in the Chanuka edition of the Jewish Welfare Board publication *Jewish Chaplain* I am given quite a bit of publicity and also learned, in a letter from Boston, that my old friend, Josh Liebman, devoted a portion of his Chanuka sermon to me. Very nice. . . .

I haven't had a chance yet to use the medicine dad sent me. However, I haven't been bothered much lately by the tachas-aches and pains and I've really got very little time to worry about myself. . . .

One of the biggest time takers right now is visiting chaplains. I had 5 of them to entertain yesterday and have just been informed that another one is on his way to the office to see me. There goes another half-hour or so. . . . Was sorry to learn of the passing of Uncle Leopold who was always so very nice to me. . . . Sure sounds as though you had a bitter winter in Columbia.

February 25th

One day later. . . . Am now at the rest center [located in Nancy, France]. The Chaplain stopped my letter-writing cold. Then left for here by jeep after lunch, a 2½ hour trip. Not a bad place at all. Hotel accommodations for the officers, gym, movies, dry cleaners, recreation centers, dames, swimming pool (heated), showers, barbers, donuts & coffee, and shows. The officers and men are now being given 4-day rests here as an extra-special reward if they have an extra-special rough time with the Jerries. However, I am not here to rest. I am here for 2 purposes; a. To arrange for Purim services tomorrow night and b. To report to the Corps HQ on ways in which chaplains can be of service to the rest center. As the first step in this direction, we have already adopted a policy of having two chaplains (Catholic & Protestant) assigned each week on detached service to the rest center from among our Corps chaplains. . . . Am trying to add some more to this letter between appointments. . . .

February 26th

One day later. . . . The above was all I was able to get written before I was dragged away from the typewriter and have not been able to get back since. I've been so danged busy that I thought it was two days since I've written the above. Spent yesterday morning conferring with some big shot about 7th Army Passover plans and most of yesterday afternoon letting the many units in town know of the Purim service which I shall hold this evening in the town's large synagogue. Then yesterday evening I went to attend a service being conducted by another Jewish chaplain, Harry Skydell,[1] and he insisted that I preach which I did. There were about 300 soldiers and 100 civilians at the service, including about 40 kids to whom the soldiers brought gifts of candy and chewing gum as Purim presents. The civilians kept on shmoosing to each other not only during the davaning but also while I preached, to the great annoyance of Skydell and the soldiers. Skydell laid them out in Yiddish. He told them that in America we observe strict decorum at services and that, since this was an American service they would have to behave as Americans behave or else they would not be allowed to come to the services. I got a big kick out of the whole thing. We then went to a civilian home and were served "latkes." . . .

Dad, I suppose the best way to send money is by money order. However, if you are thinking of sending me money for myself please do not do so as I am able to manage quite well on the approximately $100 a month which I keep for myself from each month's pay-check. Henny, I will use the money which you sent for our refugee fund and you may be sure that it will be put to good use. . . .

Dad, you asked what the men here think of the war. They all want it to come to an end, of course. Occasionally one hears speculation as to when it will end but not very often. These men, at least most of them, know by now that it is fighting and not talking that wins wars and they know further that they stand a good chance of being wounded or killed before it ends. So they go on about their business in a rather grim manner hoping for the best. There is no doubt in anyone's mind about the eventual outcome of the struggle but there is not too much guessing as to when it will end or how many more lives it will cost. I have never gone in for optimistic forecasts but I am more optimistic now than I have ever been before and I feel that there is good reason to believe that organized German resistance will have ceased by the middle of this summer although a type of guerrilla warfare may continue between die-hard Nazis and our forces for an unpredictable length of time. In our own Army sector, the defenses are so strong and the opposition so determined that we consider an advance of one mile a very good day's work. Many days our fellows have to fight like hell to hold on to what they've got. In such circumstances one is not inclined to get over-confident. The Russians are doing magnificently.[2] If they can maintain their present pressure or, perhaps, even increase it, the end of the war is most certainly in sight. Whether or not their man-power and materiel is sufficient to do this is, of course, something that is known only to Stalin, God, and perhaps, Roosevelt and Churchill. . . .

Micky, I enjoyed very much receiving and reading your letter and am glad you liked the perfume. It certainly is fine that Harry and you have been able to be together all this time and I hope that you will be lucky enough to be together until the end of the war and from there on. . . . Henny, I was very sorry to learn of your illness and hope that by now you have fully recovered. I appreciate the fine birthday greetings and wishes I received from you and the rest of your family. I was very interested in your fine account of the latest happenings among the Columbia Eichhorns.

February 27th

You guessed it. It is a day later. I am now back at Corps HQ. While trying to finish this letter yesterday, there was the usual interruption calling me to visit a local headquarters in the same town as the rest center. And when I got there, who do I bump in to, Zelda, but our wonderful friend from old Camp Croft, Chaplain Donald Henning! Boy, was that a joyful reunion. We hadn't seen or heard of each other since Henning left Camp Croft in November '42. He wanted to know all about you and the kids and said that one of the most pleasant memories of his Army life was the evenings he spent with us in Spartanburg. My goodness, that seems such a long while ago. We had lunch together and then I went back to the rest center to prepare for the evening's Purim service. We held it in the local synagogue with about 150 soldiers and civilians present. The local Chazzan read the Megilla and after each chapter, I acted out in English the story (to the great delight of all assembled),[3] and Don Henning preached the sermon in his usual marvelous manner. He is truly a great scholar and preacher. He has been through Africa, Corsica, Italy, and now France. In Corsica, for a while, there was no Jewish chaplain and Henning organized the services for the Jewish men and preached to them. He was called the "Chief Rabbi" of Corsica. And by good luck, the soldier who acted as my Chazzan last night was the same one who had been Henning's Chazzan in Corsica. Soldiers and civilians alike went wild over Henning. And who would not? He is so danged charming and just about all one could expect in a man.[4] After the service, we went to his room and drank Shenley's Black Label and shmoosed until about 1:15 a.m. and, when I tried to find my way back to the rest center I got lost and didn't land there until after 2 a.m. and I was up and about again at 7:30 a.m. and on my way back to Corps HQ at 10 a.m. and got here about noon and looked the situation over and I was so tired that I went to my room and slept from 3 p.m. to 5 p.m., a most unusual thing for me to do in my present busy state. So it is now evening and, the Lord willing, I shall be able to finish this letter. Found a couple interesting things waiting for me.

On my desk was a note from the 7th Army Chaplain informing me that I had been selected as one of 25 7th Army Chaplains who was to write a prayer for the Minute of Prayer Broadcast of the Mutual Broadcasting System. You will remember that this bunch published a prayer of mine when I was at Croft. This is pretty nice because there are over 300 chaplains in the 7th Army. The note said that I would represent the Jews. That is also very nice. We have 7 other Jewish chaplains in this area. . . .

Your news about Applebaum getting Miami was disturbing. Coleman Zwitman, their rabbi, is (or I guess I should say "was") on leave of absence from this congregation to serve as an Army chaplain and we chaplains don't like congregations to do things like that. . . .

I just received two packages, the cigars from Dad and a can with cigars, candy, and chewing gum from Zelda. Thanks very much to both of you but please don't send me any more chewing gum or Life Savers. Of these we get an ample amount. I gave away most of the candy and things which I received from all of you and from a number of others, including the Blocks of Tallahassee, to the Jewish civilian kids of this area as Purim gifts and they were thankfully received. . . .

Zelda, you ask what kind of life I have and what I eat and where I sleep and all that. . . . I think I've told you about that in past letters. For about 2 months through the first week of February, I went up and down the battle-lines through snow and ice, wind and rain, in an open jeep, conducting services, sleeping in battalion aid-stations, battalion CPs, occasionally in civilian homes, mostly in unheated and unlighted rooms, eating C rations. It wasn't exactly the most pleasant way to live but this isn't exactly a pleasant war. My only recreation was an occasional game of gin rummy, bridge, or pinochle and an occasional drink. This isn't exactly my idea of a completely filled recreational program but it's a damn sight better than was being enjoyed by those who I serve so I certainly have no kicks. And these fellows and I are in unanimous agreement that, if and when the opportunity proffers itself, we are going to [have] us one helluva good time. It is no use dwelling at too great length on the horrors of war because only those who have gone through and are going through these things fully comprehend. Two examples should suffice. Example #1: Finding a boy who had been with me in Croft and had been a loyal follower of mine all through France in a hospital with an arm off and both legs crushed. Example #2: Jerry Feenberg. I have an inner urge to work and work and work for these fellows until I can work no more. I left the lines after two months because I was ordered to do so. Both the Corps and Army Chaplains felt that too much was enough and they ordered me to the rear for a while to work in less exposed places. One does not like to write too much about these things because in writing they may sound like bragging even though they are true and also because those who are back home live in such an entirely different world that they can only vaguely understand and can not really appreciate. If everyone, by some supernatural miracle, could be made to spend just one day where the fighting is going on, there would be more understanding and appreciation. And when we read and hear some of the attitudes of some of the folks back home, we don't like it. . . .

Thanks for that wonderful poem by [Norman] Corwin. He is a truly spiritual personality and I glory that I have had a small part in the development of the religious fervor which moves him (more bragging). He has tried hard to come over here and take part in what is going on but he is not well and the doctors have not permitted him to come. . . .

I wonder just how much we are missed in Tallahassee.[5] Hyman Myers and family sent me a New Year Greeting. Al and Evelyn sent me greetings and a fine box of goodies. The Board of the Leon County Welfare Association, of which I was a member, sent me their annual report. But, after 3 years, I have yet to see any congregational publication in which my name was even mentioned. Nor, I have learned, is my name even listed on the congregational stationery. Every other congregation whose stationery I have seen lists its chaplain-rabbi in the proper place with the notation that he is in the Army on leave of absence. I wrote several times to Hyman and also once I think to Lin

Eisenson (who is now president) asking that some one be appointed to send me a monthly account of what is going on. I have yet to get the first account. Perhaps my request was unreasonable. . . .

Jonny, I got a tremendous thrill out of seeing your name in the *Temple Israel Bulletin*. I am sure that you made the Kiddush blessing in true rabbinical style. If either you or Jerry or both of you decide to become rabbis, it will please me very much. However, that is a matter which is entirely up to you. I do hope and pray that all my children will find their life's work among one of the following: doctor, nurse, teacher, scientist, philosopher, rabbi. I have always believed that these are the folks who do the really worthwhile things. My war experience has developed that belief into a feeling of certainty. . . .

Helene, I'll answer your two fine treatises when I get the chance. I certainly had a good laugh out of your health-hints, as am sure you meant I should. I've averaged about a bath a month this winter, gone a week sometimes without brushing my teeth and ages without a haircut, even couldn't wash some days even in cold water and I do mean "cold." Once I had to melt snow over a fire in order to shave. Yes, yes. . . .

And now for that request. . . . O.K. Here it comes. I've had two fountain pens. I've lost them both. So somebody please send me a fountain pen. And not an expensive one either because I'm quite likely to lose it too. Some folks here have a definite tendency of borrowing things like fountain pens and forgetting to return them.

> Love and kisses to all, big and small.
> Your husband and daddy,
> Max

[1]Though trained as an Orthodox rabbi at Yeshiva University, Harry Skydell worked as an accountant in New York before the war. Because of a shortage of Jewish chaplains, he agreed to serve in that capacity and was with the 29th Infantry Division for most of the war. This was a mistake, he says now, because the accountants got to come home in 1944, and as a chaplain he had to stay until the end of 1946. He returned to New York and resumed his work as an accountant. Skydell retired at the end of 2001, at the age of eighty-eight, and as of this writing lives in New York City.

[2]Shortly before this letter was sent, the Russians finally took Budapest after a two-and-a-half-month battle. Beginning on February 4, 1945, Churchill, Roosevelt, and Stalin met at Yalta to ponder the division of postwar Europe.

³The story of Esther is traditionally acted out (*Purimspiel*) during the Purim service, though not necessarily after each chapter, and not necessarily by the rabbi.

⁴After the war, Donald Henning served first as the headmaster of Shattuck School in Minnesota and then became pastor of Calvary Episcopal Church in Memphis, Tennessee, in 1949. In 1964 he joined St. John's Episcopal Church in Johnson City, Tennessee, and in 1966 moved to St. Michael's and All Angels Church in Dallas, Texas.

⁵At the time of his induction, Rabbi Eichhorn was on leave from Temple Israel in Tallahassee, Florida.

March 12, 1945
Somewhere in France

Dear Zelda, Jonny, Jerry, Judy, and all the rest
of the Eichhorns and Socols,

You all have been mighty nice to me and I shor' do appreciate it. Since I last wrote, I have received cigars and candies from Zelda, cigars and candy from dad and Henny, and cigars and fine things to eat and to wear from the Breckinridge Socols. For all these, I am very grateful and appreciative. Boy, the cigars have certainly piled up and I should have enough to keep me in smokes for quite a while so please don't send any more until I reach the point where I write to ask you to send me some more, which I promise to do when the time comes. . . . Also thanks for the lovely birthday greetings [January 6] and good wishes, dad, Rae and Gwendolyn. Your hopes for the best and the best of luck are most warmly reciprocated. . . . And while we are on the subject of birthdays, I hope that my two girl-friends, Zelda and Judy, had a happy joint celebration two days ago and I hope the check I sent arrived in time for each of you to get yourselves a nice birthday present.

I am enclosing a number of items which I hope you will find interesting and which I wish to have preserved. One is an account in the *Stars and Stripes* of the war in France. I have drawn on the map an ink-line of the general direction of my journey across France with the XV Corps, first as part of Patton's 3rd Army and, since November 1, part of Patch's 7th Army. Of course, the journey was far from being on as straight a line as is indicated. It was quite a zig-zag maneuver the whole way across although, up to now, it has always been in the direction of Germany and never back the way we came. We are all hoping that the record will be preserved to a victorious end. I have also indicated the battles in which the Corps has taken part and for which, thus far, we are entitled to wear 3 stars on a campaign ribbon, representing the battles of Normandy, France and Germany. I am also enclosing 2 photos and 3 negatives which you can have developed. One of the negatives shows the first service I conducted in France about the middle of July at Barneville on the Cherbourg peninsula. The other two negatives show the altar of the Lunéville synagogue as it was when I conducted services in October and November of last year. In one picture I am in the pulpit and in the other I am not. I have never received copies of 2 of these pictures. In fact, I've never even seen what they look like so my curiosity in this regard will have to wait for my home-coming, whenever that may be.

The only letters received since I last wrote have all been from Zelda and all V-mails, Jan. 16 (1), Feb. 15 (3), and Feb. 19 (6). Nice going, Zelda. The only mail which is certain of eventual delivery is V-mail. Much mail has been delayed in recent months through sea and air accidents but no V-mail is lost when an aeroplane carrying it crashes. The original letters are re-photographed in the USA and re-mailed so eventually they all get there. Also most of the sea-going mail and packages have been held up because of a crash between two mail-carrying ships. Most of this, too, will eventually reach its destination. So perhaps it is an exaggeration to write that this stuff has been lost but it most certainly has been delayed. Many letters and packages sent in December are only now about to be delivered.

I wrote a letter to the Feenbergs on the same day that Jerry died. I hope that, by now, they have received the letter. . . . Sorry to say that I do not agree with Art's optimistic statement that we could have a reunion in NY during the coming summer. Things are good but not that good. . . .

Certainly am proud of the new-found actor in the family. Just develop your talents in this direction, Mike, so that one of these days you can put on a special show just for me. . . .

I don't know why it should be that Catholic chaplains are mentioned more in public print than the others, except perhaps because they may have more expert publicity agents. Certainly all the chaplains (or at least most of them) are doing a fine job as, for that matter, is everyone in the Army (or at least most of them).

Things have been very quiet around here. Since coming back from Dijon and the General Hospital tour on February 20, I have not been out of the office very much. Chaplain Schellhase is still in the hospital and it looks as though he will remain there for some time. In his last letter, he wrote that he expects to return to us sometime before the end of the war. In the last few weeks, I have been called away for a day or two at a time on three occasions and I shall have to make three more short trips this week. I am knee-deep in preparations for Passover which is quite a good-sized job. Not knowing just what the tactical situation will be at Passover-time, it is rather difficult to know just how and what to prepare. There is a growing likelihood that, when Passover rolls around, our men will be too busy killing Germans to have time to come to a Seder. Just now things in our sector are "comparatively" quiet but we have no way of knowing just when the comparative state may become a superlative one or versa visa. . . .

My one vice at present, which I have been indulging every night, is playing bridge. We have some very good and congenial players and I really look forward to the diversion and relaxation which I have missed for so long. We play for high stakes (fifth of a cent a point) but are so evenly matched that nobody gets hurt. We've played about ten times so far and I'm about five dollars loser so far. Our four regulars are a French captain from far-off Tahiti (the best player of the lot), I rank second, and the other two are majors, Frank Smith (formerly of Tallahassee, Fla., where he played football at Leon High; I think he now lives in Jax) and Carl Woost, a Pennsylvania Dutchman from, I think, Allentown. Major Smith was at Camp Croft when we were there. He was the IRTC [Infantry Replacement Training Center] adjutant but I don't remember him and versa visa. Such is fame. Three very fine men and we really do enjoy our bridge game which, temporarily, is a nightly feature of our somewhat cramped social lives. . . .

I was given a pass to go to Paris for 48-hours last week-end and, when I had conjured up the most beautiful pictures of seeing Joe Newton and Paul Abramson and a few other folks, bang! I was ordered to attend a chaplains' conference at 7th Army Hq and the danged pass was cancelled. The war permitting, I hope to get to gay Paree for the 3rd time in the not too far distant future. I feel very much in need of a slight change of scenery for at least a little while. War has a way of making people old fast if they do not un-lax occasionally. . . .

Love and kisses to all.
Your husband and daddy, Max

March 31, 1945
Somewhere in Germany
V-mail

Dear Zelda, Jonny, Mike, Jerry and everybody,

As you can see from the heading, I've got a new address. Crossed over into Germany ten days ago and have really been on the move ever since. Have been head over heels in work preparing for Passover and now celebrating it on the soil of our enemies. It has been and is a hectic existence. Crossed the Rhine two days ago. What a disappointment that creek was! You could add its width to the Susquehanna River and never even notice the difference. Had my first Passover service on the west bank of the Rhine on Wednesday evening with about 175 men present. What a contrast with the affair last year at Croft. This year we had no food, just wine and matzos. We went through the Seder ritual just the same and, for sheer fervor, I've never had a Seder like it before and never will again probably. The men really felt in a celebrating mood. The service for the 2nd day was wiped out by the move. Yesterday I came up to a division in the front lines to hold a Passover service at the division Clearing Company this evening. Really have a front seat in a most awe-inspiring show. There is a town three miles in front of us that is clearly visible from where we are where the Jerries still are and that is really getting the business. The division arrived in front of the town 4 days ago expecting no opposition. When the first troops entered, they received a joyous greeting from the local females who welcomed them by throwing hand grenades from the second story windows. Whereupon those Americans who were still navigable hastily withdrew and the artillery and air force went to work. Never before have I stood and watched a town being blown off the map. It is not a pleasant sight. I feel a sense of horror and shame that mankind is still so perverted that such things are necessary but I feel no pity. Nor have I felt any pity in the other German towns whose ruins I have traversed nor toward any of the Herrenfolk that I have seen suffering except this morning when I comforted a little 7-year-old girl who had been shot by a stray German bullet.

Love and kisses to all, your husband and daddy, Max

At the same time he wrote the preceding letter, Rabbi Eichhorn was involved in a difficult situation involving the top brass. The following is from his autobiography.

On March 30, Major General Maurice G. Rose,[1] commanding general of the Third Armored Division, was killed while on a reconnaissance mission near Paderborn, Germany. His body was brought back to his division HQ for burial. The Third Armored Division was not then, nor at any other time during the European campaign, attached to the XV Corps. But its division chaplain, Peter Mahrer, was a good friend of our Corps Chaplain, Gustav Schellhase, and so Chaplain Mahrer called Chaplain Schellhase to get some advice with regard to the funeral service and burial of General Rose. Chaplain Mahrer explained that the Third Armored had no Jewish chaplain but that a Jewish sergeant who conducted the Jewish services for the division was insisting that General Rose was a Jew and should have a Jewish funeral service and burial. The Division Chaplain stated further that General Rose had never indicated that he was Jewish nor had he ever shown any interest in Judaism. Chaplain Schellhase turned to me, told me what Chaplain Mahrer had said, handed me the field telephone, and declared, "Brother Eichhorn, this one is all yours."

I had never heard of General Rose. I asked Chaplain Mahrer the following questions and received the following answers: What religious preference does the general's dog tag indicate? The dog tag has on it the letter "N" (meaning "no religious preference"). What religious preference is listed on the general's Form 66-1 (this was the officer's personal identification form)? His Form 66-1 states: "Religious preference — None." Is the general married? Yes. What is his wife's religion? Protestant. Has he children? Yes. In what religion have they been reared? Protestant. Did the general ever attend any of the division's Jewish services? No, except that on state occasions, such as Memorial Day or Thanksgiving, he would come with his staff.

After listening carefully to the replies of the division chaplain, I said to him: "I have no way of knowing whether General Rose is or is not a Jew; but the appropriate Army regulation is very clear: Anyone whose records indicate that he had no religious preference, and particularly one whose nearest of kin (i.e., the general's wife) is Christian, is to be given a Christian burial and a cross to mark his grave. This, therefore, is the prescribed manner in which the funeral and burial of General Rose is to be handled." And this is what was done. However, when I visited the military cemetery where General Rose was buried, I gave him the benefit of the sergeant's protestations. I sought out his grave and recited Kaddish over it.

Several weeks later, two Jewish chaplains of the type we called "Com Z commandos," i.e., spit-and-polish boys who had never smelled gunpowder, arrived at the cemetery (by this time I, of course, was far ahead with the combat troops) and raised hell because Rose' grave had a cross on it. At that time the cross was removed and a Star of David was substituted. At the end of the war, when the general's body was transferred from its temporary resting place to a permanent abode in an American military cemetery in France, a Jewish chaplain was assigned to accompany the corpse on its final trip.

(Many years later I was in Denver, Colorado, the city in which General Rose was reared. While making an official visit to the Denver VA Hospital, I happened to notice the General Rose Memorial Hospital directly across the street. I went over to the hospital and, after looking around, paid a visit to the hospital director. After I told him of my connection with the burial of the general, he said to me, "The general's father is dead but his mother, 87 years old, is still living. She has been told that her son had a Christian burial and this has grieved her very much. Would you mind telling her a bit of a white lie? Just omit the first part of your story and tell her that, as a Jewish military chaplain, you said Kaddish at the grave of her son. If you will do this, you will give great comfort to a fine old lady." I readily agreed. We got into the director's car and drove to the home of General Rose's mama, a typical pious European Orthodox Jewess. I spoke as the hospital director had suggested. The old lady's eyes filled with tears of joy. Although

General Rose does not seem to have been much of a Jew, I feel sure that this act of kindness would have had his hearty approval.)

[1]Maurice Rose (1899–1945), in some reports the son of a rabbi, joined the army as a buck private in 1916. After being wounded in World War I, he quickly rose through the ranks. He was famous for leading his men from a jeep on the front lines, and it was there, on March 30, 1945, that he rounded a bend in the road and encountered a German tank. The young German tank commander mistook the general's movement to surrender his sidearm and shot him in the head. Rose was buried in Ittenbach, Germany, and mourned by his men as "a soldier's soldier."

April 6, 1945
My Passover Diary

Dear Friends of JWB,

Thought you might be interested in taking a look at a summary of the entries in my Passover Diary, season of 1945.

The first notation is made on February 13 at Dijon, France, where a minyan of Jewish chaplains sits down with Chaplain Nadich of ETOUSA [European Theater of Operations, U.S. Army] to make plans for the Passover. It is decided that another meeting will be held at a later date to make more definite arrangements. The second meeting is held at Seventh Army Headquarters on March 9 and "more definite arrangements" are made, arrangements which are destined to be changed beyond recognition by subsequent military developments. A third meeting takes place at the same HQ on March 22, a meeting which I do not attend because I am busily engaged in traveling in the opposite direction.

On March 17, a 2½ ton truck goes bumpedy-bump along the rough roads from 7th Army HQ to XV Corps HQ. Alongside the driver sits a calloused Jewish chaplain. Inside the truck are 1,000 pounds of English Matsos and 24 bottles of French kosher wine, obtained through the joint efforts of American Jewish money, the JWB offices in New York and London, and Chaplains [Judah] Nadich, [Abraham] Hazelkorn, and [Max] Braude.

During the next few days, it becomes very evident that something big is in the offing and all plans for holding a big Corps Seder in a central location are discarded. Instead, unit chaplains are summoned to Corps HQ to get Matsos and wine for their Jewish men. Corporal Irving Levine, Jewish chaplain's assistant, becomes so fatigued from delivering Matsos to hospitals and to units which have no chaplains that he affirms that never again does he wish to behold a Matsa or a reasonable facsimile thereof.

On March 19, 1945, it happens. Since November 30, 1944, our HQ has been located in Saarebourg, Alsace, France. On March 19, off it goes "nach Deutschland." The "drang nach Osten"[1] becomes a reality but not in the way that the Junkers hoped. From now on, one lives again through a hectic series of moves reminiscent of the dash of the XV Corps across France last summer. A special truck is assigned to move the Matsos and the wine. One 50-pound crate is carried on the chaplain's jeep for the benefit of those brethren who, recognizing the Mogen David, eagerly demand a box of their favorite crackers.

The German border is crossed on March 21 at about three in the afternoon. Because he has not eaten since breakfast and because no other food is readily available, the chaplain dips into the crate and, as the little jeep with its big Mogen David moves proudly into the land of the enemy, the chaplain is munching on a crunchy sheet of you-know-what. Later there comes a realization that this unpremeditated act holds within itself the elements of that drama which men call "religious tradition."

Move follows move in rapid succession. When Kaiserslautern is reached, a city-wide pilgrimage is made in the company of T-5 Leonard Felsenthal, until 1934 a resident of Kaiserslautern and now a citizen of the United States in the Army of the United States. Together we visit what was the synagogue of Kaiserslautern. It was a gorgeous structure, erected in 1900 when Felsenthal's grandfather was Parnas and dedicated in the presence of the king of Bavaria. It is now a beautifully sown plot of grass. . . . We visit the Jewish cemetery. No one has been buried there since 1938, the year the synagogue was destroyed. The weeds are two feet high. About every tenth tomb-stone is turned on its face and broken. We pause reverently at the graves of Felsenthal's grand-parents and great-grand-parents and great-great-grand-parents. We look at many tombstones, some dating back to the 18th century. One memorial is of especial interest. It is a beautiful black marble slab

surmounted by a carved marble replica of a World War I German hel-
met. It stands over the remains of a Jewish lad, a law-student, who died
for the Fatherland in 1915. He was an only child. On the imposing
stone is an insignia of crossed swords, topped by the crest of the college law fraternity. Underneath the swords is the coat of arms of the
elite Bavarian cavalry regiment with which the lad fought and died. At
the bottom of the memorial is the German inscription: "We shall be
faithful always; we shall never rest content." In 1939, the lad's parents,
they who had erected this costly monument, both in their late 60s,
were deported to Poland. . . . Felsenthal visits the burgomeister [mayor].
He makes inquiry concerning the cigar factory which his late father
owned in Kaiserslautern. He is informed that the German government
appointed a trustee who sold the property to the government which
imposed a special tax on all monies collected from the sale of Jewish
properties, which tax in time absorbed all the money which the trustee
had in his care. Everything done in a legal and orderly fashion, the burgomeister assures Felsenthal. . . . On Sunday we are still in Kaiserslautern. Not many troops are yet in the town. No Protestant chaplain
is available to hold religious services. So the Corps' Jewish chaplain
leads a Protestant and Jewish congregation in prayer in the Protestant
church of Kaiserslautern, the first such religious convocation of the XV
Corps on German soil. Hitler won't like that.

The next day we move. Erev Pesach finds us in a small community
farther to the east [Eisenberg]. 110 Jewish soldiers travel in from miles
around to attend our "Seder." Well, yes, I suppose one may call it a
Seder. We make Kiddush and bless the Matsa and sing "Addir Hu" and
"Ki Lo Noeh." Outside of the fact that no food is served, it is a perfect
Seder. The "Mah Nishtanas" are recited by our baby, a strapping six-
footer of 19 years and the answers are given by the oldest man present, a venerable doctor who has reached the blessed age of 41. A
colonel explains to us in scholarly fashion the meaning of Matsa and
a buck-private who has been overseas for almost three years demon-
strates that he still remembers the proper response to "Moror zu al
shum maw?" It is a perfect Passover Seder, this 1945 celebration on
German soil which finds all of us chanting with unsurpassable fervor,
"Next year may all mankind be free!"

Another move cancels all plans for second-day worship. The third
day of Passover I journey forward to attempt to conduct services for a

very famous division [the 3rd Division] which has achieved distinction in Sicily, Italy, France, and Germany. When I arrive at Division HQ, the Division Chaplain informs me that a service has been arranged for the morrow at the Clearing Company's CP. He asks me with whom I should like to spend the night. Innocently I reply, "With my good friend, Major Sam Gollub of St. Louis, regimental surgeon of the –th Regiment." "Very well," says the chaplain, "Get in your jeep and follow me. We'll try to find him if we can." "Where is he?" I inquire. "On the other side of the _____ River. We've just established a bridgehead there. It isn't a very big bridge-head yet so locating Major Gollub should not be difficult." Gulp, gulp goes my throat and pitter, patter says my heart. My friendship for Sam Gollub is put to a severe test. If Chaplain M. is game, so am I. Off we go. Over the river and through the woods — but not to grandfather's house. We end up at a collecting company commanded by Captain Arthur Shainhouse of Brooklyn. His company's tents are set up at the bottom of a hill. Arthur tells us that the Jerries are dug in at the bottom of the other side of the hill and one of our infantry companies is dug in at the top of the hill. We hear a whine. "Jerry shell," Arthur cautions. He predicts the spot where it will land — about 300 yards away. His prediction comes true. "Where is Sam?" I ask. "Four towns up the road," says Arthur. "Is it kinda hot up there?" I ask "Kinda," replies Arthur. Just about then the Division Chaplain gently suggests that perhaps I had better spend the night elsewhere, which gentle suggestion is accepted with speed, finality, and relief.[2]

We go to the CP of the Clearing Company. A handsome young doctor walks up to me. "Aren't you Max Eichhorn?" "Yes." "When I heard that a Chaplain Eichhorn was coming to hold services for us, I said, 'That must be my Uncle Max.'" I look at the doctor somewhat quizzically. To the best of my knowledge, my oldest nephew is in his first year of public school. "You certainly remember me, Jesse Holland, from Camp Kirk?" Camp Kirk? Memory speedily takes me back to a glorious summer in the Catskills 17 years ago.[3] Jesse Holland? A bright-eyed, button-nosed, black-haired youngster from Brooklyn who never missed a camp religious service or a chance to have fun. "Why, Jesse, you old son of a ___!" It is a happy reunion.

I spend two days with the Clearing Company. They are days which will not be forgotten soon. Five kilometers away and clearly in view is the city of _____. It hung out the white flags of surrender four days ago. When our troops marched in, men and women hurled grenades at them from second-story windows. An immediate withdrawal was ordered. The guns of the artillery and the bombs and incendiaries of the air force began to speak in a language that even Germans understand. Four and five days later, the guns and bombs are still speaking, preaching a sermon against deceit and stupidity which all Germany will hear. From the heights overlooking the city, I hear the roar of cannon and see the burst of the shell. I watch the planes zoom down over the streets, strafing the buildings and setting them on fire. Watching a city die is not pleasant. One is filled with the same mixed feelings of horror and grim satisfaction that is in the heart of him who witnesses the execution of a hardened criminal.

The service at the Clearing Company is completed and I move on to another battle-hardened division and yet another. Black-out rides down sniper-infested roads are the order of the day. Wherever possible, the little jeep with the big Mogen David brings the message of Passover, the message of the triumph of righteousness over unrighteousness and of that perpetual spiritual vigilance which is the price of spiritual freedom. Everywhere the Jewish men who are able to leave their stations come to worship, to thank God that the enemy does not stand on our soil and that we stand on his, to pray to God that next year, at this season, each will sit with his own family at a table that has a clean white table cloth and real linen napkins and will eat real gefilte fish and knadlach and will hear a childish voice intone "Mah nishtanaw ha-layelaw ha-ze" and will celebrate the deliverance of Israel from Pharaoh and Haman, Antiochus and Hitler.[4]

> Sincerely yours,
> David Max Eichhorn

[1]*Drang Nach Osten* — the twelfth-century German desire to colonize the Slavic lands east of Germany — was resurrected by Hitler in his efforts to find *lebensraum* (living space) for the German people with a push to the east.

[2]Dr. Sam Gollub (d. 1999) returned to St. Louis after the war and became a pediatrician.

[3]Camp Kirk was a Boy Scout camp in the Catskill Mountains near Port Jervis, New York. Rabbi Eichhorn served as the camp rabbi for one summer.

[4]Pharaoh was the enslaver of the Jews and the pursuer of Moses, as recorded in Exodus. The Persian minister Haman (circa 470 B.C.E.) plotted to kill the Jews

and was hanged for it. Syrian ruler Antiochus IV attempted to kill the Jews under his power; his defeat in the Maccabean Revolt (circa 167 B.C.E.) by the Hasmoneans is celebrated in the festival of Hanukkah.

April 12, 1945
Corporal Paul Miller Family Circle

Dear Sir [Chaplain Eichhorn],

On November 14, 1944, I received a letter from you, sending a kind message that you saw my son Paul, since that date my son has passed onto oblivion my boy was killed in action 8 January 1945. I understand he is buried in Hochfelden Cemetery in Metz France. My son's name was Cpl Paul Miller 32991330 Hochfelden Cemetery Plot H — Row 19 Grave #1089. If you are in the vicinity, would you help a broken hearted mother and send me a picture of my boy's grave. And you will have the undying gratitude of a bereaved mother.

Yours truly,
Matilda Miller
Brooklyn, New York

April 19, 1945
Municipal Court of the City of New York, Borough
    of Manhattan
J. M. Roeder, Justice

Reverend Sir [Chaplain Eichhorn]:

Both Mrs. Roeder and I were delighted to receive your communication in regard to our son, John, who attended Seder services led by you on Passover evening. Not only was I delighted to hear that John himself had the urge to attend the religious services in commemoration of the oldest festival proclaiming freedom, but also that the services were led by one (of whom John wrote to me) who instilled in his hearers a feeling of pride in their ancient heritage as Jews.

I hope upon your return to your native land I may have the pleasure of personally greeting and becoming acquainted with you.

Assuring you of my esteem, and with sincere regards, I am

Cordially yours,
Jehiah. M. Roeder

April 24, 1945
Headquarters XV Corps

Dear Friends of JWB,

While it has only been a little more than two weeks since I last wrote you, several happenings in my experience during this period have been somewhat out of the ordinary and I thought that you might be interested in knowing about them.

At the conclusion of the Passover season, I journeyed by weapons carrier and train to Paris for a three-day vacation, the first break I have enjoyed since landing in France early last July. During this all-too-short Parisian interlude, a delightful lunch with Chaplains Nadich and Hyman was had.

From Paris I went to a lovely city in eastern France [Nancy], where our Corps operates rest-centers for officers and enlisted personnel. While there I conducted a memorial service for President Roosevelt[1] in the local synagogue and also addressed a meeting of Poale Zionists[2] in English, after which my remarks were translated into Yiddish and French.

During my stay in this city, I became well acquainted with the family Vischel, consisting of a charming and intelligent mother and two attractive daughters, Luisette, aged 25, and Rosette, aged 20. Luisette is an artist and Rosette a dancer. When the Nazis came in 1940, their father was among the first deported to Poland. Shortly thereafter, the conquerors began to seize Jewish girls for use in German army brothels. When Luisette and Rosette learned, through underground channels, that they were to become unwilling recipients of Wehrmacht-style love-making, they fled to the woods and joined the Maquis. For two years, they served the French guerrillas as nurses and cooks. During most of this time, they went about in tattered garments and bare-footed. Oftimes, for two or three days there was nothing to eat. Life was a continual battle of wits with the Nazis and the elements. The Maquis finally decided that the girls' looks and talents could be used more advantageously elsewhere and they were sent to the Riviera. Here they danced in the night-clubs of Nice and Cannes and, at the same time, did what they could to advance the cause of the Free French. The conquest of Southern France by the Americans[3] ended the girls' military career in that sector and, last October, they were enabled to return home. Luisette has since become engaged to an American Jewish officer-pilot.

These modern Deborahs,[4] who for four years lived constantly in the shadows of torture and death, have remained singularly steadfast to the conventional pattern in which they were reared. Their companions and hours are very closely regulated by their mother. They fear their mother's wrath much more than they ever did the Nazi rack or bullets. Unlike many of their female contemporaries, they do not seek the company of soldiers. "Too many uniformed visitors cause gossip among the neighbors," the girls explain.

After leaving the rest-center, it took me two days to locate the XV Corps, then fighting its way toward the Nazi stronghold of Nuremberg. I finally caught up with our troops at the town of Bamberg. The next day we moved on to Erlangen. In that city I sought to discover the fate of the approximately 40 families of Jews who had lived there.

The town was completely "Juden-rein" [Jewish-free] save for those who were at rest in the small Jewish cemetery, located on top of Hindenberg Hill at the edge of town. In the caretaker's house lived an elderly lady, her 18-year-old daughter, and also a woman who had fled from Nuremberg. The elderly lady and her husband had been caring for the cemetery for 24 years. They had tried without success to protect it against Nazi vandals. Practically all of the tombstones were overturned except, strangely enough, those placed over the remains of former rabbis of the community. With one exception, there had been no burials since 1936. The exception was a Hungarian Jewess, a "displaced person," who had died in Erlangen in 1939. At the time of her death, the caretaker was already away serving in a Nazi labor battalion. The local grave-diggers refused to dig a Jewish grave so the caretaker's wife and her then 12-year-old daughter dug the grave and interred the Hungarian Jewess as decently as they could. They also erected a simple headstone over the grave.

There had been a sharp fire-fight in the cemetery. A well-constructed trench ran along the edge of the hill. Three SS men had defended this post. One surrendered. Two did not. The two who would not surrender were still in the trench when I got there. The flies were buzzing over them. They had been dead for three days. They were hauled away next day to a military cemetery.

The three women in the house were vehemently anti-Nazi. While talking with the woman from Nuremberg, she told me that, in pre-Hitler days, her father had been a teacher in the same school with the notorious Jew-hater, Julius Streicher.[5] Her father and Streicher had had many controversies. In the years after 1933, her father had narrowly escaped the concentration camp. I asked her if she knew where Streicher was. She said she most certainly did. He was "hiding out" in a certain village east of Nuremberg. This information was conveyed immediately to our intelligence officer who set out post-haste to nab the Nazi gangster. Unfortunately, the information had been received just seven days too late. One week earlier, Streicher had departed for an unannounced destination.

After a week of bitter fighting, the XV Corps took Nuremberg on Hitler's birthday, Friday, April 20. The next day I went to the edge of the city to visit an Allied PW [prisoner of war] camp, Stalag 13, which our troops had overrun.[6] It was a typical German prison camp, starvation diet, unsanitary grounds and buildings, insufficient heat, poor medical care, prisoners chained, beaten and shot. There were 11,000 Allied prisoners in the camp, mostly Russian, some Jugo-slav (including 32 Jugo-slav generals), 55 Americans and 600 British. 3,000 British and Americans had been marched away when our army approached the city. Those who remained had been too sick to move.

Among the British were a number of Palestinian Jews, taken prisoner in Greece and Crete four years ago. They had been for more than two years at Oswitz [Auschwitz] in Silesia. The infamous civilian concentration camp at Oswitz was their next-door neighbor. They confirmed many of the horrible tales which have been told about this camp. They worked on the roads with the civilian victims and perfected a technique whereby they were able occasionally to sneak food from their own miserable supply to the even more under-nourished people with whom they labored. The chronicle of atrocities which they unfolded — men and women standing naked in the snow for hours for slight infractions of the rules, solitary confinement for days, forced marches, the beating, starving, shooting and cremating of their Jewish brethren, civilians and soldiers going raving mad from that which they endured and that which they beheld, soap being manufactured from the residue of cremated victims — all these things have been told before. One believes but one can never fully comprehend.

That same afternoon I went to what had been Nuremberg. As a city, Nuremberg has ceased to exist. With the sights, smells and tales of the prison camp freshly in mind, I have never beheld a more satisfying heap of ruins.

At 3 p.m., a ceremony of formal occupation was held in what had been the Adolph Hitler Platz. A token military force was assembled from all the units which had taken part in the fight for the city. The National Anthem was played and the American flag was raised.

Then Major General Wade H. Haislip, commanding general of the XV Corps, spoke to his men. His opening words were, "We stand today amid the tumbled ruins of Nuremberg, amid the ruins of a city which gave its name to the infamous laws that violated every concept of human decency. Here Hitler reigned and strutted, and here he shouted at the multitudes of adoring Germans who used to gather in propaganda-filled stupefaction. In this city fascism flourished. We have conquered Nuremberg and we have destroyed it just as thoroughly as we shall destroy fascism and every evil thing connected with it."[7]

General Haislip recounted the many outstanding achievements of the XV Corps — the exploitation of the break-through out of Normandy last summer, the creation of the first bridge-head over the Seine River, the opening of the way for the liberation of Paris, the capture of Strasbourg. In the last five weeks, the XV Corps had breached the Maginot and Siegfried Lines, crossed the Rhine, driven 260 miles into Germany, captured more than 100,000 enemy soldiers, and killed or wounded countless thousands more. Of none of these valiant deeds was the general prouder than that it had been the privilege of the troops under his command to capture and destroy the Nazi stronghold of Nuremberg.

His address was concluded as follows, "From here we are going on to victory. We must give the enemy no rest whatever. We must prove to him completely and conclusively that his way of life is not what the civilized world wants. This we shall do."

General Haislip, to you and your gallant men of the XV Corps, and especially to those who here gave their lives that this structure of bigotry and hate might crumble into dust, the Jews of the world owe an everlasting debt of gratitude and honor.

On Sunday afternoon, April 22, the little jeep with the big Magen David entered Zeppelin Stadium, the huge arena in the suburbs of Nuremberg where the Nazi Party Congresses were held and the place where, some ten evil years ago, 250,000 cheering Nazis approved the enactment of those discriminatory laws which resulted in the destruction of nearly five million of our brethren.[8] In the jeep were one American Jewish chaplain, one American Jewish chaplain's assistant, one portable Aron Ha-Kodesh, one Torah (property of the destroyed Jewish community of Hagenau, Alsace, France), and five Palestinian Jewish soldiers who had been captives of the Nazis for four long years. Behind followed a second jeep bearing five American Jewish soldiers of the 45th Infantry Division, fighting soldiers who had helped destroy the citadel of Nuremberg.

Slowly and proudly, the little procession drove around the stadium. It halted before the speaker's rostrum, a rostrum surmounted by a resplendent gold-leafed swastika, the rostrum from which der Fuehrer had, again and again, fulminated against democracy and the Jews. The soldiers got out of the jeeps and, forming a guard of honor around the holy Ark, carried it up the steps to the speakers' platform. Here the procession halted. The Ark was opened and the Torah taken out. The representatives of an eternal people offered up songs and prayers of thanksgiving to the eternal God for having once more revealed to mankind the certainty of His justice and the timelessness of His love. At the end of the service, the Americans and the Palestinians joined hands and, forming a solid ring around the rabbi, the Ark, and the Torah, pledged renewed fidelity to the cause of Israel and the worship of Israel's God.

Shortly thereafter, units of the 3rd Infantry Division, which, together with the 45th, took the city, assembled in the stadium. They listened to thrilling words of congratulation and praise from Lieutenant General Alexander M. Patch, commanding general of the Seventh Army. Then demolition charges were attached to the resplendent gold-leafed swastika atop the speakers' platform, and it was blown sky-high. Amid the thousands of cheering beholders, none, perhaps, was more deeply moved than the little group of seven Americans and the five soldiers from Palestine who were clustered around the little jeep with the big Magen David.

Sincerely yours,
David M. Eichhorn

[1]Franklin Roosevelt died April 12, 1945, in Warm Springs, Georgia.

[2]Poale Zionists, also called Proletarian Zionists, were members of the Zionist Labor Party.

[3]American and French forces invaded southern France beginning August 15, 1944, making landings between Toulon and Cannes.

[4]Deborah, called "the Mother of Israel," was a judge, prophetess, and military leader in approximately 1200 B.C.E. She helped the Israelites achieve victory over the Canaanites.

[5]Julius Streicher was a virulent antisemite, friend of Hitler, and publisher of *Der Stürmer* (The Attacker). Eventually captured, he was judged sane enough to stand trial and was convicted of crimes against humanity by the Nuremberg War Crimes Tribunal. Streicher was executed October 1, 1946.

[6]Stalag 13D near Nuremberg was specifically for airmen. At maximum capacity, the camp held 30,000 prisoners.

[7]Rabbi Eichhorn wrote General Haislip's Nuremberg speech, at the general's request.

[8]This stadium is perhaps best known as the site of Leni Reifenstahl's 1934 documentary *Triumph of the Will*, chronicling a massive Nazi rally.

In 1958, in preparation for a 100th anniversary celebration of the first Jewish chaplain in the U. S. Army (Civil War chaplain Michael Allen), Rabbi Eichhorn was commissioned to edit a book on the history and exploits of Jewish chaplains. He was forced for medical reasons to relinquish the task in 1959, but not before writing a history of Jewish chaplaincy and revising the preceding report (as well as five other reports to the Jewish Welfare Board) for inclusion in the book Rabbis in Uniform: The Story of the American Jewish Military Chaplain *(1962). The principal change in the revised version consisted of these two paragraphs.*

On March 28 (1945), the Jewish men of the XV Corps celebrated the Passover in the little village of Eisenberg, on the left bank of the Rhine.

We were advancing so rapidly at that time that there was no time to prepare any food. All we had for our Seder were wine, matzos, and Haggadas. But who cared about food on an occasion such as that? For us it was not only a remembrance of "yetsias Mitsraim"; it was also a "bias Mitsraim." We were about to assault the last main strongholds of the hated Nazis, the destroyers of millions of our brethren. Never was Passover Seder celebrated with more solemnity, more sincerity, more joy.

The next day we crossed the Rhine. By April 16, XV Corps had fought its way northeast from Worms as far as Fulda and Meiningen and then southeast to the city of Erlangen, fifteen miles northwest of Nuremberg, the city which Hitler had made the showplace of the Nazi world. [Here the original report resumes, beginning with information about the "Juden-rein" town of Erlangen.]

April 27, 1945
Somewhere in Germany

Dear Zelda, Jonny, Mike, Jerry, Judy and everybody,

It has been a long time since I have had a chance to write to you. Since the middle of March we have been on the move continuously and, in the rare moments of quiet which I have had I have been too exhausted physically and mentally to do any letter-writing. The only writing that I have done has been to send two letters to the JWB describing my activities during this period. I am enclosing copies of these letters, and, when you have read them, you will have a rather good idea of what has been happening to me during the last six weeks or so. I have all kinds of business and personal mail piled up which goodness knows when I shall get a chance to reply. A rapid glance thru the pile shows letters to be answered (among many others) from Mrs. Feenberg, Henry Grumbacher (who, it seems, is engaged to a Chicago cousin of mine, a Miss Meta Sauer, and who informs me that Uncle Max — Zivi, I suppose — is again a grandfather), Mrs. Heineman, Arele Diambo, Herman Snyder, Mrs. Fuld, Ruth Peppercorn, Norman Corwin, Ed Gruss, editor of the B'nai B'rith mag, who wants me to pursue a literary career in the post-war world, Rabbi Meyer

Marx (HUC [Hebrew Union College] summer school long time ago),
Alex Weinstein.

Thank you for the packages which I have received and the good
things which they contained. Many of the delicacies were eaten at the
end of a long day's move and tasted mighty good. Many of them I gave
away to wounded men and to freed prisoners of war and their gratitude was indeed touching. Until you hear from me further in this regard, please do not send any more packages. While we [are] actively
engaged as at present, it is difficult to move anything extra around.
The less one has to move, the better. For the present, I have plenty
cigars and the other things I can very well do without until matters
quiet down a bit. Just when that will be, goodness knows. Some of the
men are very optimistic. I think it will probably be at least two more
months here — then, after that, off to CBI [China-Burma-India theater
of war] for an indefinite period.

The mail at hand is as follows: Breckinridge, Mar. 18; Tulsa: V-mail
and air-mail (including eagerly welcomed letter from Jonny), Mar. 27;
V-mails Mar. 22, 27, 29 (2). Judging from the stamp-picture, little Gwendolyn Socol is a darling, as, I am sure, is my own beloved little Judy.
These cute little German kids that exist in such abundance in every
town we occupy certainly make me home-sick once in a while for a
sight of my own brood. I was very happy to get the pictures of Jonny
and Mike. In reply to your questions, Jonny: It looks like it will be a
very long time before we are able to get together. As to where I now
am, you should get a rather good idea about that from reading the
enclosed articles. Zelda, it certainly sounds as though you have done
quite a job on that apartment and I'm sure that your efforts and hard
work are bringing you much pleasure. You certainly have had your
hands full of sick children. It doesn't seem like there is much left for
them to get. They've about run the gamut now and I hope will stay in
good health for a while. Whenever any of the children complain about
their teeth, eyesight, or hearing, be sure that you have the complaint
checked right away. It does seem odd that one as young as Jonny
should have to have a tooth pulled. And why wait until the war is over
to get glasses, if you need them now? That is being penny-wise and
pound-foolish. Let me know what the glasses will cost and I'll send
you the extra money for them, if that is what is holding you up.

You ask about my post-war plans. I haven't any. When one is right up in it trying to help win a war and also trying to avoid getting hurt, there is enough present planning to do. The future will just have to take care of itself. While nothing has as yet been definitely decided, the indications are that I shall go to the Pacific when this is over. Quite a world traveler, from the looks of things.

The bridge game came to a rather abrupt halt when the drive started. The boys told me yesterday that they hope to get together with me tonight so maybe we'll have a little Oneg Shabas around a bottle and a bridge table. The approximately ten days' relaxation and change I had going to, about, and from Paris did me much good. I was as jittery as could be but the change, together with pleasant surroundings and companionship, helped considerably. I didn't have much time in Paris. One whole day of the three was spent in getting fluorescent light bulbs for our Signal Section. Getting them was a pain and bringing them back was even more of a nuisance. However I did get a chance to see a number of good friends. Went to a cabaret one night and to two girly shows (Folies Bergere and Casino de Paris) the other two nights. Paris is certainly going all out to entertain the Americans and take their money. Just like before the war. As a matter of fact, outside of a shortage of food, Paris and the war seem worlds apart. I have a bottle of perfume for you and some other knick-knacks of the war which you will get when I have a chance to pack them up and mail them. At the present time, Levine is in Paris taking a one-week course in teaching. When the war is over, the Army will probably use him for a while to give piano lessons to soldiers. Am sending along a couple small photos. The feller with me is Chaplain Harry Essrig of the Air Corps.[1] The photo was taken in Dijon on March 9. Not such a good picture. But it seems to indicate that I sure need a rest which, fortunately, I got.

> Lots of love and kisses from
> Your husband and Daddy, Max

[1]Rabbi Harry Essrig, age ninety at this writing, recalls having a splendid time with his friend Max Eichhorn in France. After the war, Rabbi Essrig spent a year as the Hillel director at Harvard and eventually became rabbi of Temple Emmanuel in Grand Rapids, Michigan. He moved to Los Angeles and University Synagogue in 1964. He and his wife live in retirement in San Rafael, California.

The following version of Rabbi Eichhorn's experiences at Dachau was revised from his original report to the Jewish Welfare Board for inclusion in Rabbis in Uniform. *More material from the original report can be found on page 195.*

First week of May, 1945
Dachau

The XV Corps took Nuremberg on April 20 and Munich, about 125 miles southeast, on April 30. Thus to our Corps went the honor of capturing two main centers of Nazidom. En route from Nuremberg to Munich, in the town of Treuchtlingen, I was given a large Sefer Torah which had been hidden in the town hall by a local official on the November night in 1938 when the Treuchtlingen synagogue was burned and all the Jews in Treuchtlingen were killed or driven off into the woods.

The concentration camp at Dachau, twelve miles northwest of Munich, was taken on April 29.[1] I arrived there on the afternoon of April 30. The horrors of this camp have been described by so many in detail that I shall not dwell at length upon this aspect except to record the following reactions of myself and others who were with me. We saw the 39 boxcars loaded with Jewish dead in the Dachau railway yard, 39 carloads of little, shriveled mummies that had literally been starved to death; we saw the gas chambers and the crematoria, still filled with charred bones and ashes. And we cried not merely tears of sorrow. We cried tears of hate. Combat hardened soldiers, Gentile and Jew, black and white, cried tears of hate. Then we stood aside and watched while the inmates of the camp hunted down their former guards, many of whom were trying to hide out in various places in the camp. We stood aside and watched while these guards were beaten to death, beaten so badly that their bodies were ripped open and innards protruded. We watched with less feeling than if a dog were being beaten. In truth, it might be said that we were completely without feeling. Deep anger and hate had temporarily numbed our emotions. These evil people, it seemed to us, were being treated exactly as they deserved to be treated. To such depths does human nature sink in the presence of human depravity.[2]

Soon after arriving at Dachau, I met Meyer Levin, the novelist and newspaper correspondent.[3] The next morning, he and I went to Allach, a sub-camp of Dachau, about five miles away. The Allach Camp was divided into separate sections of Gentiles and Jews, about 3,300 Jews and 6,000 Gentiles. The comparative conditions in the Jewish and Gentile sections may be understood through one simple statistic: The first day I was there, 40 Jews and 5 Gentiles died. In other words, the death rate was about 15 Jews to one Gentile.[4] Causes of death were listed as malnutrition and general debility.

Both at Allach and Dachau, death was commonplace. Naked bodies lying outside of barracks waiting to be carted away were a familiar sight. And the bodies did not smell. There was no meat left on them to rot, just skin and bones. While I was sitting on the corner of a bed in the Allach "lazarett" [hospital] talking to a Professor Schwartz, who had for six years been the only unconverted Jewish professor at the University of Warsaw, the man on whose bed I was sitting died. A doctor came along, saw that the man was dead, covered his head with a sheet and Professor Schwartz and I continued our conversation as calmly as before. Just like that. I did not even get up from the bed. "Poor fellow," said Professor Schwartz. "At any rate, his worries are ended." It was a fitting eulogy.

I presented the Torah from Treuchtlingen to the Jews of Allach. I shall never forget the presentation ceremony and the service which accompanied it. There were quite a number of rabbis and cantors in Allach, including a Czecho-Slovakian rabbi, Dr. Klein, who spoke about a dozen languages. During the service, Dr. Klein thanked me eloquently for the Torah in English, German and Hungarian. Another dramatic moment was the chanting of the "El Male Rachamin" by a cantor from Warsaw with a very beautiful voice. After the service, literally hundreds of people crowded around me, kissing my hand and begging for an "autogram." It was a very embarrassing experience. I felt that it was I who should be humbling myself before them and honoring them for that which they had suffered and surmounted. I kept reminding myself that it was not I to whom they were paying homage but to the wonderful American Army which had delivered them from certain death and from physical and mental tortures worse than death. To die from a bullet is so easy and so quick, many said. But to die slowly, in mind and in body, from torture, humiliation and hunger is much worse.

The administration of the Allach camp was in the hands of a non-Jewish American officer, Lieutenant Schreiber,[5] and a small group of American soldiers who moved heaven and earth in a mighty effort to get food and medicine quickly to the starving and the sick. They were aided greatly by a fine group of inmates who were organized within the camp into a well disciplined and smoothly functioning committee. Lieutenant Schreiber, in his early twenties, a toughened combat soldier, reacted to the situation with the mind of a brilliant executive and the heart of a saint. The tragedy of these unfortunates became his personal tragedy. To work with such a person was an exalting experience, even in the midst of misery and death.

A few paragraphs back, I wrote of deep anger and of hate. In harboring such thoughts, one must be sure that he is directing his thoughts toward those who are really guilty and not toward those whom he presumes to be guilty. Every time I hear some thoughtless person say that the only good German is a dead German, I think of the hundreds of Germans and Austrians I met inside the concentration camps, priests and ministers, lawyers and doctors, Socialists and pacifists, workers and farmers, living skeletons with eyes that burned with an imperishable prophetic fire and a boundless love for their fellow-men. I think of many Germans whom I knew who had saved Jewish lives at the risk of their own. I think especially of SS Mann Gerhardt Schmidt. Schmidt looked like the kind of man the Nazis brag about, the perfect typical Aryan, tall, blond, and handsome. He was a pilot in the Luftwaffe. He was shot down and wounded and then forced into the SS.[6] He was a patriotic German who loved his country but who hated Hitler and the Nazis and everything for which they stood with a hatred that was deep and true. In the spring of 1944, he was sent to the Jewish section of Allach as "block fuehrer," section leader. He protected his Jewish flock in every way within his power. Every evening he listened in secret to the broadcasts of the BBC and kept the hopes of the Allach Jews buoyed up by informing them of the progress of the Allied advance. When he learned that certain Jews were destined for extermination, he hid them until the danger had passed. When a Jewish inmate would contract typhus, which was a one-way ticket to the gas chamber, he would smuggle the sick person out of the camp in one of the camp's straw wagons, take him to his home in Dachau where the patient would be nursed back to health by

Schmidt's wife and then be smuggled back into the camp. Three days before the American liberators arrived, he hid two machine guns and bandoleers of ammunition in his straw-wagon, brought them into the camp and buried them in the Jewish section. He informed his Jewish brethren (and, God bless him, I write that word deliberately) that he would fight with them to the death against the other SS if they attempted to massacre the Jews before they retreated. Fortunately, the other SS left so fast that there was no attempt at massacre.

SS Mann Schmidt did not run away. He took off his uniform, put on civilian clothes and went home. Three days later, he decided to return to the Jews of the Allach camp. He and his wife walked up to the gate where they were stopped by an American guard and questioned. When Schmidt readily admitted that he had been a German soldier, he was quite naturally taken into custody and destined for a quick trip to a POW compound. His wife came into the camp office and pleaded with Lieutenant Schreiber to release her husband. Some of the Jewish leaders were summoned and they attested to the truth of the facts I have just written down. They said further that the Jews of Allach would be grateful and happy for the privilege of taking their German comrade into "protective custody" so that he could go on working with them as before. Lieutenant Schreiber secured permission from Corps HQ to have Schmidt retained as a worker in the camp. He was released by the military and placed in the care of the Jewish committee. I accompanied Herr and Frau Schmidt from the office to the Jewish compound. It was the home-coming of a hero. The Jews crowded around their beloved "fuehrer," hugging him, kissing his face, his hands, his feet. The big man broke down and cried. So did his wife. So did I. When I left Allach, Mr. and Mrs. Schmidt were living in the headquarters of the Jewish committee and Herr Schmidt was a key-figure in the manifold relief activities that were being conducted there. A few weeks later I learned that one night the Schmidts had quietly left the camp for an unannounced and unknown destination. It seems that they had heard that some of the bad Germans in the nearby community of Dachau had vowed to kill the "traitors" at the first opportunity. There were and there still are many bad Germans as well as many good ones. The same may be said of every other group of people on the face of the earth.

After two days at Allach, I returned to Dachau on May 3. I was placed on temporary duty there as a member of the camp staff and remained for four days. I roomed in an Army hospital that had been set up just outside the "lager" [camp] gates; but practically all my time was spent inside the camp compound. Because of the prevalence of typhus, I received an injection of anti-typhus serum. Every time I had to go out of the camp, which was about three or four times a day, I was dosed with anti-louse powder. By nightfall I was so full of powder that the inside of my clothes and my body were lily-white. And I certainly needed the stuff. Whether it was the son of the Gerer Rebbe or the melamed from Palestine or the merchant from Prague or the plain ordinary Jew from Lodz, all the inmates were emaciated, filthy and lice-ridden. Only the Jewish doctors were clean. In some semi-miraculous way, the physicians had maintained standards of cleanliness demanded by their profession. Another exception to this condition of disease and dirt was the barracks of Hungarian, Greek and Italian Jewish girls, 160 of them, who had been brought to Dachau just a week before. Some of them had been workers in factories and farms, some had been used in German military brothels. They had been treated with so little consideration by the Germans that most of them had lost the female's normal sense of modesty. When, from time to time, my duties brought me into their barracks, they continued to dress or undress in my presence as though I were not there. I used a room in this barracks as a sort of headquarters, not because of the situation just described but because it was the only semi-cheerful spot in all of Dachau. The girls had not been in Dachau long enough to be afflicted with typhus or with lice and, occasionally, some of them smiled. Unfortunately, when these girls were given thorough medical examinations in the ensuing weeks, it was discovered that many of them, who looked healthy outwardly, were afflicted with tuberculosis.

I did what I could, in the short time at my disposal, to bring what comfort and cheer was possible to the approximately 2,600 Jewish men and 225 Jewish women who remained among the 34,000 inmates of Dachau. I visited every barracks in which there were Jews, talked to the bed-ridden, miserable unfortunates and tried to raise their spirits. I also tried to act as a liaison between the Jews, the camp's International Prisoners' Committee and the American military authorities. At both Allach and Dachau, I supervised the gathering of a list of the names and addresses of all the Jews in the camps. The overwhelming majority of the Jews at both places were Hungarian and Polish. I met only one German Jew and a few French and Belgians.

I had a very unpleasant experience soon after being assigned to the Dachau staff. The inmates, after liberation, left the camp, invaded the town of Dachau, took whatever food they could find from the greatly frightened Germans of the town and proceeded to eat and eat and eat. Their emaciated bodies could not stand the strain. A number of them literally gorged themselves to death. The American medical authorities decided that, for the protection of the inmates, they must be forcibly detained within the compound in order to get the proper medical attention and to be fed the proper kinds and amounts of food. The effect of this on the inmates is not difficult to imagine. Many of them were not in the proper state of mind to understand the necessity for this action and they thought that their liberators had suddenly become persecutors. Since it was impossible to change many of the disagreeable features of confinement at a rate fast enough to satisfy the inmates, considerable discontent generated rapidly in the compound.

The doctors ordered me to see to it that no inmates got out of the sections in which most of the Jews were quartered. Armed guards were placed around the fences to make sure that this order was obeyed. Some of the inmates were still bringing food they had "liberated" in Dachau back to the compound by means of bicycle, wheelbarrow, donkey cart or any other type of vehicle they could commandeer. Finding the gates locked, they would scurry up to the fence, throw the food parcels over the fence to those on the other side and then quickly scurry away. I was told by the medics that this would have to be stopped. I instructed the guards to frighten away the food-bearers by shooting over their heads. This worked quite well for a while, but, when the food-bearers discovered that the soldiers were not aiming directly at them, they continued their well-meant but harmful tactic. Reluctantly I was compelled to tell the guards that they would have to actually hit one of the offenders in a non-fatal spot on his anatomy in order to protect the health of those in the compound. This was done. The next fellow who tried to throw food over the fence got a well-aimed bullet through his leg, was taken off to the hospital and eventually recovered from the wound. This drastic measure halted all further efforts to get any more food over the fence.

(I had another unpleasant experience of a somewhat similar nature a little more than a month later at the concentration camp at Ebensee, Austria.[7] The JDC [Joint Distribution Committee] bought 12 tons of food in Switzerland which was delivered to XV Corps HQ in Salzburg by the International Red Cross. Here it was loaded on Army trucks for delivery under my supervision to the camp at Ebensee. The shipment consisted of such items as raw beef, flour, cocoa, and other normally inedible items. When the camp inmates saw the trucks come through the gate of the camp, their hunger was so intense that they made a mad dash for the food shipment. I was on the lead-truck of the twelve-truck convoy sitting beside the driver. On every other truck was a driver and a guard. Feeling sure that the approaching mob would trample us to death in its determined rush for the food, I ordered the drivers and guards to get off the trucks and stand in line with fixed bayonets, with the hope that this would put a stop to the frenzied dash of those coming in our direction. Fortunately for all concerned, this did the trick. The mob came within perhaps seventy-five or an hundred yards of us, stopped uncertainly and then slowly retreated. We were able to deliver the supplies to the Ebensee kitchen without further interruption. . . . About seven or eight years later, I was visited at my office at the National Jewish Welfare Board in New York by a fine-looking young American soldier. "Remember me?" asked he. "No," I replied. "You should remember me," said he, "I tried to kill you once." "That is something I ought to remember," said I, "but I don't." He laughed. "Of course, you don't," said he. "I was one of that mob of hunger-crazed people who tried to run you down at Ebensee." His eyes lit up. "And while those trucks were being unloaded," said he, "I stole a hunk of that raw meat and carried it off to my room and ate it all by myself. Best tasting meat I ever ate in my life."

On Friday afternoon, May 4, I held a service in the women's barracks. It was, of course, a very touching experience, as were all such services which I was to hold during the months to come in many DP [displaced person][8] camps in Germany and Austria. At the end of the service, a lieutenant colonel who had been standing at the rear of the room approached me with tears streaming from his eyes. He introduced himself. "My name is George Stevens.[9] I am in charge of the Signal Corps unit which is taking the official Army pictures of Dachau. When will you hold another such service? I want to get a film of it for the historical record." I told him that a camp-wide Sabbath service was planned for the next morning, Saturday morning, and that he certainly could make a film of it if he wished.

The service was to be held at 10 a.m. in the main square of the Dachau compound. The International Committee had promised to have the platform in the square decorated with the flag of every nation represented in the camp (I think there were 28 in all) and, in addition, every nationality would send a delegation to the service as an indication of its brotherly sympathy for the Jewish people. I arrived at the square at 9 a.m. to make sure that everything was in readiness for the service. To my amazement, no preparation of any kind had been made. I sent for Charles Baum, a young Belgian, the Jewish representative on the International Committee, and asked for an explanation. Greatly embarrassed, Mr. Baum informed me that the service would not be held in the main square. The Polish non-Jewish inmates had threatened that, if a Jewish service were held in the square, they would break it up by force. (This was only one of a number of ways in which the Poles of Dachau showed hostility for their fellow Jewish sufferers. I was informed that, when the Polish Red Cross distributed food packages to the Poles of Dachau, the packages were given out on the basis of one to every Polish Christian and one to every two Polish Jews.) Rather than cause a disturbance, the Jews had decided to cancel the service in the square and to hold the service, instead, in the camp laundry, which was only big enough to accommodate about 80 people and could, therefore, hold only a very small percentage of the Jews who would want to be present. While I was not pleased with the decision, I raised no strong objection as I felt that the Jewish inmates were more knowledgeable in this particular situation than was I and should be allowed to do what they considered proper. So I set up an altar in the laundry and prepared for the limited service.

While the service was in progress, in a jam-packed room with hundreds of others outside crowded around the open doors and windows, Colonel Stevens came in, elbowed his way to my side and demanded to know why the service was not being held in the square. His cameras and crews were ready for action and he wanted the event to go on as scheduled. I stopped the "davaning" long enough to tell him that I would explain, after the service, what had happened. He waited outside until the end of the service to hear the explanation. After hearing the "inside story," he exploded in anger. "I did not give up a good job in the movie business in Hollywood," he bellowed, "to risk my life in combat for months and months in order to free the world from the threat of Fascism and then stand idly by while the very victims of Fascism seek to perpetuate its evils. I am going to do something about this." And do something about it he did. He took me to the Camp Commandant, a fine gentleman of Irish extraction who had formerly been Police Commissioner of Boston,[10] and, with loudness of voice and much banging of the table, George Stevens repeated his anti-Fascistic sentiments. The Commandant readily agreed with Colonel Stevens. It was decided that the service would be held next morning, Sunday, May 6, at 10 a.m. under the protection of an American military "guard of honor." As an added "movie" touch, Colonel Stevens requested that I teach some of the girls in the women's barracks to sing "God Bless America" at the service. I did as he asked. That Saturday night I spent about two hours teaching a choir of fifteen Hungarian Jewish girls to sing the Irving Berlin composition; and they learned to sing it quite well, even though they knew not one word of English.

And so, thanks to the decent instincts of an American movie director, the camp-wide service was held in the main square. It was attended by every Jewish male and female whose health permitted. As promised, every nationality was represented by flag and delegation. There were an estimated two thousand Jews and non-Jews at the service. And ringing the outer rim of the service with faces turned away from the platform and with loaded rifles and fixed bayonets was the American military "guard of honor." They were prepared to deal with a situation which did not develop. No untoward incident of any kind marred the service. (Meyer Levin, who was present at the service, described it in an article in the American press. It is quite likely that the incident with which Irwin Shaw concluded his novel *The Young Lions* is based on Levin's account of the Dachau happening.)

The program of the day was as follows: The opening remarks were made by Mr. Kuci, formerly Albanian Minister of Propaganda, chairman of the inmates' International Committee, who said that all the inmates of Dachau were very much aware of the exceptional intensity of Jewish suffering there and elsewhere under the Nazi yoke and that all freemen rejoiced that the Jews of Dachau were, at long last, able to resume their religious life without hindrance. The Ark was opened and I recited "Shehecheyanu" and "benshed Gomel" and went through a brief Torah service. After being formally introduced by Mr. Charles Baum, I gave a short talk. When I finished, one of the loveliest of the

Dachau girls presented me with a bouquet of flowers on behalf of Dachau Jewry. Then a Palestinian "chalutsa" came up to the platform bearing a Zionist flag and made an impromptu speech in beautiful Sephardic Hebrew to me and the assembly. Little American and Zionist flags made by the girls from their precious store of remnant materials were presented to me as priceless "souvenirs" of this never-to-be-forgotten occasion. My talk, given in English, was then translated into German by one of the inmates. He must have made what I said sound good because the crowd's response was very generous. Then my girls' choir sang "God Bless America" sweetly and enthusiastically. Then Mr. Baum spoke in French and German, thanking all the non-Jewish delegations for coming to the service and also expressing the hopes and aspirations of the Jews of Dachau. The latter part of his speech was so moving that it gave everyone a chance to have a good cry. The assembly joined in the singing of "Ha-tikva," after which I ended the program with a benediction. The entire service, about forty-five minutes in length, was filmed with sound by Colonel Stevens and his crew. While the service was in progress, a wagon-load of naked dead came past the assembly on the way to the crematorium. Colonel Stevens ordered the cameras turned on the wagon and a filmed record made of this weird though temporary addition to the audience. (Several years later I was invited to the Army Pictorial Center at Astoria, L.I., to witness a showing of the film of the Dachau service. The "staged" singing of "God Bless America" was retained in the film. The dead-wagon scene was eliminated. "We had to take it out," the movie people explained to me. "It seemed so improbable that a viewing audience would suspect that the scene had been "staged.") [11]

For an hour after the service, I was mobbed, kissed, photographed and signed so many "autographs" that I vowed then and there to give up completely and absolutely whatever chance I had of becoming a movie star. It was a tiring and, as mentioned before, highly embarrassing experience.

The next morning I attended two Polish Catholic masses also held in the main square at Dachau as memorial services for the Polish dead of Dachau. I did so for two reasons: to express my gratitude by this act to the small number of Christian Poles who had attended the Jewish service and to show their less brotherly brethren that we have greater respect for their religion than they have for ours.

On Monday afternoon, May 7, I returned to HQ XV Corps, which, in my absence, had moved with the battle-line about seventy five miles eastward from Munich, Germany, to Salzburg, Austria. Here, on May 8, the war in Europe officially ended; but die-hard Nazi units of the German forces did not cease fighting with our units until May 11. On that date, XV Corps was placed in charge of the Austrian Occupation Zone, a mission which it fulfilled until July 1. During these six weeks, I traveled constantly between Innsbruck on the west and Linz on the east, holding services for our widely scattered troops and trying to be of some help to the DPs in the many camps throughout Austria.

The text of the speech which I delivered at Dachau on May 6, 1945, follows:

My Jewish brethren of Dachau,
In the portion which we read yesterday in our holy Torah, we found these words: "Ukrawsem d'ror baw-awretz l'chawl yoshvehaw; yovel hee ti'ye lawchem; v'shavtem ish el achuzawso v'ish el mishpachto tawshuvu" which mean "Proclaim freedom through the world to all the inhabitants thereof; a day of celebration shall this be for you, a day when every man shall return to his family and to his rightful place in society."

In the United States of America, in the city of Philadelphia, upon the exact spot where 169 years ago a group of brave Americans met and decided to fight for American independence, there stands a marker upon which is written these very same words: "Proclaim freedom throughout the world to all the inhabitants thereof." From the beginning of their existence as a liberty-loving and independent people, the citizens of America understood that not until all the peoples of the world were free would they be truly free, that not until tyranny and oppression had been erased from the hearts of all men and all nations would there be a lasting peace and happiness for themselves. Thus it has been that, throughout our entire history, whenever and wherever men have been enslaved, Americans have fought to set them free, whenever and wherever dictators have endeavored to destroy democracy and justice and truth, Americans have not rested content until these despots have been overthrown.

Today I come to you in a dual capacity — as a soldier in the American Army and as a representative of the Jewish community of America.

As an American soldier, I say to you that we are proud, very proud, to be here, to know that we have had a share in the destruction of the most cruel tyranny of all time. As an American soldier, I say to you that we are proud, very proud, to be with you as comrades-in-arms, to greet you and salute you as the bravest of the brave. We know your tragedy. We know your sorrows. We know that upon you was centered the venomous hatred of power-crazed madmen, that your annihilation was decreed and planned systematically and ruthlessly. We know, too, that you refused to be destroyed, that you fought back with every weapon at your command, that you fought with your bodies, your minds and your spirit. Your faith and our faith in God and in humanity have been sustained. Our enemies lie prostrate before us. The way of life which together we have defended still lives and it will live so that all men everywhere may have freedom and happiness and peace.

I speak to you also as a Jew, as a rabbi in Israel, as a teacher of that religious philosophy which is dearer to all of us than life itself. What message of comfort and strength can I bring to you from your fellow-Jews? What can I say that will compare in depth or in intensity to that which you have suffered and overcome? Full well do I know and humbly do I confess the emptiness of mere words in this hour of mingled sadness and joy. Words will not bring the dead back to life nor right the wrongs of the past ten years. This is not time for words, you will say, and rightfully so. This is a time for deeds, deeds of justice, deeds of love. . . . Justice will be done. We have seen with our own eyes and we have heard with our own ears and we shall not forget. As long as there are Jews in the world, "Dachau" will be a term of horror and shame. Those who labored here for their evil master must be hunted down and destroyed as systematically and as ruthlessly as they sought your destruction. . . . And there will be deeds of love. It is the recognized duty of all truly religious people to bestir themselves immediately to assist you to regain health, comfort and some measure of happiness as speedily as is humanly possible. This must be done. This can be done. This will be done. You are not and you will not be forgotten men, my brothers. In every country where the lamps of religion and decency and kindness still burn, Jews and non-Jews alike will expend as much time and energy and money as is needful to make good the pledge which is written in our holy Torah and inscribed on that marker in Philadelphia, the city of Brotherly Love.

We know that abstractions embodied in proclamations and celebrations must be followed by more concrete, more helpful fulfillments.
We do not intend to brush aside the second part of the Divine promise: "V'shavtem ish el achuzawso v'ish el mishpachto tawshuvu." Every
man who has been oppressed must and will be restored to his family
and to his rightful place in society. This is a promise and a pledge
which I bring to you from your American comrades-in-arms and your
Jewish brethren across the seas.

> You shall go out with joy, and be led forth in peace;
> The mountains and the hills shall break forth before you into
>   singing;
> And all the trees of the field shall clap their hands.
> Instead of the thorn shall come up the cypress,
> And instead of brambles myrtles shall spring forth;
> And God's name will be glorified;
> This will be remembered forever,
> This will never be forgotten. [Isaiah 55:12, 13]

Amen.

[1]Dachau opened as a concentration camp in March 1933, making it the oldest of the German camps and the model for all those that followed. Although
the earliest inmates were political prisoners, the Jewish population grew rapidly, especially after Kristallnacht, the Nazis' November 1938 pogrom against
the Jews, referred to in the previous paragraph. By the time of liberation, 30 percent of Dachau's inmates were Jews, and the camp's population included representatives of more than thirty countries. Many of the Jews of Dachau had been
transferred there — often via death marches — from camps in areas where the
Germans had lost control. Thousands had worked as slave laborers in nearby
subcamps, including Allach, where, along with other companies and other military production, BMW manufactured airplane engines.

[2]In November and December 1945, forty surviving members of Dachau's SS
(Nazi security force) staff were tried by an American court at the camp; thirty-
six were sentenced to death.

[3]Meyer Levin (1905–1981) was a writer, reporter, and documentary
filmmaker whose first novels concerned immigrant Jewish life in his native
Chicago. His reportage in World War II led to the book *In Search* (1950); others
included *Eva* (1959), *My Father's House* (1947), and perhaps his best known,
Compulsion (1956), a fictionalized version of the Leopold-Loeb murder case.

[4]Clearly, the rabbi's figures are off. If the number of dead is accurate, the
death rate would have been eight Jews to one Gentile.

[5]Timorah Perel, with Reference and Information Services at the Yad Vashem Archives in Jerusalem, reports that there is no mention of a Lieutenant Schreiber in the seventy-seven records of documentation concerning Allach — mostly testimony of camp survivors in Hebrew, Yiddish, Polish, Hungarian, and English. There are, however, numerous references to Rabbi Eichhorn.

[6]Besides being a concentration camp, Dachau also housed an SS training camp and garrison, called the SS-Übungslager. Graduates of this large facility included Auschwitz commandant Rudolf Höss and Bergen-Belsen commandant Josef Kramer, as well as Adolf Eichmann, chief of the Jewish Office of the Gestapo and implementer of the "Final Solution."

[7]Ebensee, opened in November 1943, was one of the forty-nine subcamps of Mauthausen concentration camp near Linz, Austria. Ebensee's purpose was to provide slave laborers for the construction of enormous underground tunnels housing armament-manufacturing plants.

[8]For military purposes, "displaced persons" meant people outside their countries of origin who needed help to survive and to either go home or get to some other country. "Refugees" were defined as people in their own countries but in similar circumstances, trying to return home but unable to do so.

[9]George Stevens (1904–1975) began working as a director in Hollywood in the early 1930s. Both before and after the war, he directed many highly regarded films, including *Gunga Din, Alice Adams, Woman of the Year, Talk of the Town, I Remember Mama, Shane, Giant,* and *The Diary of Anne Frank.* Stevens won the 1951 Oscar for Best Director for *A Place in the Sun.*

[10]According to Donna Wells, historian for the Boston Police Department, none of the Boston police commissioners from 1906 to 1943 (Stephen O'Meara, Edwin Curtis, Herbert Wilson, Eugene Hultman, Joseph Leonard, Eugene McSweeney, and Joseph Timilty) ever served in any capacity at Dachau. According to Dr. Marcus Smith's 1995 memoir *Dachau: The Harrowing of Hell,* the first president of the Dachau International Prisoners' Committee was "Patrick O'Leary." Although it is pure conjecture, it could be that Rabbi Eichhorn was under the impression that O'Leary was from Boston. In fact, O'Leary was really Albert Guérisse, a Belgian doctor who had been a lieutenant commander in the British navy (where he could have acquired the necessary brogue). Guérisse became involved in the French underground and used the alias to prevent reprisals against his family. He was eventually captured and sent to Dachau. After the war, Guérisse became a general in the Belgian army and executive president of the Comité International de Dachau.

[11]The edited, black-and-white sound film of the Dachau service that Rabbi Eichhorn reports seeing in 1948 has apparently disappeared. The U.S. National Archives and Records Administration has five reels (out of perhaps seven original reels) of the raw, unedited footage, some of which was heard in the third program of the PBS documentary series *The Perilous Fight,* accompanying George Stevens's color film footage. The search continues for the final, edited film of Rabbi Eichhorn's Dachau service shot by the Army Signal Corps.

In the preceding report to the Jewish Welfare Board about his experiences shortly after the liberation of Dachau, Rabbi Eichhorn says little about the service he conducted at the Allach camp. But one witness to that service, Lieutenant Chester A. Kaplan, described it in detail in the September 1945 issue of Jewish Chaplain.

NEVER A MORE SOLEMN OR BEAUTIFUL SERVICE

Yes, this is another story of a concentration camp. But not of the horrors or atrocities committed there; nor of the sickness or death. It is a story of beauty and everlasting faith and devotion to God, by a few plain, simple people, just like you or I.

It was just about forty-eight hours after our American troops had routed the enemy out of the area and taken the small community of Allach, near Munich, Germany. Chaplain David M. Eichhorn, of Tallahassee, Florida, set out to investigate a report that several thousand Jews were interned in a concentration camp there. I went along more out of curiosity than official business.

In appearance, the camp at Allach is not too different from all the others. Perhaps it is a little more crowded, as it is a predominantly Jewish camp. They had no crematorium, or death chamber, since all the executions were done about ten miles away at Dachau. Therefore, the air was comparatively fresh and the smell of death was hardly discernable until one actually went inside the enclosure.

Our welcome by the internees was typical and similar in every detail to the greeting received at the previous camps. It was heart-rending and sincere as our desire to help these people, Jew and Gentile alike.

After we had spent some time exchanging greetings, attempting to make a few arrangements to obtain food, etcetera, we began to talk to some of the men who had been there for three and four years. Finally, one rather thin, stoop-shouldered, elderly-looking man (it later developed that he was the younger brother of a judge in New York) got up enough nerve to ask us what he considered a great favor. It seems that after four years of a living hell his one burning desire was to attend a real Jewish service once more.

The chaplain, feeling that such devotion could not go unrecognized, determined to give them his Torah. At this announcement such a shout for joy arose as has not been heard since the Brooklyn Dodgers won two consecutive games. Arrangements for a Guard-of-Honor to go after the Torah was made, a place picked for the service and within 30 seconds (or less) word had spread through the camp and inmates were gathering for the great occasion.

Never was a more solemn and beautiful service held in a less pretentious setting. The straw mattresses were pushed back against the wall and a table secured and covered with a once-white cloth as an altar. The afternoon sun sent enough light in through the door and one window to no more than outline the figures standing packed together, so the "synagogue" was lighted by two candles placed on either side of the table flanking the Torah. About five hundred were able to crowd into the small barracks or gather round the window or find a peephole in the paper-thin wall, while as many stood outside, straining to hear.

Rabbi Sholom Klein, a former Czechoslovakian rabbi, was in charge of the service. As they continued to read I was amazed to discover that this was no different from thousands of services at home in America. Here amongst these strangers, representing some thirty countries throughout the world, I was hearing the same words, feeling the same reactions as I had on the innumer-able Saturday mornings I had attended the synagogue with my father in Kansas City many years ago.

When the proper time had come, a small, insignificant, di-sheveled, bony-looking little man stepped before the altar and, lift-ing his head high, began to sing as if to the heavens. His face gave off a radiance as of a true halo, as his soft, clear, melodious chant rang out: "ShemaYisreal! Adonay Elohenu, Adonay Echod" . . . (Hear, O Israel: The Lord our God, the Lord is One). Yes, after four years, in which he had every reason in the world for thinking the Lord had truly forgotten them, once famous Cantor Isaac Wise of Hungary, still knew in his heart and soul that the Lord had not for-gotten the Children of Israel.

As the ceremony proceeded, many more crowded into the little room, so that when the time came to present the Torah it became necessary for the cantor to hold it high overhead as he commenced the traditional, "Ave Ho' Rachamim." I could hardly restrain myself from joining the many others who were openly weeping as he continued. . . . "For in thee alone do we trust, O King, high and exalted God, Lord of worlds." Little twelve-year old David Faegan of Poland, who had been loyal guide and companion since morning, buried his face in my jacket to hide his tears for the family he had left so many months ago.

I felt someone kneeling at my feet and kissing my hand. For a moment I could not suppress a shudder of revulsion at the sight of this dirty, lice-ridden, typhus-infected skeleton of a man kneeling before me.

But the tension of the atmosphere was irresistible. Michelangelo, himself, could hardly have done justice to the holy, radiant picture they presented in the half-light of the flickering candles.

He, and the others who followed his example, were not, in fact, bowing to any mortal. They were figuratively kissing the hand of Jews throughout the world who had kept their people and their religion alive through a decade of darkness. Yes, they knew that once again a Jew could hold his head high throughout the world.

On May 6, 1945, Rabbi Eichhorn's superior officer, Chaplain Gustave Schellhase, wrote home to his wife, Isabel, of his own experience visiting Dachau. His letter begins as follows.

Dearest Sweetheart,

I wonder if you want to hear about my visit to (Dachau)? If you don't, then put this aside. I want to tell you about it because I have figured out the real reason why I am over here. I never knew the real reason why, but I see it now and believe me I am sure my stay over here is not too long to help make sure that such treatment will never be given to any people by any nation. . . . [There follows a description of the things he saw at Dachau, concluding with:] Do you see, Sweetheart, why I have to fight to keep hate out of my heart? I don't want to hate anyone but God help me to keep from hating these Germans!

This report to the Jewish Welfare Board, dated May 17, 1945, and sent from somewhere in Austria, begins with a description of the events at Dachau almost exactly as described previously and concludes as follows.

Other remembrances of Dachau: On Friday morning, May 4, I, together with two Protestant chaplains, represented the American Army at a mass recited by the Polish priests of Dachau in honor of those American soldiers who had given their lives to liberate the prisoners. . . . On Sunday afternoon, May 6, I helped organize a Dachau Jewish committee which I hoped would continue to function after I left. . . . A girl who had been at Treblinka[1] sang for me two painfully beautiful Yiddish songs composed at Treblinka, songs of death which were sung by the condemned as they marched to the gas chambers of that hell-hole. I tried to find someone at Dachau with enough musical ability to write down the words and music but could not. I hope that whoever followed me at Dachau learned about these songs and had them written down. They are pre-eminently worthy of preservation and would take their place, I believe, alongside of "Eli Eli" and "Kol Nidre."[2] . . . I was ordered to return to the Corps on May 7 and obeyed the order very reluctantly. I knew that military necessity required me to be with my men but, for many days, my heart remained with the Jews of Allach and Dachau.[3]

On May 7 the Corps HQ moved to Salzburg, Austria, where it has been ever since. The next day came V-E. Few of us here shouted, whistled, or got drunk. Most of us prayed, each in his own way, that the deaths and sacrifices of the past ten months might bring mankind not only present release from tyranny but also might enable our children and children's children to live in a warless world. I thought of Jochanan Tartakower and Benny Migdoll and Jerry Feenberg and Harry Loeb and so many others, "alehem ha-shawlom," and I hoped that this day, spent by the unthinking and unfeeling in feasting and merriment, would be for their bereft beloved a day of pride and not a day of bitterness.

European peace has already brought us some compensations. We have our offices in a fine building on Mozart Square and live in the semi-palatial Oesterreichischer Hof. We have large rooms and bathtubs and real hot water comes out of the faucets. We sleep in big beds between clean sheets and we have maids and porters who make our beds, press our clothes, and shine our shoes. We eat in a beautiful dining room and dress up for the evening meal. There is wine on the table — and German cigars, not bad. I have been holding services in the Festspielhaus, where the famous Salzburg Music Festival is the yearly attraction. I also continue to travel around the area, holding services among the units, visiting many small concentration camps, and trying to be of some assistance to the little groups of Jews that pop up all over the place.[4] European peace has brought us a relaxing of the ever-present tension and more material comfort. It has in no way lessened the scope of our labors. And the big question of the moment in all our minds is: what next?

Cordially yours,
David Max Eichhorn

P.S. Major Joe Smith of Providence, R.I., a fine doctor who is doing typhus control work in this area, called me in this morning and told me that he has definite proof that the Nazis deliberately formed a wide ring of typhus-infested Jews in the villages and towns of this area, a ring which extends around their entire "inner redoubt" and which forms the "first line of defense" of the redoubt. Nice people, those Nazis!

[1]Treblinka, fifty miles northeast of Warsaw, began in 1941 as a penal camp. Alterations in May–June 1942 turned it into one of six extermination camps in the nation that had been Poland before 1939. Treblinka operated as such until April 1943, when a major effort was undertaken to obliterate all evidence of the dead. By the fall of 1943, the camp was closed, but not before an estimated 870,000 people had been murdered there.

[2]Bart Werb, staff musicologist of the U.S. Holocaust Memorial Museum, reports that although he is not familiar with these two specific songs, "perhaps Rabbi Eichhorn's singer had performed a song about, rather than from, Treblinka. One such piece, 'There Lies Treblinka,' was composed in the Warsaw ghetto and would also have been known in the death camp. Another possibility is that one of the songs was 'Ani Maamin' (I Believe), reportedly sung in Treblinka by pious Jews en route to execution. The text to this song is in Aramaic, though Rabbi Eichhorn conceivably identified the informant's spoken Yiddish with the language of the song."

[3]Before leaving Dachau, Rabbi Eichhorn asked Seventh Army headquarters to assign a Jewish chaplain to the camp immediately. Chaplain Abraham Klausner, in Paris awaiting assignment, was ordered to Dachau, where, according to Eichhorn's autobiography, he "functioned magnificently."

[4]Besides attending to his regular duties in Austria, Rabbi Eichhorn made frequent visits to liberated concentration camps, particularly Mauthausen, Ebensee, Leonding, Hoersching, Kammer, Landeck, Neustift, and the DP headquarters in Salzburg and Linz.

May 26, 1945
Salzburg, Austria

Dear Everybody,

I know it has been a long time since I've written but, perhaps, when you read through some of the material enclosed herein you will understand why. I have so much to do that I do not know where to turn next and I have definitely entered upon a period of all work and no play. I am swamped with requests for services from soldiers and with requests for help for soldiers and civilian refugee Jews. It would be simply impossible for me to tell you of what I have seen or what I am doing. There is only time for me to try to discuss with you some of the things mentioned in your letters and also to mention some things in my experiences that may be of interest as they occur to me.

I have had packages from the Breckinridge branch, from Zelda, and from Helene for all of which I can only say an appreciative "thank you." I also get packages from soldiers' relatives. For the present, our physical comforts are so well taken care of that much of the contents of these packages have been given away to released Allied prisoners and needy Jewish refugees.

Jonny, for a long time I have been carrying around the address of a little girl in Alsace at whose home I stayed a number of times. I promised her that you will write to her and, when she gets your letter, she will answer you. She is very sweet and bright and is ten years old. She is not Jewish. Her name and address: Mademoiselle Hugette Houp, Cocheren 90, bei Forbach, Moselle, France. I know that she will be glad to hear from you and that you will be delighted to hear from her.[1] She and her folks were very kind to your daddy last winter when her home was right in the front lines. When I was at her house, the Germans were less than five miles away.

Roosevelt's death was a great shock to all of us but Truman seems to be off to a good start.

Yes, V-E day has finally come and the war in Europe is over. Now we must stay here and try to win the peace as well and it is not very likely that I shall return to the States very soon. There is too much work of reconstruction to be done here in which we must play a part.

If I am finally sent to the Pacific, which is quite possible, I hope to be sent by way of the States on a 30- or 45-day leave so that I can see you all enroute. But do not think in terms of my getting out of the Army very soon. From all indications, that is simply not to be. We are still short of Jewish chaplains. I am enclosing a statement from the JWB that it has been asked to secure 36 more Jewish chaplains.

You, like everyone else, are probably interested in the matter of points.[2] These apply primarily to enlisted men. With officers, there are many considerations. I shall list them as they are and the manner in which they apply to me.

1. Does the Army need you? Answer: The Army says YES very emphatically in my case.

2. Are you in good health? Answer: The Army says that I am. However, those officers who have had considerable combat experience, in which category I am now included, will be given a breather in Europe and possibly in the US before being sent to the Pacific so I may be spared that trip.

3. Do you wish to remain in the Army until the end of the national emergency? My answer to that was YES. I came in voluntarily and have no wish to take off the uniform until the job is completely done. We are still at war. The emergency is far from over.

4. Have you made a good officer? The perfect score on this question is 50, a practically unattainable score held by a very, very few. The ratings are listed as Superior 50, Excellent 40, Very Satisfactory 30, Satisfactory 20, Unsatisfactory 10 or less. My score on this is 41.3, which I can say without conceit is above average.

5. How many points have you? I have 106, which is way above average also and may result in my getting out of the Army a little quicker than some, although we have been told that chaplains will be among the last ones out. These points of mine were computed as follows:

Children	36
Months In Service	34
Months overseas	11
4 major campaigns (2 in France, and 2 in Germany)	20
1 decoration for bravery	5
Total	106

The last entry leads me to tell you that I have been awarded the Bronze Star Medal "for meritorious service, above and beyond the call of duty, in the military service from July 25, 1944, to May 7, 1945," the period during which the XV Corps was in active combat.[3] I was told some time ago that I had been recommended for this but it was not awarded to me until the end of the war. The ribbon was pinned on me yesterday at a public ceremony and review by Lt. Gen. Wade H. Haislip, our Corps commander, who said of me publicly, "You have done a swell job. You have been a great help to me." Naturally, I felt very proud. Chaplains Schellhase and Laning were also awarded the Bronze Star and, in addition, Schellhase was awarded the Croix de Guerre[4] by the French government, as were all our Corps section Chiefs. I do not have the medal or the official citation yet. When I get them I shall send them to you. About half the officers in our Hq have been decorated and about 10% of the enlisted men. I feel very happy about this for two reasons, A. Our Corps, while not highly publicized, probably has more major achievements to its credit in the war than any other Corps in the Army. This has been officially recognized in that our Corps is one of three in the entire Army (there are about 30 Corps in the Army) which is commanded by a Lieutenant General. The other commanders have only two stars. B. I have always thought of myself as somewhat of a coward and I still am very much of that opinion but I know now that, when the chips are down, coward or no, I manage to do my share of the work. So our kids can now get some satisfaction from knowing that, although their daddy did not kill any Germans, he did manage to get hold of a medal.

Jonny and Mike, I enjoyed your letters very much and hope that you will keep on writing. And news about Jerry and Judy and all of you is always welcome. It looks as though I won't be home to help you celebrate next month's anniversaries, for which I am very sorry, but there is some unfinished business around the world that will have to be taken care of before I can join in such celebrations in the flesh.

Yes, Henny, I am in your beloved Austria with the Alps looking down on me through the window. It is a very lovely country. Scenically, I like Germany and Austria better than England or France but I like the people in the other countries more. I haven't had time to do much sight-seeing. Hitler's Berchtesgaden is only 15 miles away but I have not had a chance to take a look at it.[5] Was sorry to hear about

Solomon's son. Please express my sympathy to them. Many fine young men will not return and many more will return crippled.

I certainly wish I could remember people's names. I meet so many whose names I can not recall. I've gotten to the point now where even faces do not mean much unless I see them often.

Zelda, don't worry about the fact that you are putting on weight. That is much better than having things the other way around. I've seen what folks look like when they lose too much weight and the sight is not exactly a pleasant one.

Corwin is making a wonderful name for himself and doing a magnificent job. I have not had a chance to write to him for a long while.

Dad, I was very happy to get your letter. I hope you will soon have an opportunity to visit Zelda and the kids. They do get to see Grandpop Socol occasionally and they should also get a chance to know you.

Henny, don't you worry about us treating the Huns as equals. They are getting the business in a very cold, business-like way. It is not pleasant to give back unto them just a little of the kind of stuff they dished out but it has to be done. The kind of life we are leading is very unnatural. All the conquered are so subservient, crawling up to you, especially the pretty gals, in a way which is very hard to resist. However, the non-fraternization policy is being enforced very strictly. We have to work like hell and have no chance for any kind of gayety. Trips are now available to Brussels, the Riviera, London, Paris, and all over the place but I've got too much to do to take advantage of them. Some of our chaplains are also being allowed to make pilgrimages to Rome and Palestine. For the present, that ain't for me. . . .

We are eating strictly Army food prepared by Austrian cooks. They do an excellent job. There is also much wine and champagne. But I don't drink very much. I run from 7 in the morning until 11 at night 7 days a week. Doesn't give me much time for drinking. I've gotten drunk just once since I landed over here. That was about a month ago back in Germany. Five of us were so danged tired of moving and being shot at and living like little pigs that one day, back the other side of Nuremberg, we sat down and drank our lunch. We drank and drank. I never went back to the office that afternoon and slept like a log until the next morning. But nobody said anything to me about it and I guess that they sort of understood how I felt.

We finally caught Julius Streicher about 12 miles south of here a couple days ago. He was hauled in by one of our Jewish officers, a refugee from Nuremberg who, at the age of 12, was accused of Rassenshande [racial dishonor] in *Der Stuermer.* You can imagine how Julius fared in his hands. Also caught with Streicher was Ritter von Epp, one of the original Nazis.[6]

I held a service a few days ago at Garmitsch Parten-kirchen. It is very beautiful there.

That's all for now.

> Love and kisses from your husband, daddy, brother,
> and son,
> Max

[1]When asked whether he had ever corresponded with Hugette Houp, Jonathan Eichhorn replied, "I don't remember being asked if I was interested in writing to this young lady, but I am sure I would not have written to her. At that age, I was very, very shy, especially re girls."

[2]The separation point system, devised by the War Department (and almost universally disliked by GIs), translated each soldier's service and home life into numbers. Points were awarded for length of time in uniform, battles fought, medals won, size of family, and so forth. But commanding officers had the power to deem anyone or any job classification (such as chaplain) *essential,* in which case points meant little. The point system was dropped after the Japanese surrender.

[3]The Bronze Star was awarded "to any person who, while serving in any capacity in or with the military of the United States after 6 December 1941, distinguished himself or herself by heroic or meritorious achievement or service, not involving participation in aerial flight, while engaged in an action against an enemy of the United States. . . . Awards may be made for acts of heroism, performed under circumstances described above, which are of lesser degree than required for the award of the Silver Star."

[4]Instituted in September 1939 by Edouard Daladier, this was the World War II equivalent of the World War I Croix de Guerre. It was awarded for bravery to soldiers and citizens of any nationality.

[5]Berchtesgaden, in the Obersalzberg area of Bavaria, was where Hitler completed *Mein Kampf* in 1925. When he became chancellor of Germany eight years later, he purchased and rebuilt the house, renamed it the Berghof, and used it as both a retreat and a place to entertain guests, who included the Duke and Duchess of Windsor, Neville Chamberlain, Mussolini, and Lloyd George. Hermann Goering, Martin Bormann, and Albert Speer moved in down the road. At war's end, the U.S. Army turned the area into an Armed Forces Recreation Center.

[6]Franz Ritter von Epp (1868–1947) was a professional soldier and early supporter of the Nazi Party. He spent the war as the governor of Bavaria and head of

the Colonial Policy Office of the Reich leadership. He died in an American internment camp.

[May 1945]
Headquarters, XV Corps, United States Army
Office of the Corps Chaplain
Subject: Jewish Religious Services
To: All unit chaplains, XV Corps

1. It is desired that the time of the Jewish Chaplain at XV Corps Hq be utilized in a manner which will enable him to reach the men of the Jewish faith within the area assigned to the XV Corps and its attached units as often as possible. To achieve this end, the following plan is now in effect:
2. Until further notice, the Jewish Chaplain will conduct services in Salzburg in the auditorium of the U.S. Army Post Office, located on Bismarckstrasse, next door to the Mozart Theater, according to the following schedule:

Friday   2000
Saturday 0930
Sunday   0930

It is desirable that all units in this area acquaint their Jewish personnel with the time and place of these services and provide transportation for those who wish to attend.
3. It will be possible for those units whose Jewish men are unable to attend the services at Salzburg to have an occasional service in their immediate area conducted by the Jewish Chaplain if the arrangements for such a service are completed one week in advance. Where such a service is requested, it is desired that the unit Chaplain make a reasonable effort [to] ensure the maximum attendance of those Jewish men who may wish to attend.

G. A. Schellhase
Chaplain (Colonel), USA
Corps Chaplain

The following is from Rabbi Eichhorn's postwar report to the Jewish Welfare Board under the title "Contacts with the Great and Near-Great."

My notes say that on the evening of May 29, 1945, I conferred with two chaplains at Seventh Army HQ in Augsburg, Germany. That is, factually, a correct statement. However, it does not tell the whole truth. In the morning I had journeyed 125 miles from our HQ in Salzburg, Austria, to the Dachau concentration camp. In the afternoon I had conducted a service at Dachau. Toward evening I traveled an additional thirty miles to Augsburg to "confer" with two highly regarded colleagues, Chaplain Max Braude[1] of Seventh Army HQ and Chaplain Aryeh Lev, in from the States as military aide accompanying a truly great Chief of Chaplains, William Arnold, on an inspection tour of the ETO. Purpose of the conference (I confess it unashamedly now, although at the time it was a closely guarded military secret): to play pinochle. I do not remember who won. What happened next morning has completely obliterated from my mind the details of the game of the night before.

Next morning I was up early for breakfast (early for me, that is) in order to get back to Dachau as soon as possible. Seated across from me at the breakfast table was an Englishman who introduced himself most politely but whose name I failed to get. He began to query me about the number of current morale problems, including the problem of the fraternization of American troops with German nationals. At that time, it was militarily "verboten" for an American soldier to have anything whatsoever to do with a German girl. Most of the chaplains, including myself, thought this was a ridiculous state of affairs, since war is war and boys will be boys and girls will be girls and, "verboten" or not, the American boys, in large and uncontrollable numbers, were sneaking out of their barracks after taps and into the arms of willing German "schatzis" [sweethearts]. I felt, as did many others, that this situation demanded not unenforceable prohibition but properly supervised regulation. I expressed my viewpoint quite vigorously to the Englishman.

A few minutes later a distinguished looking American gentleman came in and sat down to my right. "Ed," said the Englishman to the American, "you will be interested in some of the comments the chaplain has been making to me, especially with regard to the ban on fraternization." He then proceeded to repeat some of my remarks on the latter subject. When he concluded, the American pounded the table and said, "There you are. This is what I've been saying all along. If a Jewish chaplain feels this way about this thing, you can just imagine how the average GI must feel. I'm going to take this up with Harry the minute we get back to Washington and, by golly, I'm not going to stop talking until this silly regulation is changed." From the conversation which followed between the two men, I gathered that this "Harry" to whom the American gentleman referred was the President of the United States. When this thought had penetrated deeply and sufficiently, I thought it about time to inquire: "Just with whom am I having the pleasure of breakfasting?"

The American gentleman at my right laughed and said: "Forgive us for not introducing ourselves properly before asking for your opinions. The gentleman seated across the table from you is Lord Halifax,[2] British ambassador to the United States, and my name is Edwin Pauley,[3] Mr. Truman's special representative on the matter of reparations. We just stopped here for breakfast. We are flying from Washington to Moscow to visit Mr. Stalin. Your candor has been most helpful and is greatly appreciated."

The ban on fraternization was revoked less than a month later. Presumably, the point of view held by Mr. Pauley and myself had found quick acceptance in the White House and elsewhere.

[1]Max Braude was stationed with the International Refugee Organization after the war and became involved with ORT (a Russian entity founded in 1880; the acronym now stands for Organization for Rehabilitation and Training), a nonprofit, nonpolitical, educational organization. In 1956, he became director general of World ORT Union. Braude College of Engineering in Karmiel, Israel, is named in his honor.

[2]Edward Wood, 3rd Viscount Halifax (1881–1959), held many important positions in the British government between his election to the House of Commons in 1910 and his resignation as British ambassador to the United Nations in 1946, including minister of agriculture, viceroy of India, secretary of war, leader of the House of Lords, and, under Chamberlain and Churchill, foreign secretary. He spent much of the war as the ambassador to the United States, was one of the founders of the United Nations, and wrote a 1957 memoir titled Fulness of Days.

[3]Edwin Pauley (1903–1981), a California oil man, was the U.S. representative to the Allied Reparations Committee. He also served under President Truman as petroleum coordinator of lend-lease supplies for the Soviet Union and Britain. He chaired the University of California Board of Regents as well. Pauley Pavilion at UCLA is named in his honor.

June 7, 1945
Salzburg, Austria

Dear Jonathan and Zelda,

I appreciated very much the lovely letters which you sent me. I am very sorry that I shall not be with you to celebrate the anniversaries which occur this month. I am enclosing money-orders for each of you with which I hope you will buy yourselves something in order to make the celebrations somewhat more pleasant.

I am very busy here and have not much time for letter-writing. At the present time, I am engaged in arranging the distribution of 12 tons of food which the Joint Distribution Committee sent in from Switzerland through the International Red Cross for the Jewish displaced persons in this area. It seems to be quite definite now that we shall not be sent to the Pacific area but that our Corps will remain here as occupational troops in charge of all American-occupied Austria. This, it seems, will take in a territory of three provinces, Tyrol, Salzburg, and Oberdonau, extending roughly from Innsbruck to Linz. The Corps chaplains had a conference yesterday with our new general, a very fine person, and it seems that I am, for the present, to be Chief Rabbi of all this area, charged with caring not only for the thousands of American Jewish soldiers who will be here but also the tens of thousands of wandering Jewish civilians. Rather a big assignment. And, believe you me, plenty of headaches.

My Bronze Star citation, official seal and all, arrived a few days ago. This is what it says:

CITATION FOR AWARD OF THE BRONZE STAR MEDAL

DAVID M. EICHHORN, O-482124, Captain, Chaplain Corps, Headquarters XV Corps, United States Army, for meritorious service in connection with military operations against an enemy of the United States during the period 25 July 1944 to 9 May 1945. During this period while the XV Corps was actively engaged against the enemy, Chaplain EICHHORN made many visits to the front with the troops, sharing their dangers and hardships and serving them most efficiently as Chaplain. He visited hospitals and remained there with the wounded and dying, giving them both physical and spiritual assistance and comforting them in every way possible. His services were available on all occasions and, in the performance of his duties, he labored untiringly with no thought of self. His spiritual direction and untiring efforts were a contributing factor in the development of the high state of morale existant [sic] within this Corps. Such enthusiasm and devotion to duty reflects great credit upon himself and merits the highest praise. Entered military service from Tallahassee, Florida.

Sounds good. This plus five cents will now buy me a cup of coffee. That's all for now. Lots of love and kisses from

>   Your daddy and husband,
>   Max

P.S. One extra ration of love and kisses is also to be added for each of the following: Mike, Jerry, and Judy.
P.P.S. The photos which are enclosed are pictures of my service in the stadium in Nuremberg, a service held on the very spot where the infamous Nuremberg laws were promulgated and where Hitler delivered his most important speeches.

In a letter sent to Rabbi Judah Nadich after the war, Rabbi Eichhorn discussed the challenges he faced working with displaced persons (DPs) and concentration camp survivors in Austria, and where he found help.

There was a multiplicity of problems, of course — how to raise the DP's morale, how to restore his confidence and faith in his fellow man, how to keep him alive, keep him sufficiently housed, clothed and fed; but in one major area, support from the American Army, there was no problem of any kind. The military personnel, officers and men alike, were simply superb. They never turned down a request; they never refused to lend a hand; they simply paid no attention to what the AR [Army Regulations] said or did not say. As far as I am concerned: The JDC [Joint Distribution Committee] and the Palestine Brigade [Jewish volunteers in the British army] and all that got the headlines and the glory; but, to a very great extent, the American

Armed Forces, officially and through the individual GI and the Jewish chaplain, did the job without fanfare and without headlines and without asking the American Jewish community to shell out tens of millions of dollars. The Jewish chaplains and the Jewish GIs, especially, begged, pilfered and provided more food and clothing and bedding and medicine and many other things for the DPs than they got from a number of other sources who have gotten the credit and the publicity; and it is high time that this fact be made known in the history books.

July 16, 1945
Dear Zelda, Jonny, Mike, Jerry, Judy, Helene,
    Pop, and everybody:

I know that I should have written a long time ago but the plain truth is that this has been one of those periods which come upon me every now and then when I just have not felt like writing. I worked myself to a frazzle, I guess, trying to take care of all the Jewish DPs in Austria, in addition to my other duties, and I must have overdone it. At any rate, about two weeks ago, I had another one of those things like I had back at Camp Croft in March, 1944, when the doctor said that if he was not certain I was a male he should surmise that I was going through menopause — hot and cold flushes, ringing noises in the head, sleepless nights, listlessness, no ambition. This time the doctor said it was a plain case of nerves caused by overwork and inability to relax properly. So his prescription was: a minimum amount of work, as much rest as possible (for which purpose he had me take sleeping tablets night and day), and as often as possible I should get away some place where I can forget the war and Jews as much as possible. He said it was either that or else going on working to a point where I would not be much good to anyone including myself — so I took that — and for the last two weeks I have been the Army's champion goldbrick and have tried to do as little as the law allowed.

I've got a boss, God bless him, who is a fine man but who is very conscientious about taking care of his Jews and, since from the very beginning, I've been practically the only Jewish chaplain around, he's been very niggardly about granting me permission to take vacations.

He's always been very generous about letting me go places on business but strictly for pleasure — no. He has been very consistent as far as his end of it is concerned. He has never gone any place either, says he has no desire, but I think he would also admit that he has not worked nearly as hard or as long hours or under such arduous physical conditions as have I. At any rate, I was asked to go to London to a rabbinical conference at the end of June to make a speech and, in a polite way, Chaplain Schellhase said "No" and I was asked to go to Paris this week to join in a conference on future JWB policies in Europe and once again Chaplain Schellhase felt he was forced to reply in the negative. But now, out of a clear blue sky, we have discovered that there are five more Jewish chaplains within a hundred miles and there came an opportunity for me to go to our Rest Center in Nancy for six days and this time the boss said "Yes." So I'm leaving for Nancy Wednesday and will be gone from here until the following Friday.

Had a pleasant surprise two days ago. The provost marshal of Nuremberg, an MP captain, walked in on me and he was none other than my old Florida student, Murray (Micky) Weintraub, of Miami, a very fine boy whom you may remember and who mentioned to me over and over again that he wants to be remembered to you, Zelda, and all the kids. He married Gladys Wolf of FSCW [Florida State College for Women] a couple years ago and they have a little girl whom Micky has never seen. He brought me some bad news about our Florida boys which dampened the pleasure of seeing him: Nathan Aronowitz of Miami, my brilliant Nate, a sweet loveable boy, killed in Luxembourg; Louis Dwoskin, another fine member of our Hillel Council from Jax, killed leading his company in Brittany; Bob Richter of Miami, little Alfy Cohen of Miami, another brilliant boy who was editor of the university newspaper and in the Army was a correspondent for the *Stars and Stripes*, Si Rothstein, Phi Beta Kappa and future sociologist of Jax, and many others whom I remembered more dimly, all dead. These sad tidings must be expected but when they come they can not be taken easily.

Yesterday I made my first aeroplane flight in Europe. I had a service in Aschaffenburg which is 110 miles from Bamberg by jeep and 80 miles by air and I asked for and was granted permission to go there in a Piper Cub to save the five hour jeep trip over rough roads. It took us an hour to go and 1½ hours to come back. Coming back we bucked high winds and it was so rough that even the pilot, a regular Army Air Force pilot, got a little uneasy in the stomach. The pilot warned me in advance that the return trip would be bumpy, and so I took elaborate precautions; ate no solid food for lunch, stuffed cotton in my ears, took off my specs, and tied a handkerchief around my eyes — so that as far as possible I was deafened and blinded — and I didn't get the least bit sick. It wasn't exactly enjoyable. One had the feeling, at least I did, of a long journey in a giant elevator. And I just don't enjoy being up high. Never did.

The pictures of the children are wonderful, thank you very much for sending them to me. I have them in my office, placed on display on either side of the Ark and they have been greatly admired. Jonny looks like a little man. Mike has that impish grin which gives him a wistful and attractive countenance. Jerry is certainly turning into a handsome youngster. And little prize-package Judy is a little dream-girl. She looks like a sweet but determined young lady. I am sending you herewith some pictures which up till now I have not been allowed to send. They date from January to June 1945. The four taken in January were taken in areas where shells were coming in while the services were going on. While they were taken under adverse photographic circumstances it is easy to see that the looks on the faces of the men and myself indicate that we were under something of a strain. When one is not sure but what the next one may land right on top of him, it is not too easy to smile.

I have in front of me the following home-communiqués: V-mails from Zelda, 2 undated, June 17, 25 (2), 30, and air-mail, June 18; from Jonny, June 1; from Helene, 2 V-mails, 1 undated and the other June 29; from dad, June 13 (already answered); and from Henny, July 2. Thank you all for writing; the letters are always heartily welcomed. Sorry that I can't write as often and individually.

Reactions to said letters: Well, Jonny, I guess you know by now that daddy just was not able to be there in the flesh for your birthday, although when the day rolled around, he certainly was thinking of you. From your picture, you are developing into quite a young man and, according to most of those who see your picture, you are very much a counterpart of me in appearance. You have my deepest sympathy. I always did think that in thought and in action, you and I are very much alike. I don't know if that is good but that is the way it is, for better or for worse. . . .

I was surprised to learn, Zelda, that the American radio had said that the XV Corps would be in Europe until December. There is a strong rumor around here, which must always be discounted strongly, of course, that the Corps is leaving Europe in September. There is also a very strong likelihood that I shall be left behind. As a matter of fact, the Corps has so recommended to Supreme HQ. A letter went out from here to the "higher ups" on July 9 stating that, because of the fine job I have done with Jewish refugees in France, Germany, and Austria, I should be retained with a "Higher headquarters" in Europe as a liaison officer between the American Army and Jewish welfare agencies. What the result will be is anyone's guess. Of the 81 Jewish chaplains who were in Europe when the war ended, 13 have already gone to the Pacific or returned to the USA, 11 are definitely to stay behind with the occupation forces, and the other 57, including myself, are waiting around to find out what is going to happen. You might also be interested to know that, of the 81, 11 including me were decorated. . . .

Jonny, I hope that your tooth trouble and that of Jerry and everybody is now fixed up. I think the YMCA idea is wonderful and I am very happy that you and Mike get a chance to go there and to enjoy all the fine things there. I am happy too, that you all get a chance to go swimming together. You must all try to get as much exercise as you can. There is nothing which is more helpful in finding happiness in life than to have a strong and healthy body. This helps also to give you a strong and healthy mind.

Most of the things which were in the box that you received at the end of June are war souvenirs. They are not to be used. They are to be saved for me until I get back. As I remember it (it has been so long since I sent it), the perfume was for you and the little necklace for Judy. Glad to learn that Marty is going to get to go home soon. If you write to Ruth, tell her I said "Thank you" for all the magazines she has been sending me. I read them all and then pass them on to the boys. But as a letter-writer, I just don't have the patience any more to sit down and bang out a lot of letters. Guess it is just part of the post-war "let-down." After the tension of the past year, most of us around here aren't interested in much of anything except, when possible, having a good time.

Dad, I've already written you about the impossibility of getting around Germany either personally or by mail. I don't know who in the world is giving my name out all over the USA but I'm being flooded with requests from all over the country to locate missing relatives, which I am utterly powerless to do. I can only work in my own particular area which in itself is too much for one person. In the city of Bamberg alone, I've got about 500 Jews on my hands from all over Europe. I wish I were a miracle-worker but I'm not. I can understand the anxiety of people in America and their desire to discover and be of help to their loved ones. While it is true that the Jewish army chaplains have done more so far to help the remaining Jews than all the Jewish relief organizations combined in Germany and Austria, the fact remains that the chaplains are soldiers and are tied down to their Army duties and the relief work is definitely a civilian job and a civilian responsibility. You can tell anyone who asks you that; if one's relative is alive, he will be so informed as quickly as possible by the JDC or the International Red Cross. If one does not receive such information in, let us say, at most a year, the overwhelming possibility is that the person is dead. Out of 6½ million Jews in Hitler's Europe, less than a million remain. The chance of any particular person being alive is less than 1 in 7. And practically all of these Jews, when they left their homes, became *numbers* and were no longer names and lie buried in nameless graves. That is the bitter fact and no amount of frantic inquiry will add to it or detract from it. . . .

Henny, these last remarks will tell you of the present situation that I have to face with regard to getting any information about anyone's family. It is absolutely impossible for me to go to Vienna or to write to anyone there. My hands are completely tied, except for the area over which our Corps have jurisdiction. In that particular area, so far as Jewish matters are concerned, I do all that I can to be of help to the civilians. For example, I spent all of yesterday afternoon and this morning working with local Jews and the military government on purely civilian matters. . . . Much as I should like to procure for you the items you desire, that, too, I can not do. These countries are stripped of everything except the barest necessities and to try to find anything is also out of the question. Much of that which was beautiful and worthwhile has been taken by looters or destroyed by the war. We did not come here nor do we stay here as tourists. I was in all the places in Austria that you mention and never went swimming or sight-seeing once. Hitler's Berchtesgaden was 15 miles from Salzburg, where I was for almost two months, and I never went to see it. I was at Chiem See and went within a half-mile of Mad King Ludwig's Castle and didn't spend a minute looking at it.[1] I held a service at Garmisch and didn't go near the Zugspitze.[2] The only thing all of us noticed and enjoyed was that, beyond a doubt, the Austrian women are the prettiest in Europe. The only ones that come near them are the French city-dwellers and they only because they know how to dress and make-up. The Austrian beauty is more natural. The Czechs are also OK for looks. Also the northern Italians. Most of the rest look and act like hicks. I didn't find Linz quite as unattractive as you make it. Probably because the demi-monde of Vienna had fled there from the Russians. The American soldiers liked that. From all that we can gather, the Americans in America are much more concerned about the political opinions of the women over here than the American soldiers over here are. The soldiers over here may be rather peculiar animals but, from all that I have observed and overheard, it is my guess that when a soldier over here seeks and obtains the company of a native female, there isn't much political discussion. As a matter of fact, usually neither can speak the other's language so there isn't much discussion (period). But somehow they still seem to manage to get along and enjoy each other's company. The fact that, through most of Europe, there are 2 or 3 young females for every healthy young male may have something to do with it. Another peculiar fact is that many of these healthy young males who actually killed Germans do not hate them nearly as much as many of those who did most of their fighting with their vocal cords.

So long for now. Lots of love and kisses to all.
Your husband, daddy, son, and brother,
Max

[1]Chiem See, called Herren Chiemsee, was King Ludwig II's third and largest castle, a replica of Versailles on an island named Herreninsel in Lake Chiemsee. The king lived in the castle for just ten days. He was eventually declared insane by his brothers and died shortly thereafter.
[2]Garmisch, eighty-five miles south of Munich near the Austrian border, was the site of the 1936 Winter Olympics and is one of Europe's foremost winter sports areas. The nearby Zugspitze is Germany's highest mountain (9,739 feet).

August 10, 1945
Bad Wildungen, Germany
Dear dad, Henny, Helene, Zelda, Jonny, Mike, Jerry,
    Judy, and everybody,

I am sending this letter first to Columbia and then want it sent on to West Orange and Tulsa because it contains news that I know will be of especial interest to the Columbia and New Jersey branches of the Eichhorn mishpacha. I have not written sooner because, for the last two weeks, my affairs have been in a very unsettled state and I waited, hoping to have more definite information when I wrote. I finally decided to wait no longer and to write, even though I can not yet give you absolutely definite news concerning my immediate future.

I last wrote just prior to going on a leave to Nancy, France, on the 18th of July. I'll carry on with the story from there. I left Bamberg on July 18 and headed for Nancy. The first night was spent in Alsace in Hagenau. There I made the acquaintance of the family of a retired French Army officer and spent two days with them very enjoyably. One day was spent touring Strasbourg and I have some very lovely pictures of this beautiful city. Unfortunately, the famous cathedral clock was not operating, so that was one sight that I was unable to see. I arrived in Nancy on July 20 and spent three days there. I then received an invitation to spend the rest of my vacation at Lake Constance (Boden See) on the Swiss border. So I left Nancy on July 23 and spent that night in Colmar. The next day I headed for Muelheim and arrived in Mama Selig's birthplace at noon on July 24. The rest of the day I was the guest of the French commandant of the town, a captain from Metz, and he really showed me a grand time. We tried to locate mama's parents in the town records so that I could visit their graves but there were so many Zivis (and I didn't know my grandparents' first names) that we finally had to give up. I did see Laura and Hugo's names on the list and the captain and I believed that my particular grandfather was one of the four who were named Isaac Joseph but that was as far as we got. One Jew by the name of Dreyfuss had returned to Muelheim but I did not meet him. The town is in very good shape. The war left its mark in destroyed buildings here and there but, as a whole, it survived quite well, considering its proximity to the war zone. Alt-Breisach, for example, through which we passed, was practically completely destroyed. The

Jewish cemetery in Muelheim is being put back in good shape by the French authorities. I left Muelheim at about 5 p.m. and headed for Ueberlingen on Boden See, arriving there at 8:30, and learned that my friends had moved on to Siegmaringen, about 30 miles away. We (two enlisted men, Levine and a friend of his, and myself) then went on to Siegmaringen and located my friends at about 10 p.m. Siegmaringen has become the center of a very fine French project in which my friends are taking part. The French government has requisitioned all the castles in this area as recreation centers and is sending 10,000 children from Paris to these castles for 3-week vacations. 5,000 of the children are Jewish. In charge of the project are 2 rabbis, 3 priests, 1 minister, and a group of social workers, all French. I stayed with these folks until the morning of July 27 and then returned to Bamberg, about 150 miles away. During this time, I was the guest of the French army there and they really wined and dined me. I sure do like the French.

When we returned to XV Corps, some startling news awaited Levine and myself. We had both been transferred! Levine was to leave for the re-deployment center at Rheims, France, where he was to be an instructor in the Music School at the center and I was to go to HQ XXIII Corps at Bad Wildungen, Germany. What had happened was this: On July 9, the Corps sent a letter to Supreme HQ stating that, since XV Corps would soon return to the States and since I was to be retained in the Army, it was felt that I should be used in a spot where I would be most helpful. Because of the great number of refugee matters which I had handled, the Corps felt that I should be kept in Europe with a higher headquarters to continue to work along these lines. Therefore, the Corps made a strong recommendation to Supreme HQ that I should not return to the States but should remain in Europe. After I had left for Nancy, a letter arrived from Supreme HQ stating that, in accordance with the Corps recommendation, I was to be transferred to HQ XXIII Corps, which was to remain in Europe, and that I should be transferred to a higher HQ if and when an opening occurred. When the transfer orders arrived, I was away on leave and so, when I got back, I had a farewell service, packed, and went off to Bad Wildungen on July 30.

When I arrived at HQ XXIII Corps, I was informed that the situation was "snafu."[1] Supreme HQ had not followed the usual procedure of consulting XXIII Corps before making the transfer and, not knowing I was coming, XXIII Corps had, in a private deal, secured the Jewish chaplain

of the XIX Corps, which was also leaving for the States. The result was
that when I got here I found another chaplain in the job which I was sup-
posed to fill. Since my orders came from the highest HQ, I could have
insisted on the other gentleman being kicked out but I did not want to
do this and asked to be returned to the XV Corps. This the XXIII Corps
promised to do and so all I could do and have been doing was wait
around and hope. However, in the meantime a notice has arrived from
Supreme HQ that orders were requested on me by them on August 2
transferring me from HQ XXIII Corps to the staff of the 197th General
Hospital, which, so far as I can learn, is located in or near Rheims,
France. The orders have not yet arrived and I'm still waiting and doing
nothing except to hold an occasional service here and there. The last ten
days, therefore, have been very boring and very trying.

However, one very important thing has happened. Chaplain Ernst
Lorge, who succeeded me for two years at Tallahassee and then came
on into the Army, was transferred from the 69th Division to the 3rd
Division, which is also in Bad Wildungen. Ernst is a very fine boy and
we have been spending as much time together as possible. He told me
that the HQ of the 69th Division was in Rotenburg and that Richelsdorf was occupied by troops of this division, the last town before the
Russian zone! So, contrary to my previous information, the town was
in American hands and we could go there. By a strange coincidence,
Lorge's father comes from the same neighborhood. His father was
rabbi in Mainz but he (the father of Ernst) was born and reared in Har-
muth-sachsen bei Waldkoppel, which is about 20 miles from Richelsdorf. In fact, he had a cousin, a woman who had lived in Sontra who
was married to a Loewenstein who was related to the Richelsdorf
Loewensteins! Rabbi Lorge's folks now live in Cincinnati.

So Lorge and I planned a trip to Richelsdorf together and we went
there two days ago on August 8th. On the way, we had lunch at the
69th HQ at Rotenburg and there I met an old dear friend of mine,
Chaplain Poole (now a major) who had been in the same chapel with
me at Camp Croft and who has been overseas since September, 1942.
We went to the burgomeister at Richelsdorf and gave him the letter,
dad, which you had written. I am enclosing his reply. Also several
people who knew you and Uncle Leopold jotted down greetings in the
note-book I had and I am enclosing these brief messages. As you will
learn from the burgomeister's letter and as I am sure you must have

felt, Uncle Max is no longer among the living. From 1939 until August, 1942, he and Aunt Caroline were the only Jews left in Richelsdorf. On August 4, 1942, Aunt Caroline was ordered to report to Gestapo head-quarters in Cassel. She has not been heard from since. On August 12, 1942, Uncle Max received a similar order. The next news the Richels-dorf community received was that Uncle Max had died of dysentery in the Dachau Concentration Camp on Oct. 4, 1942. As I have written you previously, my own knowledge of what has transpired here led me to expect just such sad news. I hope you will understand when I write that it was a blessing that his period of confinement at Dachau was of such brief duration.

I visited the house where you were born, the synagogue, and David's house. The synagogue was being used as a stable.

I visited the cemetery. Every stone was overthrown, some broken. The burgomeister promised me that, as soon as he could obtain cement, he would put the stones and the cemetery in good order. I could not locate grandfather's grave but I did find grandmother's grave and I had the stone reset immediately. It was not broken and it and the grave are in good condition.

Rabbi Lorge took pictures of both the house and the cemetery and if they come out well, I shall send them to you. It was a dismal, cloudy day and they may not come out. All the people I met wanted to know about Uncle Leopold and Julius and Albert. They did not know that these Eichhorns had succeeded in getting to America or that the Joseph Loewensteins were also in America. They asked me about oth-ers of the Jewish community there, a Dr. Stanner (?), and others but I knew nothing of them. There were 39 Jews in Richelsdorf in 1933. Now there are none. The newest grave in the cemetery was that of a Handstein, who had died in 1934.

I am glad that, because of this mix-up in assignments, I was able to visit Richelsdorf and to find out what had happened there. Like the thousands of similar little villages and towns scattered throughout Ger-many, as a Jewish community it no longer exists except in memory.

Now I am still waiting for my orders which, in all likelihood, will send me to the 197th General Hospital in Rheims, France. Exactly what kind of work awaits me there, I do not know. Boy, will old Cor-poral Levine be surprised to see me! We thought we should not meet again on this side of the Atlantic.

Mail from America has been very sparse lately. In the last five weeks, I have received two V-mails from Zelda (one undated and the other July 19) and one from Helene (July 6). I received all three this afternoon and they furnished the necessary final push to get me to sit down and write. The unsettled situation of the last ten days has put me in no mood for letter-writing and I've got a mountain of business mail that has been similarly neglected.

The reason, Helene, why I listed only 36 points for children is that that is the maximum allowed for kids. Points or no points, Judy is still daddy's little angel-chil' and counts a-plenty. You are right about the hardness that has come over us, certainly over me. Just how much I've changed is something, of course, that it is not possible for me to judge but of one thing I am certain — for better or worse, I have changed. I think I have become more impatient with human selfishness and more tender towards those who genuinely suffer.

I am certainly looking forward to a checker game with you, Jonny. You will probably beat me to a frazzle. I've developed lately into a pretty good ping-pong player. So if you beat me in checkers, maybe I'll be able to beat you in ping-pong.

It looks from here as though Japan is about ready to call it quits.[2] That should hasten the home-coming of many of our men. How soon I may expect to get back to the States is a matter of pure conjecture. The Army seems to feel that I am needed here — and here I shall stay until the Army changes its opinion.

> Love and kisses to all from
> Your hubby, son, father, and brother,
> Max

P.S. Don't write to me until I get my new address, which I shall send you as soon as I know what it is.

---

[1]"Snafu" derives from a famous military acronym; the G-rated version is "situation normal, all fouled up."

[2]This letter was written the day after the atomic bomb fell on Nagasaki, two days after the Soviet Union declared war on Japan and began a major offensive in Manchuria. The Japanese would formally surrender, on board the USS *Missouri*, on September 2.

September 12, 1945
Assembly Area, Rheims, France

Dear Zelda and everybody,

I have delayed and delayed writing this letter in the hope that I could tell you something definite about the Army's plans for me for the immediate future. Since July 30, I have been moved around and around until I was dizzy — due to no fault of my own but just general stupidity and laziness on the part of certain of the administrative chaplains and others. Now, however, things have shaped up to the extent that I have been told that I shall be ordered to a unit which will return to the States in the very near future which is all right with me as I am completely fed up with this "snafu" situation. I should have been willing to remain in Germany for a time to help the Jews there if the Army had not balled up the whole business. I have not had any mail in from anyone for a month. Doesn't seem to be much use in writing to me now as I'll probably be on my way back to the States shortly. When I know something more definite, I'll write again. Love and kisses to all

Max

The following is from Rabbi Eichhorn's 1969 autobiography.

On July 1, XV HQ moved back to Bamberg, Germany, as a preparatory for deployment to the Pacific theatre of operations. The Corps was scheduled to leave Europe in September. Because of my experience with Displaced Persons work, the Corps CG recommended to Eisenhower's HQ that I be retained in Europe as a "liaison officer between the American Army and American Jewish welfare agencies." The higher HQ approved this recommendation. Accordingly, I was transferred to HQ XXIII Corps, Bad Wildungen, Germany, on July 24. However, because the Pacific war ended on September 2, XV Corps was sent back to the USA and deactivated and, because I, on the basis of my combat record and my large family, had a very large number of "separation points," I was relieved of my assignment and started toward home on August 15. But because of lack of adequate shipping facilities, I did not get home very quickly. I was sent to Camp Philadelphia, Rheims, France, on August 22; and then on September 14 to the 46th General Hospital at Besançon, France, and, at long last, on October 21, to the Port of Embarkation at Camp Calas, Marseilles, France.

October 27, 1945
Port of Marseilles

Dear Zelda, Jonny, Mike, Jerry, Judy and everybody,

Well, I've finally gotten this far and it looks like I'll soon be back in the U.S.A. Rumor has it that we go on board of a Victory ship, the "Lincoln," on Monday the 29th and we should be in some American port before November 15th. I have asked to be discharged in New York City so that I can visit my dad and Helene and can also consult the Jewish Welfare Board with regard to my future. Of course, there is also a chance that I may not be discharged and may have to remain in the Army for a while longer.

I have not yet written to Tallahassee and shall not do so until I arrive in the U.S. and get a clearer picture of just what lies ahead. I rather suspect that I may end up in Tallahassee but that will depend on a number of circumstances which are unpredictable at the present time.

That's all for now. Next time you hear from me will probably be on your side of the Atlantic.

Love and kisses to all
Your hubby and papa,
Max

P.S. I haven't received any mail for a heck of a long while.

The following is from a recent correspondence with Rabbi Jonathan Eichhorn.

Dad was reunited with the kids in New York City at Grand Central Station on December 25, 1945, when we got off the train from Tulsa. This was after being overseas at war one year, six months, and 19 days. Mike and I gave him a big hug and kisses. It was truly a joyful moment! However, it did take Jerry and Judy a few days to readjust to his return. Judy was only a year old and Jerry only two years old when he left for Europe. The kids had chocolate cake every night to celebrate. After our return, we stayed at a hotel for a week to ten days, while mom and dad searched for an adequate apartment in the metropolitan area.

David Max Eichhorn began his terminal leave from the U.S. Army on November 11, 1945, although, because of accrued leave, his active duty did not technically end until February 21, 1946. On January 19, 1946, he was promoted to major. He reenlisted in the U.S. Army Reserve in August 1948 and continued on active reserve status until reaching mandatory retirement age in February 1966. He retired from the reserve with the rank of lieutenant colonel.

Soon after returning to the United States, Rabbi Eichhorn became director of field operations of the Commission on Jewish Chaplaincy of the National Jewish Welfare Board, a position he held until 1968. He described his duties in his autobiography as "supervising all these full-time and part-time Jewish chaplains ecclesiastically." He was also one of the organizers of the Association of Jewish Chaplains of the Armed Forces, founded in March 1946, and was president from 1953 to 1955. He then became part-time rabbi of Temple Israel in Merritt Island, Florida, and Jewish civilian chaplain for the Kennedy Space Center. In his postwar life he wrote a variety of both popular and scholarly books, including Cain: Son of the Serpent *(1957);* Musings of the Old Professor *(1963), a new translation of the Book of Ecclesiastes;* Conversion to Judaism: A History and Analysis *(1966);* Evangelizing the American Jews *(1978);* Jewish Intermarriages: Fact and Fiction *(1974); and* Joys of Jewish Folklore: A Journey from New Amsterdam to Beverly Hills and Beyond *(1981), reissued in 1996 and still in print as* Jewish Folklore in America, *all published by Jonathan David.*

At the time of his death in 1986, Rabbi Eichhorn and his wife of fifty-two years, Zelda, lived in Satellite Beach, Florida. Jonathan Eichhorn served as a rabbi in Kingston, New York, for thirty-five years and is now retired and living in Silver Spring, Maryland. Michael and Jerry are businessmen in Florida. All three sons of Rabbi Eichhorn had three children. Judy married businessman Ronald Zaid, had two children, and now lives on Long Island, New York.

Rabbi Abraham Shusterman, a classmate of Rabbi Eichhorn's at Hebrew Union College, wrote a memorial tribute to the man who had been his close friend for more than six decades. He said in part:

David Max Eichhorn did not need the glamour of the pulpit or the applause of an admiring congregation to feel fulfilled. He possessed inner security. He was a genuine universalist. The child of affluent parents, he was never demanding, but always modest in his way of living. He traveled everywhere, but at heart remained a small-town boy from Columbia, Pennsylvania. His two closest boyhood companions became a Catholic priest and a Protestant minister.

He was conditioned by a natural love for all people and a feeling of at-homeness with everybody. He edited a book on conversion to Judaism. He was a prolific writer. Among his books was one on the joys of American Jewish folklore, reflecting his undying enthusiasm for the Jewish experience in the country he loved so truly. Here was a rabbi who lived in harmony with his Judaism and his Americanism. In his life, one enriched the other. . . . I thank God that this man of unique personality and rare qualities of character lived and walked among us for more than fourscore years.

October 24, 1986
Los Angeles

Dear Helene [Tash]:

. . . Though I saw far too little of Max since I came to California in the 40s, I never forgot those indelible days when I was lucky enough to have him as a neighbor — a marvelous neighbor — wise, witty, with an easy charm and erudition from which I profited. Over the years we exchanged letters, books, and greetings. My last letter to him, a few months back, was to inquire whether a star pitcher for the Toronto Bluejays, named Mark Eichhorn, was related. Max replied with his usual charm . . . that he had never heard of the young man, and [went] on to explain the derivation of the Eichhorn name. The last paragraph of his letter read, "All factors considered, Zelda and I have no grounds for complaint."

Everyone who knew Max has grounds to lament his loss, and I join you in mourning him. . . .

As for me, I continue to fire from all turrets. I teach at USC, I just wrote another book, I am caught up in all too many pro bono publico matters, and I loathe Reagan and his administration. That's enough of an agenda for a septuagenarian only three years this side of octogenarian country. What the hell, it's better than all suggested alternatives.

> Sincerely,
> Norm [Corwin]

Finally, there is this excerpt from Rabbi Eichhorn's autobiography.

In May 1966 I presented to the United States government the Torah and Ark which I had used in conducting services in Europe during combat operations in World War II and also in the DP camps after the war. This Torah and Ark will be on display in the American Museum of Immigration on Bedloe's Island in New York harbor, if and when the museum is completed.

President Richard Nixon opened the American Museum of Immigration at the base of the Statue of Liberty on September 26, 1972. The Torah and Ark were part of the display, although the donor was unidentified. In the mid-1970s, Rabbi Eichhorn's daughter Judy visited the Statue of Liberty and recognized the Torah as the one her father had brought back from the war. As a small child, she had played with the tassels and pulled off all the beads.

The museum was closed in 1990. The Torah and Ark were moved to the Museum of Immigration on Ellis Island and put in storage. They were subsequently loaned and then given to the Museum of Jewish Heritage, 36 Battery Place, Battery Park City, in New York City. They are on display there now, properly credited along with photographs, papers, and handmade flags that were presented to Rabbi Eichhorn by the newly liberated residents of Dachau.

David Max Eichhorn, circa 1908

Eichhorn and sister Helene, circa 1910

Eichhorn (front row, fourth from right) in a school photo, circa 1910

Eichhorn and sister Helene, circa 1912

Eichhorn, circa 1919

Eichhorn, circa 1920s

Eichhorn (third from left) with fellow rabbinical students at Hebrew Union College, Cincinnati, Ohio, circa 1931

Rabbi David Max Eichhorn, 1936

Eichhorn and wife Zelda at Seder supper, Temple Israel, Tallahassee, Florida, 1941

Eichhorn's official military photo, Camp Croft Army Base, South Carolina, July 1942

Eichhorn, wife Zelda, sons Jonathan (directly in front of his father), Michael (in front of Jon), and Jeremiah, and daughter Judith, Spartanburg, South Carolina, 1943

Rabbi Eichhorn conducting Sabbath services with the Reverend John Elias Jones of Richmond, Indiana, at Camp Croft Army Base, South Carolina, October 13, 1943

Eichhorn leading Seder supper services, Camp Croft Army Base, South Carolina, April 7, 1944

Eichhorn leading Passover Seder services, accompanied by Zelda, Jonathan, and Michael (on the right), Camp Croft Army Base, South Carolina, April 1944

Eichhorn (back row, second from left) and nine other Jewish chaplains traveling to their European posts aboard the Queen Mary, *June 6–11, 1944*

Exterior of the synagogue in Lunéville, France, September 1944

Eichhorn leading Yom Kippur services for American forces at the synagogue in Lunéville, France, September 1944. The Torah and Ark in the picture were later donated by Eichhorn and placed on display at the Statue of Liberty.

*Eichhorn conducting Yom Kippur services for American forces at the
synagogue in Lunéville, France, September 27, 1944*

American troops attending Yom Kippur services led by Eichhorn at the synagogue in Lunéville, France, September 27, 1944

Eichhorn, center, speaking with injured U.S. servicemen, circa 1944

Eichhorn conducting services under combat conditions somewhere in France or Germany, 1944–1945

Eichhorn and Zelda, December 7, 1946

Eichhorn after war in New York City, circa 1947

Eichhorn and Zelda, July 1962

Eichhorn, circa late 1970s

Eichhorn, circa early 1980s

My grandfather, Chaplain David Max Eichhorn — or "Poppa," as I knew him — was my mother's father. During my childhood years, he and my grandmother spent their time shuttling between Rego Park, New York — approximately thirty minutes from my home on Long Island — and Satellite Beach, Florida, which is near the Kennedy Space Center. By the early 1980s, my grandparents were living year-round in Satellite Beach, where they remained until his death in July 1986, when I was nineteen years old.

My memories of him center primarily around family events. There were the usual family visits over the years, mostly at holidays (such as winter break, when we traveled to Florida), bar and bat mitzvahs (he had eleven grandchildren in total), and other milestone events such as my grandparents' fiftieth anniversary celebration, which was held at my childhood home in Jericho, New York.

I especially recall the back room in my grandparents' Florida condominium that served as Poppa's office. There, cluttered among numerous books and papers, he frequently played gin rummy with my father and smoked cigars. A very personal recollection is my grandfather's avid assistance with my stamp collecting. He would often send me stamps that he and my grandmother obtained during their international travels. One such gift was notable, given the subject of this book. In 1981, he secured for me a block of stamps denoting the tragic deaths in 1943 of four chaplains—George Fox, Clark Poling, John Washington, and Alexander Goode—who had been lost in the sinking of the army transport ship *Dorchester*. Rabbi Goode had been a close friend of my grandfather's, and they had spent an evening together in Boston shortly before the ill-fated voyage.

Among his many talents, which I recognized even as a small child, was my grandfather's prolific writing. In less than a twenty-five-year span, he authored or edited seven major works pertaining to Judaism. I possess a copy of each, but only two bear personal inscriptions. In *Jewish Intermarriages: Fact and Fiction* (1974), my grandfather wrote that I should "show this to any of your friends who may, at some future time, be faced with this 'problem.'" Seven years later, he inscribed in

Joys of Jewish Folklore: From New Amsterdam to Beverly Hills and Beyond (1981) that the book was presented to me "with the hope that you will find in scientific research the deep satisfaction and success that comes to all who devote themselves sacrificially to this arduous endeavor."

Although he finished his career as a congregational rabbi, the bulk of my grandfather's work was for Jewish organizations, primarily the Jewish Welfare Board. He was prominent within the rabbinical community, particularly the Reform community. For example, he was asked to lead the memorial services at Patrick Air Force Base after the January 1986 space shuttle *Challenger* tragedy (he was the Jewish civilian chaplain for the Kennedy Space Center). Most of all, my grandfather was an intellectual—and quite intimidating on that level, at least to one as young as I. Educational achievement was extremely important to him. In one letter to me, written in 1982, he acknowledged an academic award I had recently received and noted, "there is no personal satisfaction more deeply satisfying than that of learning and then of putting one's learning into deeds that continue this personal satisfaction by bringing great benefit to others." This sentiment is certainly reflective of the man I knew.

The message and tone of my grandfather's World War II correspondence reveal a person who was a husband to one, a father to four, and a colleague to many. When I first read his letters and reports, and even when I reread them, I could not quite equate their contents with the individual I had known. I think that, in many ways, the person who wrote those documents never returned to the United States; the man who came home was different somehow. In that sense, no doubt he was like many of his fellow soldiers. War has an effect on people, and those who have not had the experience simply cannot understand it. I cannot begin to imagine what my grandfather felt at the time. Nor can I detail what he felt after the years had passed.

Like many concentration camp survivors and liberating soldiers, my grandfather rarely discussed with his family the horrors he had seen at Dachau and elsewhere in Europe. To some extent, I have always found that surprising. I would have thought that, as a rabbi and a prominent public figure within his community, my grandfather would have openly shared his experiences, for a variety of reasons. Indeed, he wrote about what he had witnessed not only in his military reports to the Jewish Welfare Board but also in *Rabbis in Uniform* (1962). His experiences were also documented in *Deliverance Day: The Last Hours of Dachau* (1978). Yet with his family, he was remarkably silent on this episode of history.

I had only one substantive discussion with him regarding the Holocaust, and that was in writing. Just months before his death in July 1986, I queried him for a paper I was writing in college about the origins of the Holocaust and why it had occurred in Germany. His response was terse—just one typewritten page that reflected some personal thoughts and factual recitations. Unfortunately, before we had an opportunity to discuss this and related topics in more depth, he passed away.

Fortunately, history does not allow certain events or persons to be forgotten, and my grandfather falls in that category. The work my grandfather performed for tens of thousands of soldiers and victims of the Nazis during World War II merits a permanent marker of remembrance. Indeed, the U.S. Holocaust Memorial Museum in Washington, D.C., which opened in 1993, continuously displays a small segment of the film taken by George Stevens on May 6, 1945, as my grandfather led the first Jewish service held in the main square at Dachau. Additional color footage that had probably not been shown publicly for nearly forty years—incorporated with sound from a corresponding black-and-white version—aired in February 2003 as part of the PBS series *The Perilous Fight: America's World War II in Color.* It was this series, as my coeditor Greg Palmer explained in the Preface, that served as the impetus for this book.

To today's reader, it is no doubt my grandfather's experiences at Dachau that resonate with the most familiarity or recognition. It was certainly his most "famous" involvement with the Holocaust. In struggling to arrive at a title for this book, we briefly considered *The Dachau Rabbi*. However, we quickly, and appropriately, rejected this title, because frankly, my grandfather did much more important work during the war: holding Yom Kippur services, practically under fire, in Lunéville, France; discovering and helping Jewish refugees hidden in French villages; and especially performing his basic daily work as a chaplain with the XV Corps. He was, as my coeditor likes to say, the soldier in the jeep with the big Star of David painted on it who had a carton of matzos in the backseat. He drove from foxhole to foxhole

along the front lines, bringing his faith and his friendship to countless soldiers. I think of those men, many of them still in their teens or
early twenties, hunkered down in the dirt, terrified that the next
moment would be their last. My grandfather brought undeniable comfort to them, whether they lived or died, in a way that I hope never to
experience. Although he likely never fired a weapon at the enemy, his
interactions with the troops gave them the necessary spiritual courage
and conviction to fire theirs and win the war.

I have little doubt that although the several days he spent at
Dachau understandably changed him forever (especially after learning that his own uncle had died in the camp), these are not the experiences my grandfather would choose to reflect his contributions to
the U.S. military or the Jewish community worldwide. In fact, my
guess is that he would view his entire wartime service as the time of
his greatest contribution as an American, rather than as a Jew.

With respect to his rabbinical career, one of his primary interests
was interfaith marriage. As he noted in his unpublished autobiography, completed in 1969, he "came to the conclusion that the Rabbinic
practice of making non-Jews convert to Judaism before rabbis would
marry said non-Jews to Jews was spiritually, ethically and psychologically wrong." Instead, my grandfather would perform "intermarriages with no requirement of conversion but with a requirement that
word-of-honor commitments be given by the marrying couple that
they would rear their children as Jews, give them a formal Jewish religious education, and carry out in their homes the pattern of Jewish
religious life that their children would be taught in the religious
school." Although this thinking may be the norm among most Reform
rabbis today, my grandfather's advocacy of this position fifty-plus
years ago was far ahead of its time. It would have been interesting to
see how time and events would have shaped my grandfather's
thoughts on this controversial topic.

Editing this book was an important project, on both a personal and
a professional level. That the original letters authored by my grandfather sixty years ago were saved by my family is remarkable. To actually hold and read letters penned when he was my age certainly
taught me of a man I would otherwise never have known.

Of course, like everyone, my grandfather had his faults. This book
is not intended to create a false image of him. His many letters, how-

ever, open a doorway to a time long ago and recount in contemporaneous language what a young, spiritual soldier was thinking and feeling as he faced numerous daunting and sometimes life-threatening tasks. To some, the portrait presented in this book might not be a true reflection of the man my grandfather was before or after the war, but it is an image of him during one historical period that will now be preserved forever.

Mark S. Zaid

Appendix

Rabbi Eichhorn kept a journal consisting of a terse record of his activities for the last thirteen months of his army service. It was written in longhand and is difficult to decipher in places, with a number of unreadable words. He was also less meticulous about spelling than he was in his letters. The following transcription reproduces the original document as closely as possible. A handwritten note on the first page indicated that his journal for the period prior to September 1, 1944, had been lost.

Day-by-Day Account of Official Activities,
September 1, 1944, to November 14, 1945

Friday Sept 1 and Sat Sept 2 1944: Spent in office and contacting units.

Sunday Sept 3: Service, p.m. 989 FA and 3rd FOB, 30 present. 5 personal conferences.

Monday Sept 4: Went to Paris to see Nadich to make arrangements for High Holydays.

Tuesday 9/5: Conferred with ghetto leaders in Paris; got information for CIC about Gestapo activities in Paris; together with Nadich and John Sills again conferred with ghetto leaders.

Wed 9/6: Spent day with John Sills of JWB.

Thursday 9/7: Meet leaders of Paris Einheitscomite, p.m. Attended first religious service in Paris since its liberation in synagogue on Rue de la Victoire, Temple Rothschild, 3,500 present, at which Nadich presided.

Friday 9/8: Returned from Paris to Rear Ech, XV Corps.

Sat 9/9: Spent in office.

Sun 9/10: Service, Rear Ech, XV Corps, a.m. 10 present. Service, Fwd Ech, XV Corps, p.m., 15 present.

Monday 9/11: Visited 3rd Army chaplains with Cl Schellhase and Lanning.

Tues 9/12 and Wed 9/13: Spent in office.

Thurs 9/14/44: Went to Verdun for Rosh Hashana.

Fri 9/15 and Sat 9/16: Prepared for Rosh Hashana.

Sun 9/17: Rosh Hashana service, Verdun, p.m. 450 present. Pidyon Haben, Verdun, 10 present.

Mon 9/18: Rosh Hashana service, Verdun, a.m. 600 present. (same) p.m. 250 present.

Tues 9/19: Returned to Hq, XV Corps. Rosh Hashana service, Diaville, p.m., 70 present. Rosh Hashana service, XV Rear, p.m. 65 present.

Wed 9/20: Spent in office.

Thurs 9/21 and Fri 9/22: Spent at concentration camp in Vittel.

Sat 9/23: Spent in office.

Sun 9/24: Service, Fwd Ech, XV Corps, 15 present. (Same) Rear Ech, 8 present.

Mon 9/25: Went to Luneville for Yom Kippur.

Tues 9/26: Yom Kippur service, Luneville, p.m., 350 present.

Wed 9/27: Yom Kippur service, Luneville, a.m., 250 present (Same) p.m., 150 present.

Thurs 9/28: Returned to Hq, XV Corps.

Fri 9/29: Went to Vittel and collected religious articles and got documents for JDC and started for Paris.

Sat 9/30: Traveled toward Paris.

Sun 10/1: Arrived Paris, turned religious articles over to Chief Rabbi, and conferred with Ch. Nadich.

Mon 10/2: Conferred with Mr. Brewer of JDC.

Tues 10/3: Took a rest, waiting for Yom Kippur photos.

Wed 10/4: Left Paris and started for Hq, XV Corps.

Thurs 10/5 and Fri 10/6: Got to Hq, XV Corps, via concentration camp at Vittel.

Sat 10/7: Spent in office.

Sun 10/8: Service, XV Corps, 162 present. 5 personal conferences with chaplains.

Mon 10/9: Visited chaplains at 7th Army Hq. 3 letters to relatives. Service, Hq. XV Corps, 35 present.

Tues 10/10: 1 welfare case. 4 personal conferences.

Wed 10/11: Conferred with chaplain, 2nd French Armored Div. Service, 79th Replacement Pool, 5 present. Conferred with 2 chaplains in office.

Thurs 10/12: Conferred with chaplain. Conducted 10 committal services for 42 Jewish soldiers buried in military cemetery, Antilly, near Toul.

Fri 10/13: 5 conferences with chaplains. 2 letters to relatives.

Sat 10/14: 4 conferences with chaplains. 3 letters to relatives.

Sun 10/15: Service, XV Corps, 90 present. 2 personal conferences.

Mon 10/16: 43 letters to relatives. 5 conferences with chaplains.

Tues 10/17: 3 conferences with chaplains. 2 letters to relatives.

Wed 10/18: 2 conferences with chaplains. 1 letter to relatives.

Thurs 10/19: Service, 3rd Bn, 324 Inf, 44th Div, 16 present.

Fri 10/20: 16 letters to relatives. 1 conference with EM [enlisted men]. 5 conferences with chaplains.

Sat 10/21: Service, Hz. 2nd French Armored Div, 17 present.

Sun 10/22: Service, Hq, XV Corps, 28 present. Bible Class, Hq, XV Corps, 5 present.

Mon 10/23: 4 personal conferences with EM. 8 hospital visits, 51st Evac Hosp. 33 letters to relatives.

Tues 10/24: 4 letters to relatives. 8 hospital visits, 11th Evac Hosp. 13 personal conferences with EM.

Wed 10/25: 18 letters to relatives. 4 conferences with EM. 4 conferences with chaplains.

Thurs 10/26: 6 letters to relatives. 2 letters to relatives. Arranged for services in 79th Division rest areas.

Fri 10/27: 1 letter to relatives. Service, 108th AAA Bn, 6:30 p.m., 18 present.

Sat 10/28: Services, 315th Infantry, Bayon, 9 a.m., 36 present. Services, 79th Artillery, Blainville, 1 p.m., 17 present. Services, 2nd French Armored Division, 3 p.m., 28 present.

Sun 10/29: Service, Hq, XV Corps, 270 present, 10 a.m. 6 personal conferences with EM.

Mon 10/30: 2 letters to relatives. Service, 313 Inf Regt, Rosies (Theatre #1), 1 p.m., 25 present. Funeral, Mme Marie Mathilde Brille, 97 years of age; Civilian cemetery, [unreadable], 3 p.m., 10 present. Conferred with Chaplain Harald Saperstein of 2nd Replacement Center, 7th Army. Furnished relief for 1 refugee family, Rosieres.

Tues 10/31: Went to Nancy to arrange for military funeral for dead soldier in 2nd French Armored Div.

Wed 11/1: Furnished relief to 20 old Jewish ladies at Rosieres-aux-Salines.

Thurs 11/2: Funeral service, Roland Zebib, North African Jew, 20 years old, 16th Co, 13th Bn of Engineers, 2nd French Armored Division, buried in civilian cemetery near Chatel, 75 people present. 6 hospital visits. 51st Evac. Hosp.

Fri 11/3: 2 interviews with Civil Affairs officers on refugees and repair of synagogue. 1 conference with chaplain. 2 conferences with EM. 2 letters to relatives. Service, 108th AAA Bn, 25 present.

Sat 11/4: Service, 315 Inf, Bayon, 9 a.m., 70 present. (Next week will be Sunday at 1:30 p.m.) 6 hospital visits, 11th Evac Hosp. Said funeral prayers for Leon Elboz, 3rd R.M.T., 2nd Fr. Armored Div, 20 years old, wounded at [unreadable] and died this day at 11th Evac Hosp. Was native of Morocco. Service, 79th Div. Arty, Blainville, 26 present. Visited Civil Affairs officers at St. Nicholas and Dombasle in interest of refugees. Conference with Ch Emanuel Schenk of 4th Armored Div. 3 letters to relatives.

Sun 11/5: Joint Service, Hq XV Corps, 10 a.m., 372 present. Collected at this service, 37,500 francs for Jewish refugees in area. Ch. Emanuel Schenk of 4th Armored Division delivered sermon. Service, 1101 Engineers, 7 present. 2 personal conferences with EM. 10 letters to relatives.

Mon 11/6: 35 letters to relatives. 2 conferences with civilians on refugee matters. Service, 313th Inf. Rgt, 13 present. (Promised, if possible, to hold another service for same, Sunday, 12 November, at 4 p.m.)

Tues 11/7: 22 letters to relatives. Funeral — Aspirant Lucien Loufrani, (Algerian Jew), 3rd Co, 13th Medical Bn, 2nd French Armored Division,

buried in civilian cemetery at Chenvieres, 12 kilometers east of Luneville, 300 present.

Wed 11/8: 17 letters to relatives. 1 conference with EM. Funeral — Aspirant (2nd Lt) Raymond Raccah, native of Tunisia, 4th Co., 13th BN of
Engineers, buried in civilian cemetery at Chenvieres, 75 present.

Thurs 11/9: 4 letters to relatives. Discussion group, 10th Ordinance Bn, 7
present.

Fri 11/10: Service, 108th AAA Bn, 17 present

Sat 11/11: Service, 2nd French Armored Division, 11 present. Armistice
Day Service, Hq XV Corps, 26 present.

Sun 11/12: Service, Hq XV Corps, 354 present. 9 conferences with EM. 9
visits at 11th Evac Hospital. 2 visits at 7th N.P. Center.

Mon 11/13: 17 letters to relatives, Visit to 21st Genrl. Hospital, and conference with Chaplain Cook. Funeral — Rene Bourgel, native of Algiers,
1st Co., 13th Battalion of Engineers, 2nd French Armored Division;
buried in civilian cemetery at Vincy, near Charmes, France, 30 present.
8 hospital visits, 51st Evac Hospital. 1 welfare case. (Took Pvt. Louis
Goodman, 23rd AAA Group, to 7th Army N.P. Center #1, [unreadable],
from whence he was removed to 21st General Hospital and points west.)
7 letters to relatives.

Tues 11/14: 36 letters to relatives. 1 welfare case.

Wed 11/15: 40 letters to relatives. 2 conferences with EM. 1 conference
with chaplain.

Thurs 11/16: 14 hospital visits, 54th Field Hosp and 119th Clearing Co. 12
hospital visits, 9th Evac Hospital. 1 conference with chaplain. 1 conference with Jewish officer. 6 letters to relatives.

Fri 11/17: 16 hospital visits, 11th Evac Hosp. Service, 108th AAA, 23 present.

Sat 11/18: 27 hospital visits, 51st Evac Hosp. 1 personal conference with EM.

Sun 11/19: Service, Hq, XV Corps, 130 present. Traveled to 23rd Gen Hosp,
Vittel.

Mon 11/20: 38 hospital visits, 23rd General Hospital. 15 letters to relatives.

Tues 11/21: 29 hospital visits, 23rd General Hospital.

Wed 11/22: 12 hospital visits, 21st General Hospital. Service, Hq, 6th Army
Group, 14 present. 4 letters to relatives.

Thurs 11/23: 20 hospital visits, 21st General Hospital. Participated in
Thanksgiving service, Officers mess, 21st Gen Hosp, 200 present, with
Chaplains Hook of 21st Gen Hosp and Richards of 79th Div Arty. Ser-
vice, 21st General Hospital, 36 present. 2 personal conferences with EM.

Fri 11/24: 20 hospital visits, 21st General Hospital. Returned to Hq, XV Corps.

Sat 11/25: Went 14 kilometers beyond Blamont to get 2 children of Ms.
Marx of Luneville and returned them to their parents after they had
been hidden for 19 months.

Sun 11/26: Service, Hq XV Corps, 70 present. 15 hospital visits, 9th Evac.
Hosp. 101 letters to parents and relatives.

Mon 11/27: 23 letters to relatives. 1 conference with chaplain. 1 welfare case. 3 hospital visits, 9th Evac Hosp.

Tues 11/28: Attended conference of 7th Army chaplains at Epinal.

Wed 11/29: 53 letters to relatives. 1 conference with EM.

Thurs 11/30: Moved from Luneville to Saarburg.

Fri 12/1: Did routine work in Saarburg

Sat 12/2: 11 hospital visits, 11th Evac Hosp. 3 hospital visits, 116th Evac Hosp.

Sun 12/3: Service, Hq XV Corps, 80 present. 14 hospital visits, 116th Evac Hosp.

Mon 12/4: 8 hospital visits, 117th Evac. Hosp. 21 letters to relatives.

Tues 12/5: Spent day in office. 1 letter to relatives.

Wed 12/6: Got 8 damaged Torahs from synagogue at Shulsberg. 3 letters to relatives.

Thurs 12/7: Visited headquarters, 12th Armored Div, and left information for division chaplain. Conferred with battalion chaplain. Visited 7th Army VD Hospital — no Jewish patients among approximately 150 patients.

Fri 12/8: 9 hospital visits, 116th Evac Hosp. Joint Sabbath service, synagogue, Saarbourg, with Ch. Herbert Eskin, 100th Inf. Div, 40 present.

Sat 12/9: Conference with 12th Armored Div chaplain. 30 hospital visits, 116th Evac Hosp. (20 of visits to non-Jews). 10 hospital visits, 11th Evac Hosp.

Sun 12/10: Joint service with Ch. Eskin, 50 present. Joint Chanuka service with Ch Eskin and Ch Schellhase, 451 present. 10 letters to relatives.

Mon 12/11: 5 hospital visits, 7th Army NP hospital. 6 hospital visits, 11th Evac. Hosp.

Tues 12/12: 22 hospital visits, 11th Evac Hosp. 20 letters to relatives.

Wed 12/13: 11 hospital visits, 117th Evac Hosp. 22 letters to relatives. Conference with Chaplains Engelberg and Eskin.

Thurs 12/14: 14 letters to relatives. Conference with Chaplain Eskin. 1 welfare case.

Fri 12/15: 46 letters to relatives. Service with Ch Eskin and Engelberg, 48 present. 2 conferences with chaplains.

Sat 12/16: Service with Ch Eskin and Engelberg, 10 present. 16 hospital visits, 9th and 116th Evac Hosp.

Sun 12/17: Service with Ch Eskin and Engelberg, 61 present. Distributed 8 Chanuka packages to hospital patients. 18 letters to relatives. Service, 12th Administrative Center, 10 present.

Mon 12/18: 8 hospital visits, 11th Evac Hosp. 14 letters to relatives.

Tues 12/19: 4 letters to relatives. 5 hospital visits, 117th Evac Hosp. 2 conferences with chaplains.

Wed 12/20: 9 hospital visits, 116th Evac Hosp. 5 letters to relatives.

Thurs 12/21: 1 conference with EM. 5 conferences with chaplains. Sex morality lecture, 217th MP Co, 100 present. Lecture to Bible Class, 11 present.

Fri 12/22: 1 letter to relatives. Joint service with Eskin and Engleberg, Saarbourg synagogue, 31 present.

Sat 12/23: Joint service with Eskin and Engelberg, 14 present. 7 hospital visits, 9th Evac Hosp.

Sun 12/24: Joint service with Eskin and Engleberg, 61 present. 1 letter to relatives.

Mon 12/25: 12 hospital visits, 11th Evac Hosp.

Tues 12/26: 8 hospital visits, 117th Evac Hosp. 2 letters to relatives.

Wed 12/27: 12 hospital visits, 116th Evac Hosp.

Thurs 12/28: 15 hospital visits, 9th Evac Hosp.

Fri 12/29: 15 hospital visits. 9th Evac Hosp. 1 letter to relatives. Visited service of Ch. Engelberg, Saarburg.

Sat 12/30: Journeyed to Hq, 103rd Inf. Div.

Sun 12/31: Service, Rear Ech, 103rd Div; 14 present. Service, Fwd Ech, 103rd Div; 7 present.

Mon 1/1/45: Service, Div Arty, 103 Div; 16 present. Service, 3rd Bn, 409 Inf Rgt; 12 present.

Tues 1/2: 2 services, Hq 12th Armored Div, 61 present. Returned to Hq, XV Corps.

Wed 1/3: Conferred with Div Chaplain, 36th Inf Div and also with chaplain of Special Troops. Service, Rear Ech, 36th Inf. Div, 14 present.

Thurs 1/4: 1 stockade visit, 36th Inf Div. 2 welfare cases. 1 conference with chaplain. 6 conferences with EM. 1 hospital visit, 111th Med Bn.

Fri 1/5: 5 hospital visits; 111 Evac Hosp. Ret to Hq, XV Corps. 24 letters to relatives.

Sat 1/6: 2 letters to relatives. Moved to Hq, 103 Inf Div.

Sun 1/7: Service, Rear Ech, 103rd Inf Div, 16 present. Service, 328th Med Bn Clearing Station, 9 present. Attended evening song-service of Ch. Kinlow at Fwd Ech, 103rd Inf Div.

Mon 1/8: Conference with Ch. Walton, 410th Inf. Rgt. Service, 1st Bn, 410 Inf. Rgt, 11 present.

Tues 1/9: Service, 2nd and 3rd Bns, 410th Inf Rgt, 16 present. 3 conf with EM.

Wed 1/10: 2 conf with chaplains, 411th Inf Rgt. 3 conf with enlisted men.

Thurs 1/11: No services, 411th Inf. Rgt. 41 letters to relatives.

Fri 1/12: Service, Fwd CP, 103rd Arty Div, 16 present. 2 conf with chaplains. 2 letters to relatives.

Sat 1/13: Service, 103rd Div Arty, 19 present. Service, 103rd Inf. Rgt, 3rd Bn, 16 present. Service, 103rd Inf. Rgt, 2nd Bn. 12 present.

Sun 1/14: Service, 103rd Div Rear Hq, 9 present. 11 letters to relatives. Returned to XV Corps Hq.

Mon 1/15: 2 Sex Morality lectures, 3253 Signal Co., 126 present. Service, 3253 Signal Co., 14 present.

Tues 1/16: 3 personal contacts with EM. Service, 71st Inf. Rgt, 44th Div, 39 present.

Wed 1/17: Service, 749 Tank Bn, 11 present. 11 letters to relatives.

Thurs 1/18: Service, Fwd Ech, 44th Div, 20 present. Service, Fwd Ech, 44th Div, 8 present.

Fri 1/19: Service, 108th AAA Bn, 27 present. 1 conference with EM.

Sat 1/20: 20 letters to relatives. 1 conf with EM.

Sun 1/21: Service, 7th Army Rear, 40 present. 2 conf with chaplains.

Mon 1/22: 18 letters to relatives. 2 letters to relatives (condolence).

Tues 1/23: 1 conf with chaplain. Discussion group, Fed CP, 101st Airborn Div, 8 present.

Wed 1/24: 2 personal contacts with military personnel. Left 101st Airborn Div and went to 1109 Eng. C Group.

Thurs 1/25: 26 letters to relatives. Service, 1109 Engineer Bn, 41 present (Chaplains Morris and O'Connor).

Fri 1/26: Conf with Ch Stephen Balogh, 1117 Engineer Gr. Service, 1117 Engineer Group, 12 present.

Sat 1/27: Returned to XV Corps Hq. 15 letters to relatives. 3 hospital visits, 1117th Evac Hosp.

Sun 1/28: Attended service of Ch Eskin, 100th Inf Div, at Saarburg. Service, Fwd CP, XV Corps, 8 present. 4 letters to relatives.

Mon 1/29: Visited Hq, 42nd Div. 5 personal conferences with chaplains. 7 hospital visits, 93rd Evac Hosp.

Tues 1/30: 3 hospital visits, 93rd Evac Hosp. Service, 93rd Evac Hosp, 8 present (Ch McMullen and Ch Rush). 1 letter of condolence to Jerome Feenberg's parents.

Wed 1/31: Service, 650th Collecting Co. (Ch Haynes), 14 present. Went to 275th Inf. Regt, 70th Div.

Thurs 2/1: 2 services, 275th Inf Rgt, (Ch McPhalen), 20 present. 6 hospital visits, 132nd Evac Hosp.

Fri 2/2: 2 services, 276th Inf Rgt (Chaplains Powell and Vandergrift), 13 present. 8 hospital visits, 97th Evac Hosp. 1 welfare case.

Sat 2/3: Service, 276th Inf Rgt, 9 present. 2 personal conf with EM. 13 hospital visits, 116th Evac Hosp.

Sun 2/4: Service, T.F. Standish (10th Armored), 6 present. 3 letters to relatives.

Mon 2/5: Service, 1185th Eng G (Ch Ackerman) and 106th Cavalry (Ch Bristow), 14 present. 2 conferences with chaplains.

Tues 2/6: 1 conf with chaplain. Service, 433rd AAA Bn, 14 present.

Wed 2/7: Service, Rear CP, 45th Div, 16 present (Chaplains Rechter and Matheny). 119 letters to relatives.

Thurs 2/8: 2 conferences with chaplains. Service, 180th Inf, 2nd and 1st Bns, 28 present.

Fri 2/9: Service, 180th Inf, 3rd Bn; 8 present. Service, 45th Div Fwd CP, 14 present. Service, 103rd Div Rear CP, 16 present. 2 conf with chaplains.

Sat 2/10: 3 conf with chaplains. 2 hospital visits, 21st General Hospital.

Sun 2/11: 1 visit, 21st General Hospital.

Mon 2/12: Proceeded to Dijon to attend regional Jewish Chaplains' conference.

Tues 2/13: Attended service, a.m., Dijon. Attended regional Jewish chaplains conference conducted by Chaplain Nadich. On D.S.: Authority: Letter order, Hz Seventh Army, dated 1 Feb 1945. File no AG 200.4 Misc-3.

Wed 2/14: 18 hospital visits, 36th General Hospital, Dijon. 61 letters to relatives.

Thurs 2/15: Went from Dijon to 46th General Hospital.

Fri 2/16: 10 hospital visits, 46th General Hospital. Service, 46th General Hospital, 22 present.

Sat 2/17: 6 hospital visits, 46th General Hospital. Visited 236th General Hospital, Epinal. Visited service, 2nd Reinforce Depot, p.m.

Sun 2/18: Joint service, 2nd Reinf Depot, (Ch Saperstein) a.m., 40 present. Joint service, 23rd Gen Hospital, Vittel, 18 present.

Mon 2/19: Conference with 7th Army Chaplain, Luneville. From Luneville went to 5th Army Hosp Toul.

Tues 2/20: 20 hospital visits, 5th Gen Hosp, Toul. Returned to Hq, XV Corps.

Wed 2/21: Worked in office.

Thurs 2/22: 63 letters to relatives. 3 conf with Jewish soldiers.

Fri 2/23: 6 conferences with chaplains. 6 letters to relatives. Joint service, Saarburg, with Ch Eskin, 50 present.

Sat 2/24: 10 hospital visits, 116th Evac Hosp. Went to XV Corps Rest Center, Nancy. 2 conferences with chaplains.

Sun 2/25: Joint service with Ch Skydell, Nancy Synagogue, 350 present.

Mon 2/26: 3 conferences with chaplains. Purim service, Nancy synagogue, 125 present. 6 hospital visits, 95th Evac Hosp.

Tues 2/27: Returned to Hq XV Corps.

Wed 2/28: 3 hospital visits, 132nd Evac Hosp. 3 hospital visits, 95th Evac Hosp. 2 conf with chaplains. 1 conf with Jewish military personnel. 2 letters to relatives.

Thurs 3/1: 11 hospital visits, 132nd Evac Hosp. 3 hospital visits, 95th Evac Hosp. 2 conf with chaplains. 1 conf with Jewish military personnel. 2 letters to relatives.

Fri 3/2: 2 conferences with chaplains. 4 letters to relatives. 1 personal conference. 8 hospital visits, 117th Evac Hosp. Service, 117th Evac Hosp, 19 present.

Sat 3/3: 4 letters to relatives. 4 conferences with chaplains.

Sun 3/4: 3 letters to relatives. 6 hospital visits, 116th Evac Hosp.

Mon 3/5: 4 letters to relatives. 5 conferences with chaplains. 7 hospital visits, 95th Evac.

Tues 3/6: 1 hospital visit, 116th Evac Hosp. 8 hospital visits, 132nd Evac Hosp. 2 conferences with chaplains. 8 letters to relatives.

Wed 3/7: 1 hospital visit, 117th Evac Hosp. 8 letters to relatives. 2 conferences with chaplains. 2 hospital visits, 112th Evac Hosp.

Thurs 3/8: 1 conf with chaplain. 10 hospital visits, 116th Evac Hosp.

Fri 3/9: Attended conference with supervising chaplains, 7th Army Hq,
Rear. Joint service with Ch Skydell, 21st General Hospital, 31 present.

Sat 3/10: Returned XV Corps Hq.

Sun 3/11: Worked in office. 4 letters to relatives.

Mon 3/12: 11 hospital visits, 95th and 112th Evac Hosp. 2 conf with chaplains. 2 letters to relatives.

Tues 3/13: 14 hospital visits, 116th and 132nd Evac Hosp. 3 conf with
chaplains.

Wed 3/14: Sex morality lecture, 3355 QM Truck Co, 75 present. 1 hospital
visit, 112th Evac Hosp.

Thurs 3/15: 3 conf with chaplains. 2 letters to relatives.

Fri 3/16: Conf with 7th Army Jewish Chaplain. Service, 21st Gen Hospital,
35 present.

Sat 3/17: Brought matzos from Luneville to Saarburg.

Sun 3/18: Spent day in office.

Mon 3/19: Distributed matzos to 3 hospitals. Moved from Saarburg to
[unreadable]

Tues 3/20: Distributed matzos to 4 hospitals.

Wed 3/21: Left [unreadable] and this day entered Germany, proceeding to
Zweibrucken.

Thurs 3/22: Distributed matzos to 4 hospitals. Sent letters to chaplains on
Passover preparations.

Fri 3/23: Sent 4 letters to chaplains about Passover. Worked in office.

Sat 3/24: Moved from Zweibrucken to Kaiserlautern.

Sun 3/25: Service, Prot and Jews, XV Corps Rear, 26 present. Service, Prot
and Jews, XV Corps Fwd, 31 present. 4 conferences at Corps Fwd on
Passover plans.

Mon 3/26: 7 conferences with chaplains. Moved from Kaiserlautern to
Eisenberg.

Tues 3/27: 6 conferences with chaplains. Continued preparation for Passover.

Wed 3/28: Passover service, XV Corps Rear, 110 present.

Thurs 3/29: Passover service, 27th Evac Hosp, 10 present. No Passover
service because of Corps Hq move from Eisenberg to Bensheim.

Fri 3/30: Corps Hq moves to Gross Umstadt. I move to Clearing Station,
45th Div.

Sat 3/31: 2 conferences with chaplains. Passover Service, 120th Clearing
Co, 45th Div, 35 present.

Sun 4/1: Travel to 3rd Division. 1 conf with chaplain.

Mon 4/2: Passover service, Rear CP, 3 Div, 6 present. Passover service, 30th
Inf Rgt, 20 present. 3 conf with chaplains.

Tues 4/3: 2 conf with chaplains. Passover service, Fwd CP. 44th Div, 12 present.

Wed 4/4: 6 hospital visits, 93rd and 116th Evac Hosp. Passover service, Fwd CP, XV Corps, 34 present.

Thurs 4/5: Spent day in office.

Fri 4/6: Left Gross Umstadt (XV Fwd) and Reinheim (XV Rear) for 72-hour leave in Paris. While I was gone, XV Corps moved to Lohr, Bad Neustadt, and Bamberg.

Sat 4/7 to Tues 4/10: In Paris. Lunched with Chaplain Nadich. Conference with 2 other chaplains. Left in afternoon for Nancy.

Wed 4/11: 2 conferences with chaplains in Nancy.

Thurs 4/12: 2 conferences with chaplains in Nancy.

Fri 4/13: Memorial service for President Roosevelt, Nancy Synagogue, 200 present.

Sat 4/14: Attended civilian service, Nancy Synagogue. Addressed Zionist meeting, Nancy, 15 present.

Sun 4/15: Attended EM dance, XV Corps Rest Center Nancy.

Mon 4/16: Left Nancy. Spent night at Bensheim with Med Bn of 103rd Div.

Tues 4/17: Rejoined XV Corps near Bamberg.

Wed 4/18: Moved to Erlangen.

Thurs 4/19: Worked in office.

 Fri 4/20: Worked in office.

Sat 4/21: Visited prison camp at Nuremberg. Attended flag-raising ceremony in Hitler Platz, Nuremberg.

Sun 4/22: Visited prison camp, Nuremberg. Service, Nazi Party Stadium, Nuremberg, 12 present, including 5 Palestinian Jews from prison camp and 5 officers and soldiers from 180th Inf Rgt, 45th Division. XV Corps moved to Schwabach.

Mon 4/23: 1 conference with EM. 1 conference with chaplain.

Tues 4/24: Worked in office.

Wed 4/25: 1 conference with EM. 1 conference with chaplain.

Thurs 4/26: Moved from Schwabach to Treuchtlingen.

Fri 4/27: Service, XV Corps Rear, 4 present.

Sat 4/28: Worked in office.

Sun 4/29: 3 letters to relatives.

Mon 4/30: Moved from Treuchtlingen to Allach.

Tues 5/1: Went to concentration camps at Dachau and Allach.

Wed 5/2: Service, Allach Concentration Camp, 300 present.

Thurs 5/3: Spent working at Dachau Concentration Camp.

Fri 5/4: Service, Women's Barracks, Dachau, 165 present. Discussion group, 116th Evac Hospital, 8 present.

Sat 5/5: Service, Dachau Concentration Camp, 80 present.

Sun 5/6: Service, Dachau Concentration Camp (filmed by Army Pictorial

Service), 2000 (estimated) present. Meeting with representative Jewish committee of Dachau.

Mon 5/7: Visited Allach Concentration Camp. During past week had an estimated minimum of 20 conferences with American military personnel on matters pertaining to Jewish prisoners in concentration camps of Dachau and Allach. Also had an estimated minimum of 55 personal conferences with Jewish inmates of these camps. Also attended 2 Polish Catholic masses at Dachau. Returned to XV Corps Hq which this day moved from Munich to Salzburg.

Tues 5/8: Worked in office.

Wed 5/9: Worked in office.

Thurs 5/10: 3 conferences with chaplains.

Fri 5/11: Service, 839 AAA Bn, 17 present.

Sat 5/12: Service, XV Corps Rear, 60 present. 2 conf with EM.

Sun 5/13: Service, XV Corps Rear, 98 present.

Mon 5/14: 3 conf with chaplains.

Tues 5/15: Service, CCB, 20th Armored Div, 8 present. 1 welfare case (for civilians).

Wed 5/16: Returned to XV Corps Hq.

Thurs 5/17: Service, 20th Armored Div, 11 present.

Fri 5/18: 1 welfare case (civilian).

Sat 5/19: Service, XV Corps, Salzburg, 61 present. 1 welfare case.

Sun 5/20: Service, XV Corps, Salzburg, 57 present. 12 conferences with EM.

Mon 5/21: 5 hospital visits (civilian), Salzburg. 2 conferences with EM.

Tues 5/22: Worked in office.

Wed 5/23: Worked in office.

Thurs 5/24: Service, 10th Armored Div, Garmisch-Partenkirchen, 35 present. 3 personal conferences. Awarded Bronze Star Medal, G.O. No. 67, Par II, Hq XV Corps, 24 May 1945.

Fri 5/25: Service, XV Corps, 18 present.

Sat 5/26: Service, XV Corps, 47 present. 4 conferences with EM. 2 welfare cases (civilian).

Sun 5/27: Service, XV Corps, 60 present.

Mon 5/28: Worked in office. 2 conf with chaplains. 2 conf with EM.

Tues 5/29: Service 112th Evac Hosp, 18 present. 2 conf with chaplains.

Wed 5/30: Met with former Chief of Chaplains Arnold at a conference in Augsburg. 5 conf with chaplains.

Thurs 5/31: Spent at Dachau. Service, 180th Inf Rgt, 18 present.

Fri 6/1: Service, XV Corps, 22 present.

Sat 6/2: Service, XV Corps, 27 present. 3 conf with chaplains. 3 conf with EM.

Sun 6/3: Service, XV Corps, 77 present.

Mon 6/4: Worked in office.

Tues 6/5: Held service, Ebensee Concentration Camp, 800 present. Visited 38 patients, Ebensee Hospital. 11 conferences with Ebensee officials.

Wed 6/6: Service, 1101 Engineer Group, 11 present.

Thurs 6/7: Conferred with International Red Cross over food distribution from J.D.C. Worked in office.

Fri 6/8: Service, XV Corps Hq, 44 present.

Sat 6/9: Service, XV Corps Hq, 27 present. Delivered 12 tons of food, brought by J.D.C. and brought to Salzburg by International Red Cross to concentration camp at Ebensee.

Sun 6/10: Service, XV Corps Hq, 47 present.

Mon 6/11: Delivered 3 tons more food to camp at Ebensee. Delivered 2 tons to Women's Camp at Kammer Bei Gmunden. Delivered ton to Jewish DPs, Salzburg.

Tues 6/12: Service, Women's Camp, Kammer, 125 present. Went to Concentration Camp at Horsching [unreadable].

Wed 6/13: Visited Concentration Camp at Leonding. Service, Concentration Camp, Horsching, 300 present.

Thurs 6/14: Visited Concentration Camp, Mauthausen. Met with Jewish DP Committee, Linz.

Fri 6/15: Service, XV Corps Hq, 41 present.

Sat 6/16: Service, XV Corps Hq, 23 present.

Sun 6/17: Service, XV Corps Hq, 51 present. 7 conferences with EM. Conference with Jewish committee from Ebensee.

Mon 6/18: Left for Innsbruck.

Tues 6/19: Visited 2 concentration camps and held services at camp at Landeck, 31 present.

Wed 6/20: Spent day in Italy, visiting Merano, Bolzano, and Bessanone.

Thurs 6/21: Visited 2 concentration camps at Neustift, conducted service, Innsbruck, for 103rd Div and 1101 Engineering Group, 70 present.

Fri 6/22: Service, XV Corps Hq, 34 present. Conference with Chaplain Bohner of 42nd Div.

Sat 6/23: Service, XV Corps Hq, 18 present.

Sun 6/24: Service, XV Corps Hq, 60 present.

Mon 6/25: Service, 11th Armored Div, 28 present.

Tues 6/26: Service, 11th Armored Div, 16 present. Visited DP camp at Kammer.

Wed 6/27: Service, 11th Armored Div, 9 present.

Thurs 6/28: Service, 11th Armored Div, 11 present. Visited Linz — 2 conf with chaplains.

Fri 6/29: Began journey to new Hq, XV Corps, at Bamberg, Germany. Spent night with 110th Evac Hospital.

Sat 6/30: 3 conf with chaplains. Arrived at new Hq, XV Corps, Bamberg, Germany.

Sun 7/1: Attempted without success to hold service at 35th Evac Hosp.

Mon 7/2: Worked in office.

Tues 7/3: 1 conference with chaplain.

Wed 7/4: Worked in office.

Thurs 7/5: 3 conferences with chaplains. 2 conferences with EM.

Fri 7/6: Service, XII Tactical Air Force, Erlangen, 6 present.

Sat 7/7: Service, Furth, 105 present

Sun 7/8: Attempted without success to hold service for artillery group in Weissenberg.

Mon 7/9: 3 conferences with chaplains.

Tues 7/10: 3 conferences with chaplains.

Wed 7/11: Worked in office.

Thurs 7/12: 1 conference with chaplain.

Fri 7/13: Worked in office.

Sat 7/14: Service, Bamberg, Germany, 200 present.

Sun 7/15: Flew to Aschoffenberg, 6th Arm Div, for service, 10 present.

Mon 7/16: Two conferences with chaplains. Conference with Jewish committee of Bamberg.

Tues 7/17: Conference with Bamberg Jewish committee.

Wed 7/18: Left for XV Corps Rest Center, Nancy. Authority: S.O. No. 164, Par. 8, 17 July 1945, Hq XV Corps. Spent night in Hogenau.

Thurs 7/19: Hogenau and Strassbourg.

Fri 7/20: Arrived Nancy. Preached at service of Chaplain Aaron Tofield, Nancy Synagogue. 210 present.

Sat 7/21: Attended service, a.m., Nancy Synagogue.

Sun 7/22: Nancy XV Corps Rest Center.

Mon 7/23: Left for Mullheim. Spent night at Colwer.

Tues 7/24: Went to Mullheim and then on to Siegmaringen.

Wed 7/25: Siegmaringen.

Thurs 7/26: During this period, 6 conferences with chaplains.

Fri 7/27: Returned to Hq, XV Corps, Bamberg.

Sat 7/28: Service, Hq XV Corps, 217 present.

Sun 7/29: Met with refugee committee, Bamberg.

Mon 7/30: Transferred from Hq, XV Corps to Hq XXIII Corps, Bad Wildungen. Authority: S.O. 200; par. 6, Hq U.S. Forces, European Theatre, 18 July 1945. Effective date, 24 July 1945.

Tues 7/31: Spent at Hq XXIII Corps, Bad Wildungen.

Wed 8/1: Spent at Hq XXIII Corps, Bad Wildungen.

Thurs 8/2: Spent at Hq XXIII Corps, Bad Wildungen.

Fri 8/3: Service, HQ XXIII Corps, 12 present.

Sat 8/4 to Tues 8/7: Waited around doing nothing, HQ XXIII Corps.

Wed 8/8: Visited Richelsdorf.

Thurs 8/9: Still waiting.

Fri 8/10: Service, Ha XXIII Corps, 11 present.

Sat 8/11: Wasted, XXIII Corps.

Sun 8/12: Service, Hq 78th Div, 32 present.

Mon 8/13: Wasted, Hq XXIII Corps.

Tues 8/14 to Sat 8/18: Wasted, Hq XXIII Corps.

Sun 8/19: Left for new assignment with 197th General Hospital. Spent night at Kochen, Germany.

Mon 8/20: Spent night at Esch, Luxembourg.

Tues 8/21: Spent night at Arlow, Belgium.

Wed 8/22: Reported for duty, Hq 197th General Hospital, Camp Philadelphia, Rheims Assembly Area. Authority: Par 26, S.O. 223, Hq USFET, 11 August 1945. Effective date: 15 Aug 1945.

Thurs 8/23: Loafed.

Fri 8/24: Service, joint, with Chaplains Dembowitz, 179th General Hosp, and Elefant, 201 Gen Hosp, 32 present, Camp Philadelphia.

Sat 8/25: Service, joint, with Chaplains Dembowitz and Elefant, Camp Philadelphia, 15 present. 11 contacts with military personnel.

Sun 8/26: Loafed.

Mon 8/27: Conference with Chaplains Lorge and Brodey, Rheims.

Tues 8/28: Distributed High Holyday materials, Camp Philadelphia — 17 personal contacts — seven conferences with chaplains.

Wed 8/29 and Thurs 8/30: Distributed Holyday materials to Camps St. Louis, Carlisle, Pittsburgh. 5 conferences with chaplains.

Fri 8/31: Attended 1st anniversary celebration of liberation of Verdun. Conducted civilian service, a.m., 25 present. Attended Prot and Cath civilian service, Conducted service, p.m., 23 present. 3 conf with military personnel on personal problems.

Sat 9/1: Service, Camp Philadelphia, 10 present. Conf with EM.

Sun 9/2: Rested, Camp Philadelphia.

Mon 9/3: Rested, Camp Philadelphia.

Tues 9/4: Rested, Camp Philadelphia.

Wed 9/5: Went to Paris. Jeep Driver Long went AWOL and left me flat. Came back to camp by train.

Thurs 9/6: Rested, Camp Philadelphia.

Fri 9/7: Attended Rosh Hashana service, [unreadable], 94th Gen Hosp, Ch Jacob Segal.

Sat 9/8: Traveled to Nancy, France. Attended Rosh Hashana service, synagogue, Nancy.

Sun 9/9: Joint service with Ch Aaron Tofield, Rosh Hashana, Nancy, France — 350 present.

Mon 9/10: Went for [unreadable] to 197th Gen Hosp, now at Miracourt, France.

Tues 9/11: Returned to Camp Philadelphia.

Wed 9/12: Rested, Camp Philadelphia.

Thurs 9/13: Rested, Camp Philadelphia.

Fri 9/14: Set out for 46th General Hospital, Besancon, France, via 197th General Hospital, Mirocourt. Spent night at Neufchatel.

Sat 9/15: En route. Spent night at Luxemil.

Sun 9/16: Reported for duty, 46th General Hospital. Transferred from 197th Gen Hospital. Authority: S.O. #252, Par. 1, Hq Oise Intermediate Section, TSFET, dated 9 September 1945. Effective date: 12 September. Attended Yom Kippur services, Besancon synagogue.

Mon 9/17: Attended Yom Kippur services, Besancon synagogue.

Tues 9/18: Attended Mingon, Besancon synagogue.

Wed 9/19: Rested, 46th General Hospital.

Thurs 9/20: Rested, 46th General Hospital.

Fri 9/21: Attended service, Besancon synagogue.

Sat 9/22: Rested.

Sun 9/23 to Thurs 9/27: Rested.

Fri 9/28: Services, 46th General Hosp, 11 present.

Sat 9/29: Rested.

Sun 9/30: Took group of 39 men on tour to source of [unreadable] River.

Mon 10/1 to Thurs 10/4: Rested.

Fri 10/5: Visited civilian service, Besancon. Dance, officers and nurses, 46th Gen Hosp, 60 present.

Sat 10/6: Rested.

Sun 10/7: Rested.

Mon 10/8: Umpired ball game. Dance, officers and nurses, 46th Gen Hosp, 70 present.

Tues 10/9: Umpired ball game.

Wed 10/10: Rested.

Thurs 10/11: Took enlisted men on tour, 10 present.

Fri 10/12: Dance, officers and nurses, 100 present.

Sat 10/13: Dance, enlisted men, 150 present.

Sun 10/14: Tour, officers and nurses, 30 present.

Mon 10/15: Rested.

Tues 10/16 to Thurs 10/18: Had helluva good time in Paris — 6th and, for present, last visit.

Fri 10/19: Dance, officers and nurses, 46th Gen Hosp, 30 present.

Sat 10/20/45: Left Besoncon for Marseilles P.O.E.

Sun 10/21: Arrived Camp Calas, Marseilles.

Mon 10/22 to Fri 10/26: Rested, Camp Calas.

Sat 10/27: Service, Camp Calas, 21 present.

Sun 10/28: Left Camp Calas for "Lincoln Liberty," ship which will return us to the U.S.A.

Mon 10/29/45: Sailed for U.S.A., 1:30 p.m.

Fri 11/2/45: Service aboard ship, 30 present.

Thurs 11/8/45: Arrived Boston, U.S.A.

Wed 11/14/45: Began terminal leave.

Throughout his letters, Rabbi Eichhorn used English versions of Hebrew and Yiddish words and phrases. His anglicizations were not always the most commonly recognized spellings, and in fact, he did not always spell them the same way each time. To remain true to his intent, we left these terms as he wrote them and provide their definitions here.

Addir Hu and *Ki Lo Noeh:* Songs in the Haggadah, the book read on Passover evening.

Alehem ha-shawlom (or shalom): Phrase equivalent to "rest in peace," traditionally said immediately after mentioning the name of someone who has died.

Aliyahs: Literally, "to go up"; the act of being called up to the bimah (the raised platform at the front of a synagogue) to recite the blessing before and after the Torah reading.

Al kiddush ha-Shem: "Sanctification of the Name," referring to any prayer, conduct, or — the ultimate expression — martyrdom that brings honor to God's name.

Ark (or Aron Ha-Kodesh): Cabinet holding the Torah scrolls, usually set into or against a wall facing east toward Jerusalem.

Aron Ha-Kodesh: See *Ark.*

Bar Mitsvah: Literally, "son of the commandment." When a Jewish boy becomes thirteen, he is bound by "the commandment" and is thereafter responsible for fulfilling Jewish law, whether he has the bar mitzvah ceremony or not.

Benshed Gomel: Blessing of thanksgiving recited during a service, after surviving a dangerous or life-threatening situation.

Bias Mitsraim: See *Yetsias Mitsraim.*

"Bist du a Yid?": Yiddish for "Are you Jewish?"

Chaium (or Chaiium): Hebrew for "life" — the joke in the letter being that even the dead have life.

Chalutsa (or Halutz): Pioneer; specifically, a pre-1948 settler in Palestine.

Chanuka (or Chanukah, Hanukah, Hanukkah, Hannukkah): See *Hanukkah.*

Chazzan (or Hazzan): Hebrew word for cantor, the official at a synagogue who leads the congregation in prayer and song.

Davaning: Praying.

El Male Rachamin: "God full of compassion." A memorial prayer that asks for the repose of the souls of the departed.

Erev Pesach: The evening before Passover, the joyous holiday that celebrates the Angel of Death's "passing over" Jewish homes during the last of the ten plagues that forced Pharoah to free his Jewish slaves.

Erev Rosh Hashanah: Rosh Hashanah eve.

Geniza (or Genizah): Space in a synagogue or religious institution where old religious articles and prayer books are stored until they can be buried. Jewish law requires that objects containing the word of God be properly interred when they are no longer in use.

Gerer Rebbe: Gerer, or Gur, is a city in Poland; rebbe is the rabbi leader of a Hasidic sect or a teacher in a traditional school.

Goyim: Plural of *goy,* a biblical word meaning "nation" or "people," but usually used by Jews to mean non-Jews.

Haggadas: Book of prayers, songs, rituals, and liturgy used at a Passover Seder.

Hanukkah: Literally, "dedication." A joyous holiday, also called the Festival of Lights, that begins on the twenty-fifth of Kislev, generally in late November, and celebrates the victory of the Maccabees over the Syrians and the rededication of the Second Temple in Jerusalem in ancient times. Hanukkah is celebrated for eight days and involves exchanging gifts, eating traditional foods cooked in oil (such as latkes), and, each day, lighting another candle in an eight-branched candelabra called a menorah or hannukkiah.

Ha-tikva: "The hope." Before 1948, a popular song of the Zionist movement that would become the national anthem of the State of Israel.

Kaddish: From the Hebrew word for "holy," an ancient prayer recited by mourners.

Kiddush: Blessing recited over wine before all Jewish holidays and celebratory meals.

Knadlach: Matzo balls.

Koheles: Hebrew name for Ecclesiastes. The Scrolls of Koheles are read on Shabbos (the Sabbath) during Succos, an eight-day festival of thanksgiving.

Kol Nidre: "All vows." The name of the synagogue service on the eve of Yom Kippur, as well as the ancient Aramaic prayer recited at that service, in which one asks to be released from vows made but not kept during the previous year and the year to come.

Krishma: Kriat Sh'ma, three paragraphs from the Book of Deuteronomy, required by the Torah to be recited every morning and evening.

Latkes: Fried pancakes, the most common being potato latkes. During Passover, latkes are traditionally made from matzo meal.

Magen David (or Mogen David): Hebrew for "Star of David." Rabbi Eichhorn had Stars of David painted on his jeep.

Mah Nishtanas: The Four Questions recited at the Passover Seder by the youngest person present. The answers — from the oldest person present — explain the meaning and symbols of the holiday. The Four Questions are: (1) On all other nights we eat bread or matzah. Why tonight do we eat only matzah? (2) On all other nights we eat many vegetables. Why tonight do we eat bitter herbs? (3) On all other nights we do not dip our food. Why tonight do we dip our food twice? (4) On all other nights we can sit any way. Why tonight do we recline?

"Mah nishtanaw ha-layelaw ha-ze?": The first of the Four Questions. See *Mah Nishtanas.*

Matsos (or Matzos; singular, Matzah, Matzo, Matza): Unleavened, flat crackers made from flour and wheat and eaten during Passover to symbolize the haste with which the Israelites fled from slavery in ancient Egypt: they did not have time to let the bread rise.

Mawshiach: Mashiach is the Hebrew word for "messiah" and literally means "the anointed one," the person who will usher in the time of universal peace. In spelling the word as he does, Rabbi Eichhorn may be making fun of the French pronunciation.

Megilla: Literally, "scroll." Refers to five books of the Bible — Esther, Song of Songs, Ruth, Lamentations, and Ecclesiastes — but often used to refer solely to the Book of Esther.

Melamed: Children's teacher.

Mesheberachs (or Mi She-Berakh): Prayers recited at a service for life events related to health and happiness, marriage, and so forth. A special form is recited for the recovery of the sick.

Midrashim (singular, Midrash): Written interpretations and discussions of the laws, customs, and rituals of Jewish life mentioned in the Torah.

Minyan: Literally, "number." Refers to the minimum necessary for a communal religious service (ten people) according to Jewish law. For traditional Jews, a minyan is composed of men only.

Mishpacha (or Mishpachah): Literally, "family"; the whole clan.

"Moror zu al shum maw?": The second of the Four Questions (see *Mah Nishtanas*). Moror (or maror) is a bitter herb, usually horseradish, placed on the Seder plate at Passover to symbolize the bitterness of slavery.

Motsi (or ha-Motzi): A common bracha, or blessing, recited over bread before a meal is eaten. The translation is: "Blessed are you, Adonai our God, Ruler of the Universe, who brings forth bread from the earth."

Ner Tamid: "Eternal light"; the light fixture that is constantly lit in front of the Ark in every synagogue.

Nosherei: Food for snacks.

Oneg Shabas (or Oneg Shabbat): Snack, including wine, juice, and pastries, offered after Shabbat and holiday services in a synagogue.

Parnas: Leader, such as the head of a congregation.

Peroches (or Parochet, Perochet): Curtain that covers the Sefer Torah inside the Ark.

Purim: Holiday commemorating Haman's defeat by Mordecai and Queen Esther, celebrated by reading the Scroll of Esther, participating in home festivities, exchanging gifts, and giving aid to the poor. Purim symbolizes to Jews that they will be victorious over their enemies and that the spirit of bigotry will disappear.

Rosh Hashana (or Rosh Hashanah): Literally, "head of the year"; the Jewish New Year. Rosh Hashanah, which usually falls in September, begins the ten-day period of prayer and self-examination called the Days of Awe (Yamim Noraim) that concludes with Yom Kippur, or the Day of Atonement, the most solemn day on the Jewish calendar.

Seder: Traditional Passover dinner, including prayers, songs, and a retelling of the Passover story from Exodus.

Sefer Torah (plural, Sifre Torah): The actual parchment scroll.

S'farim: Books, but particularly holy books of Judaic content.

Shabbat: Jewish Sabbath.

She'erit: Leftovers, as in the leftover Jews of France.

Shehecheyanu: Blessing that translates as "Blessed are you, Adonai our God, Ruler of the Universe, who has given us life, sustained us, and brought us to this moment."

Shmoosing (or Shmoozing): Chatting.

Shofar: Hollowed-out ram's horn, blown like a trumpet and used for communication and celebration. It is blown on Rosh Hashanah and at the end of Yom Kippur as part of the prayer services.

Shul: Synagogue, but can also refer to a school.

Siddur: Book containing the set of prayers to be recited on Shabbat and during festivals.

Tachas (or Tuchis): Yiddish for "underneath"; slightly vulgar term for the rear end. (The gentler version is tushee.)

Torah: First five books of the Bible, also called the Five Books of Moses or the Pentateuch.

Yalkut Shemoni: A specific book of Midrash.

Yamim Noraim: "Days of Awe," the ten-day period of introspection and repentance beginning with Rosh Hashanah and ending with Yom Kippur.

Yetsias Mitsraim and *Bias Mitsraim:* Escape from Egypt, and, in essence, arrival in Egypt. Rabbi Eichhorn seems to be implying that they celebrated escape from bondage as they arrived in Germany, the modern place of bondage.

Yiddlach: Affectionate Yiddish term for Jews.

Yom Kippur: Day of Atonement; end of the ten-day period (see *Yamim Noraim*) that begins with Rosh Hashanah.

Index